FFmpeg Basics

Multimedia handling with a
fast audio and video encoder

Frantisek Korbel

FFmpeg Basics

Book index, user forum and other resources
are available on the website ffmpeg.tv.

ISBN: 1479327832
ISBN-13: 978-1479327836

Acknowledgements

The greatest thanks belongs to the developers of excellent FFmpeg tools and libraries and to the whole FFmpeg community that drives this project forward. The project documentation was the main source for the book.
Another great source was the Wikipedia, especially articles about color spaces, quantization, sampling, etc.

Thank you very much and best wishes.

Brief Contents

Introduction 12

1. FFmpeg Fundamentals 15

2. Displaying Help and Features 29

3. Bit Rate, Frame Rate and File Size 60

4. Resizing and Scaling Video 64

5. Cropping Video 69

6. Padding Video 73

7. Flipping and Rotating Video 77

8. Blur, Sharpen and Other Denoising 81

9. Overlay - Picture in Picture 87

10. Adding Text on Video 93

11. Conversion Between Formats 99

12. Time Operations 108

13. Mathematical Functions 113

14. Metadata and Subtitles 117

15. Image Processing 122

16. Digital Audio 128

17. Presets for Codecs 138

18. Interlaced Video 142

19. FFmpeg Components and Projects 147

20. Microphone and Webcam 154

21. Batch Files 159

22. Color Corrections 164

23. Advanced Techniques 179

24. Video on Web 193

25. Debugging and Tests 200

Glossary 207

About the author 216

Table of Contents

Introduction 12
    Welcome...12
    First steps...12
    Dedicated website...12
    Conventions..13
    Your feedback is important 14

1. FFmpeg Fundamentals 15
    FFmpeg introduction...15
    Developers of FFmpeg...16
    Participation in FFmpeg development 16
    FFmpeg download 17
    Command line syntax..17
    Windows Command Prompt and its alternatives....................................18
    Path setting..19
    Renaming to shortened form 20
    Displaying output preview...21
        Preview with FFplay media player 21
        Preview with SDL output device 21
    SI prefixes available in FFmpeg 21
    Transcoding with ffmpeg 22
    Filters, filterchains and filtergraphs 23
    Selection of media streams..25
    Lavfi virtual device 27
    Color names..27

2. Displaying Help and Features 29
    Text help in FFmpeg tools..29
    Available bitstream filters..29
    Available codecs 30
    Available decoders 36
    Available encoders 43
    Available filters 46
    Available formats 48
    Available layouts of audio channels 52
    FFmpeg license 54
    Available pixel formats..54
    Available protocols 57
    Available audio sample formats 58
    FFmpeg version..58
    Using MORE command for output formatting 59
    Redirecting output to file 59

3. Bit Rate, Frame Rate and File Size 60
    Frame (frequency) rate introduction 60
    Frame rate setting...61
        Using -r option 61
        Using fps filter..61
    Predefined values for frame rate..61
    Bit (data) rate introduction..62

Setting bit rate 62
Constant bit rate (CBR) setting 62
Setting maximum size of output file 63
File size calculation 63

4. Resizing and Scaling Video 64

Resizing video 64
Predefined video frame sizes 64
Considerations when resizing - Nyquist sampling theorem 66
Special enlarging filter 67
Advanced scaling 67
Scaling video proportionately to input 68
Scaling to predefined width or height 68

5. Cropping Video 69

Cropping basics 69
Cropping frame center 70
Automatic detection of cropping area 71
Cropping of timer 71

6. Padding Video 73

Padding basics 73
Padding videos from 4:3 to 16:9 75
Padding videos from 16:9 to 4:3 75
Padding from and to various aspect ratios 76
   Pillarboxing - adding boxes horizontally 76
   Letterboxing - adding boxes vertically 76

7. Flipping and Rotating Video 77

Horizontal flip 77
Vertical flip 77
Introduction to rotating 78
Rotation by 90 degrees counterclockwise and flip vertically 79
Rotation by 90 degrees clockwise 79
Rotation by 90 degrees counterclockwise 80
Rotation by 90 degrees clockwise and flip vertically 80

8. Blur, Sharpen and Other Denoising 81

Blur video effect 81
Sharpen video 83
Noise reduction with denoise3d 84
Noise reduction with hqdn3d 85
Noise reduction with nr option 86

9. Overlay - Picture in Picture 87

Introduction to overlay 87
Command structure for overlay 87
Logo in one of corners 88
   Logo in top-left corner 89
   Logo in top-right corner 89
   Logo in bottom-right corner 89

Logo in bottom-left corner 90

Logo shows in specified moment **90**

Video with timer **91**

Other overlay examples **92**

10. Adding Text on Video 93

Introduction to adding text on video **93**

Text positioning **95**

Horizontal location setting 95

Vertical location setting 95

Font size and color setting **96**

Dynamic text **97**

Horizontal text movement 97

Vertical text movement 98

11. Conversion Between Formats 99

Introduction to media formats **99**

File formats 99

Media containers 99

Transcoding and conversion **99**

Introduction to codecs **100**

Overwriting same named output files **101**

Generic options for conversion **102**

Private options for conversion **105**

MPEG-1 video encoder 105

MPEG-2 video encoder 106

MPEG-4 video encoder 106

libvpx video encoder 106

AC-3 audio encoder 107

Simplified encoding of VCD, SVCD, DVD, DV and DV50 .... **107**

12. Time Operations 108

Duration of audio and video **108**

Setting with -t option 108

Setting with number of frames 108

Setting delay from start **108**

Extracting specific part from media file **108**

Delay between input streams **109**

One input file 109

Two or more input files 109

Limit for processing time **109**

Shortest stream determines encoding time **109**

Timestamp and time bases **110**

Encoder timebase setting **110**

Audio and video speed modifications **111**

Video speed change 111

Audio speed change 112

Synchronizing audio data with timestamps **112**

13. Mathematical Functions 113

Expressions that can use mathematical functions...113
Built-in arithmetic operators 114
Built-in constants 114
Table of built-in mathematical functions...114
Examples of using functions...116

14. Metadata and Subtitles 117
Introduction to metadata 117
Creating metadata 117
Saving and loading metadata to/from the file 119
Deletion of metadata 119
Introduction to subtitles 119
Subtitles encoded directly to video 121

15. Image Processing 122
Supported image formats..122
Creating images...123
    Screenshots from videos...123
    Animated GIFs from videos 123
    Images from FFmpeg video sources..123
    Video conversion to images 124
Resizing, cropping and padding images...125
Flipping, rotating and overlaying images 126
Conversion between image types 127
Creating video from images 127
    Video from one image 127
    Video from many images 127

16. Digital Audio 128
Introduction to digital audio 128
    Audio quantization and sampling...128
Audio file formats 130
Sound synthesis 130
Stereo and more complex sounds 132
    Binaural tones for stress reduction...132
Sound volume settings 133
Multiple sounds mixed to one output..133
Downmixing stereo to mono, surround to stereo 134
Simple audio analyzer..135
Adjusting audio for listening with headphones 136
Audio modifications with -map_channel option 136
    Switching audio channels in stereo input..137
    Splitting stereo sound to 2 separate streams..137
    Muting one channel from stereo input 137
Merging 2 audio streams to 1 multichannel stream 137
Audio stream forwarding with buffer order control 137

17. Presets for Codecs 138
Introduction to preset files 138
Examples of preset files 139

Preset file libvpx-1080p.ffpreset...139
Preset file libvpx-1080p50_60.ffpreset...139
Preset file libvpx-360p.ffpreset...140
Preset file libvpx-720p.ffpreset...140
Preset file libvpx-720p50_60.ffpreset...141

18. Interlaced Video..142
NTSC, PAL and SECAM TV standards 142
Interlaced frame type setting..143
Field order change of interlaced video 143
Deinterlacing 144
yadif filter...144
Option -deinterlace..144
Deinterlacing filters from MPlayer project 144
Pullup filter...145
Interlaced video and digital television 145

19. FFmpeg Components and Projects 147
FFplay introduction..147
Key and mouse controls during playback 148
FFplay show modes..148
FFprobe introduction 149
FFserver introduction 150
FFmpeg software libraries 150
libavcodec 150
libavdevice 150
libavfilter 151
libavformat 151
libavutil 151
libpostproc 151
libswresample...151
libswscale 151
Projects using FFmpeg components..152
HTML5 support in Google Chrome..152
Videoprocessing on YouTube and Facebook 152
Multimedia frameworks utilizing FFmpeg 152
Video editors 152
Audio editors 152
Media players using FFmpeg 153

20. Microphone and Webcam..154
Introduction to input devices..154
List of available cameras and microphones 154
Available options for webcam 155
Displaying and recording webcam input...156
Using two webcams...156
Recording sound and sending it to loudspeakers.......................................158

21. Batch Files 159
Advantages of batch files..159

Batch file commands..159
Typical usage of batch files 161
Tone generator 161
Creating Jingle Bells..162
Simplified conversion 163

22. Color Corrections..164
Video modifications with lookup table...164
   Conversion to monochrome (black-and-white) image 164
Introduction to color spaces..165
YUV color space and its derivatives..166
   Luma (luminance) and chroma (chrominance) 166
Pixel formats...166
RGB pixel format modifications...167
   Color balance...168
Modifications of YUV pixel format...169
   Brightness correction...170
Hue and saturation setting...171
Comparison in 2 windows 172
   2 windows compared horizontally 172
   2 windows compared vertically...173
   Space between windows..173
   Modified version first..174
   2 modified versions without input...174
Comparison in 3 windows 175
   3 windows compared horizontally 175
   3 windows compared vertically...175
   Input in the middle window...176
Brightness correction in 2 and 3 windows 176
Comparison in 4 windows 178

23. Advanced Techniques 179
Joining audio and video files...179
   Concatenation with shell command 179
   Concatenation with concat protocol...180
   Concatenation with concat filter 180
   Other types of joining..180
Removing logo 181
   delogo filter 181
Fixing of shaking video parts...182
Adding color box to video..183
Number of frames detection..183
Detection of ads, section transitions or corrupted encoding 184
   Detection with blackframe filter 185
Selecting only specified frames to output 186
Scaling input by changing aspect ratios...187
Screen grabbing 188
Detailed video frame information 188

Audio frequency spectrum...189
Audio waves visualization 190
Voice synthesis 190
Saving output to multiple formats at once 191
Additional media input to filtergraph..192

24. Video on Web 193
HTML5 support on main browsers 193
Adding audio with HTML5 194
Adding video with HTML5...195
Adding video for Flash Player 196
Video sharing websites 196
Videoprocessing on webserver..198
Monetizing video uploads..199

25. Debugging and Tests 200
debug, debug_ts and fdebug options 200
Flags for error detection 202
Logging level setting 202
Timebase configuration test..203
Testing encoding features..203
Test patterns..205
    RGB test pattern 205
    Color pattern with scrolling gradient and timestamp.......................205
    SMPTE bars pattern 205
Simple packet dumping or with payload (hexadecimally) 205
CPU time used and memory consumption 206

Glossary 207

About the author..216

Introduction

Welcome

Dear reader,

welcome to the book that will try to make you familiar with many interesting features of the FFmpeg project. Its quality indicates several FFmpeg users:

- Facebook, the largest social network, handles videos from users with ffmpeg tool
- Google Chrome, popular web browser, uses FFmpeg libraries for HTML5 audio and video support
- YouTube, the biggest video sharing website, converts uploaded videos with ffmpeg.

The book's focus is to explain the basic video editing like resizing, cropping, padding, denoising, overlay, etc., but included are instructions for more complex processing and experiments.

The chapter Digital Audio describes how to convert and create audio, advanced sound processing is in the chapters Batch Files and Advanced Techniques.

First steps

The first step is to download FFmpeg binaries, if not already done, the details are in the first chapter or on the dedicated website. Many Linux distributions already have FFmpeg tools installed or advanced users can compile their own binaries.

The first chapter contains basic information about FFmpeg project and how to simplify the work with its tools. If already familiar with these data or if it looks too technical for the start, you can move to the second chapter and start to enter various ffmpeg commands.

Please note, that many commands in this book are simplified to illustrate the currently explained feature and some parameters are omitted, especially in conversions, the details are in the chapter Conversion Between Formats.

Dedicated website

For the book was created a special website on **ffmpeg.tv** that contains:

- book index, table of contents and description of the book
- examples from the book in the video format, videos are located in the particular chapters
- user forum to discuss the book topics and various ideas
- list of found errors (errata)
- contact form
- 40 last articles from 6 FFmpeg mailing lists (constantly updated)

Conventions

Text that should be entered on the command line is printed in a serif proportional typeface, for example:

ffmpeg -i input.mpg -q 1 output.avi

The part of the command that should be replaced with a particular text is printed in italics, for example:

ffmpeg -i *input* -vf mp=denoise3d -s vga *output*

The console output is printed in a sans serif proportional typeface:

```
Muxer avi [AVI (Audio Video Interleaved)]:
    Common extensions: avi.
    Mime type: video/x-msvideo.
    Default video codec: mpeg4.
    Default audio codec: mp3.
```

The blue caret ^ indicates that the command is too long to be printed on one line in the book and continues on another, but on computer it remains a 1-line command, for example:

**ffplay -f lavfi -i color=c=white ^
-vf drawtext=fontfile=/Windows/Fonts/arial.ttf:text=Welcome**

Please note a space between the word **white** and ^ in the previous example, the space indicates that there will be space also on the command line. This form of notation is required in the batch files that will be explained in the chapter Batch Files.

Important

Many examples in the book are simplified to explain the current item, so some parameters are omitted and used are defaults, details are in the chapter Conversion Between Formats.

Common omitted options include bitrate, codec, frame rate, etc.

For a better orientation the book contains a colored differentiation of FFmpeg elements like the filters, devices, sources and other items.

Colored differentiation of devices, filters, etc. related to audio and video	
audio only	
video only	
both audio and video	

Please note
FFmpeg tools and libraries are often updated and some commands used in the book or other information will be changed.

Please visit www.ffmpeg.tv for the list of updated items. e-mail: book@ffmpeg.tv

Your feedback is important
Many options and parameters of FFmpeg tools cannot be described in the book with about 200 pages and your opinion what can be improved and included in the next edition is welcome.

Please before sending a query by e-mail, visit www.ffmpeg.tv and search on the forum or FAQ, it will prevent repeated questions and in some cases it will provide instant help.

Thank you very much and best wishes.

1. FFmpeg Fundamentals

To use optimally the great variety of FFmpeg components it is useful to properly understand the basic facts and features. If it is too technical for the start, you can continue with the next chapter and return later.

FFmpeg introduction

FFmpeg is a name of a free software project for the multimedia handling licensed under GNU General Public License. The most popular part of the project is **ffmpeg** command line tool for video and audio encoding/decoding and its main features are the high speed, quality of output and small file sizes. "FF" from FFmpeg means Fast Forward - a control button on media players, and "mpeg" is an abbreviation of the Moving Pictures Experts Group. The FFmpeg logo contains a zig-zag pattern, that is characteristic for the entropy coding scheme illustrated with 8x8 block in the picture.

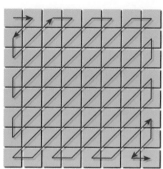

FFmpeg command-line tools	
ffmpeg	fast audio and video encoder/decoder
ffplay	media player
ffprobe	shows media files characteristics
ffserver	broadcast server for multimedia streaming using HTTP and RTSP protocols
FFmpeg software libraries	
libavcodec	software library for various multimedia codecs
libavdevice	software library for devices
libavfilter	software library containing filters
libavformat	software library for media formats
libavutil	software library containing various utilities
libpostproc	software library for post processing
libswresample	software library for audio resampling
libswscale	software library for media scaling

The programming language for all components is **C** and the source code can be compiled on Linux/Unix, Windows, Mac OS X, etc.

The book was created on the Microsoft Windows using official binary builds, but almost all instructions and examples should work without any change on other operating systems. Please see the **FFmpeg configuration** entry in the Glossary for the details about enabled options.

Developers of FFmpeg

The project was started in 2000 by Fabrice Bellard, excellent programmer known also as a creator of QEMU and Tiny C Compiler. Now the project is maintained by the FFmpeg team and developers are from many countries, main developers available for contracting work are in the table:

Name	Location	Specialization
Baptiste Coudurier	Los Angeles, USA	He has special expertise in broadcast codecs (ProRes, DNxHD, IMX/D-10, AVC-Intra), formats (MXF, GXF, MOV) and usages (Avid, FCP, Interlacing, Time Code, Metadata).
Benjamin Larsson	Stockholm, Sweden	Main area of his expertise is audio codecs.
Diego Biurrun	Aachen, Germany	He has special expertise in license compliance engineering and build systems.
Jason Garrett-Glaser	Los Angeles, USA	He is the lead x264 developer and has special expertise in H.264 and other modern lossy video formats, as well as x86 SIMD assembly optimization.
Luca Barbato	Torino, Italy	He has special expertise in streaming protocols.
Michael Niedermayer	Vienna, Austria	He is an expert in all areas of video coding as well as x86 assembly.
Stefano Sabatini	Cagliari, Italy	He has special expertise in libavfilter, ff* tools usage and usability issues.

Participation in FFmpeg development

Anyone can participate by joining particular mailing list on the webpage

`http://www.ffmpeg.org/contact.html`

Available mailing lists are in the table:

FFmpeg mailing lists	
ffmpeg-user	for regular user questions like compilation troubles, command-line issues and similar
ffserver-user	for ffserver user questions like configuration and streaming issues
libav-user	for application developer questions about development using the FFmpeg libraries
ffmpeg-devel	for development of FFmpeg itself, it is not for development of software that use the FFmpeg libraries and not for bug reports
ffmpeg-cvslog	for all changes to the FFmpeg sources / main git repository
ffmpeg-trac	for all changes to the FFmpeg Trac issuetracker

FFmpeg download

The primary download source is located on the webpage:
`http://ffmpeg.org/download.html`
The users of Windows can download the binaries (static builds are recommended) from the webpage
`http://ffmpeg.zeranoe.com/builds`
Many Linux distributions have FFmpeg tools already installed, otherwise they can be compiled, this is possible also on the OS X, or the OS X binaries can be downloaded from the webpages
`http://www.evermeet.cx/ffmpeg` or `http://ffmpegmac.net`

Command line syntax

The syntax of ffmpeg command line tool is relatively simple, important is to type required parameters in the correct position and not to mix options between various inputs and outputs. The general structure of **ffmpeg** command follows, **global options** affect all inputs and outputs:

```
ffmpeg [global options] [input file options] -i input_file [output file
options] output_file
```

Command Syntax of **ffmpeg**

ffmpeg

   global options

      input1_options **-i input1**

         input2_options -i input2

            ... additional input files, streams, etc.

               output1_options **output1**

                  output2_options output2

                     ... additional output files, streams...

Example: **ffmpeg** **-y** **-i video.avi** **-s vga** **video.mp4**

| | global option | input 1 | output 1 option | output 1 |

items in blue - required, **items in green** - optional
items in italic style - will be replaced with actual data
input1 ... inputN, output1 ... outputN - strings specifying files, pipes, network streams, grabbing devices, etc.

Windows Command Prompt and its alternatives

The **ffmpeg** command line tool on Windows is managed via Command Prompt, that is available via Windows -> All Programs -> Accessories -> Command Prompt. It can be also started with a shortcut **Win+R** , then typing **cmd** followed by Enter.

Windows Command Prompt does not save the history of used commands when it is closed and because there are free applications with additional features like the file management, editing, macros, FTP client, etc., it is recommended to select advanced program for FFmpeg tools. The next table describes several free alternatives.

Windows Command Prompt alternatives		
Name	**Download**	**Description**
FAR Manager	farmanager.com	- file manager with shell, editor, ftp client - command line completion, shortcuts, macros, plugins - 2 windows, customizable interface
PyCmd	sourceforge.net/projects/pycmd	- tab completion, persistent history...
Console	sourceforge.net/projects/console	- multiple tabs, configurable
Gregs DOS Shell	gammadyne.com/cmdline.htm#gs	- improved editing, command history, support for Aero Glass, etc.
TCC/LE	jpsoft.com/all-downloads/downloads.html	- includes 111 internal commands, 103 internal variables, 140 variable functions

The next lines describes the best alternative FAR Manager, on Linux it can be substituted with a similar application Midnight Commander, if installed, it is started with an **mc** command from the console.

FAR Manager is a popular file manager, editor and FTP client that supports macros, plugins and other advanced features. User interface is highly customizable and was translated to many languages. The next picture illustrates its command history window, that is displayed during typing a new command, so the user can easily select the command used previously and edit it eventually.

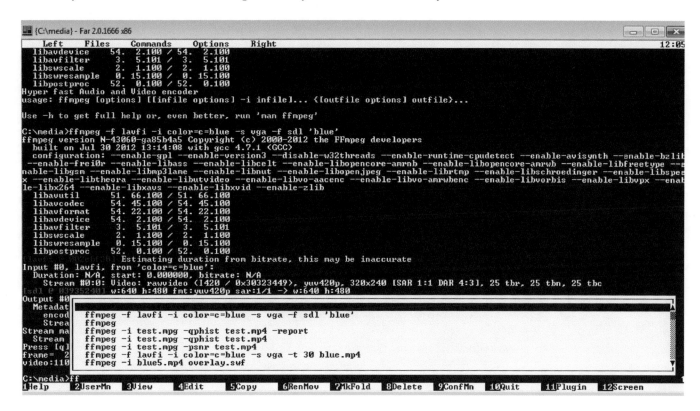

For its advanced file editor, FAR Manager will be useful when creating ffmpeg batches, what is described in the chapter Batch Files. File editor is needed also for including media files on the web page, what is the topic of the Video on Web chapter. Customization of the interface is started with F9 key and selecting the Options tab.

Path setting

It is practical to copy downloaded FFmpeg command line utilities (ffmpeg.exe, ffplay.exe, ffprobe.exe) to the directory, which is included in an Environment Variables, section Path, so they can be invoked from any directory without writing the complete path to them.

Alternatively you can copy FFmpeg programs to other directory, for example C:\media and then add this folder to the system path via Control Panel -> System and Security -> System -> Advanced System Settings. Please click here on the button **Environment Variables**, scroll down the scroll bar of System Variables, click on the line Path and then on the button **Edit**. In a pop-up window **Edit System Variable** click on the field Variable Value, move the cursor at the end of line, add the text

`;C:\media`

and click on **OK** button. The semicolon separates particular directories, it should not be duplicated.

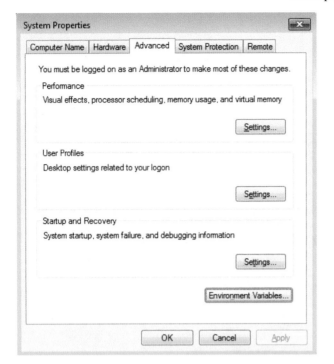
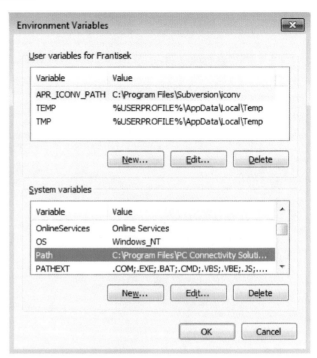

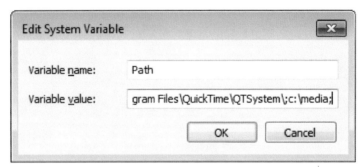

For the current session of the Command Prompt, the path can be set with the command:

```
set path=%path%;C:\path_to_ffmpeg.exe
```

For example, if the file ffmpeg.exe was copied to the directory C:\media, the command is:

```
set path=%path%;C:\media
```

Renaming to shortened form

The command name **ffmpeg** has 6 characters and to type it frequently is not very comfortable, so it is recommended to rename the file ffmpeg.exe to f.exe (ffplay.exe to fp.exe, etc.) or similar short form to save time and prevent mistyping. In the Command Prompt you can use the command:

```
ren ffmpeg.exe f.exe
```

For the clarity in this book is always used the complete command form **ffmpeg**.

Displaying output preview

During various video tests, we can save plenty of time by displaying the command output screen and not to save it to the file and than preview it in a media player.

Preview with FFplay media player

Instead of generating a new file with ffmpeg tool using the simplified command

```
ffmpeg -i input_file ... test_options ... output_file
```

we can use the ffplay that will show exactly the same as ffmpeg saves to the file using the command

```
ffplay -i input_file ... test_options
```

Preview with SDL output device

This preview is generated by an SDL (Simple DirectMedia Layer) output device described in the table:

Output device: sdl	
Description	Shows a video stream in an SDL window, requires libsdl library installed.
Syntax	[-icon_title *i_title*] [-window_size *w_size*] [-window_title *w_title*] -f sdl *output*
Description of device's options	
icon_title	name of the iconified SDL window, defaults to the value of window_title
window_size	SDL window size, widthxheight or abbreviation, default is the size of the input video
window_title	window title, defaults to the filename specified for the output device

Please note, that SDL device can display only output with a yuv420p pixel format and with other input type the option **-pix_fmt** with a value yuv420p must be prepended, otherwise an error is displayed, for example:

```
ffmpeg -f lavfi -i rgbtestsrc -pix_fmt yuv420p -f sdl Example
```

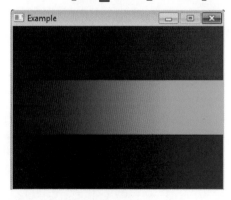

SI prefixes available in FFmpeg

When specifying numeric values to various ffmpeg options like bitrate or maximal file size you can use common SI postfixes: K for kilo (10^3), M for mega (10^6), G for giga (10^9), etc. The next example specifies a new bitrate 1.5 megabits per second for the output file, all commands give the same result:

```
ffmpeg -i input.avi -b:v 1500000 output.mp4
ffmpeg -i input.avi -b:v 1500K output.mp4
ffmpeg -i input.avi -b:v 1.5M output.mp4
ffmpeg -i input.avi -b:v 0.0015G output.mp4
```

Please note that in FFmpeg documentation SI prefixes are called postfixes, because they must be entered immediately after the numeric value.

Postfix **B** (byte) can be used in ffmpeg options with numeric values and multiplies the value by number 8. It can be combined with other prefixes to denote kilobytes (KB), megabytes (MB), etc. For example to set the maximal file size of 10 megabytes for the output file, the next command can be used:

```
ffmpeg -i input.mpg -fs 10MB output.mp4
```

SI prefixes available in FFmpeg							
for parts (negative)				for multiples (positive)			
Symbol	Prefix	decimal base 10	binary base 2	Symbol	Prefix	decimal base 10	binary base 2
y	yocto-	-24	-80	h	hecto-	2	
z	zepto-	-21	-70	k, K	kilo-	3	10
a	atto-	-18	-60	M	mega-	6	20
f	femto-	-15	-50	G	giga-	9	30
p	piko-	-12	-40	T	tera-	12	40
n	nano-	-9	-30	P	peta-	15	50
μ	mikro-	-6	-20	E	exa-	18	60
m	milli-	-3	-10	Z	zetta-	21	70
c	centi-	-2		Y	yotta-	24	80
d	deci-	-1					

Transcoding with ffmpeg

The ffmpeg program reads into memory the content of any number of inputs specified with **-i** option, processes it according to the entered parameters or program defaults and writes the result to any number of outputs. Inputs and outputs can be computer files, pipes, network streams, grabbing devices, etc.

In transcoding process, ffmpeg calls demuxers in libavformat library to read inputs and get from them packets with encoded data. If there are more inputs, ffmpeg keeps them synchronized by tracking lowest timestamp on any active input stream. Then decoder produces uncompressed frames from encoded packets and after optional filtering, the frames are sent to the encoder. Encoder produces new encoded packet, that are sent to the muxer and written to the output.

The important part of FFmpeg tools are filters, that can be organized to filterchains and filtergraphs. Filtergraphs can be simple or complex. Filtering process is realized between decoding the source and encoding the output. The transcoding process is illustrated in the next diagram.

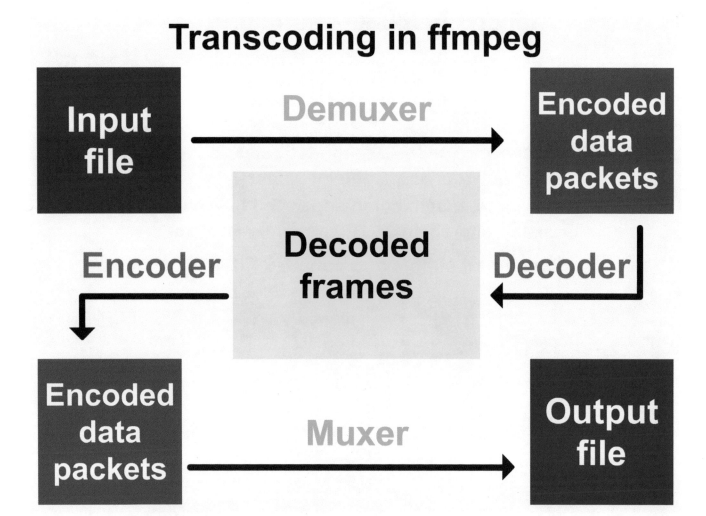

Filters, filterchains and filtergraphs

In multimedia processing, the term filter means a software tool that modifies input before it is encoded to the output. Filters are divided to audio and video filters (please see also **filter** in Glossary). FFmpeg has built-in many multimedia filters and enables to combine them in many ways. Commands with a complex syntax direct decoded frames from one filter to another according to specified parameters. This simplifies the media processing, because multiple decoding and encoding of media streams with lossy codecs decreases overall quality. Filtering API (Application Programming Interface) of FFmpeg is the **libavfilter** software library that enables filters to have multiple inputs and outputs. Filters are included between inputs and outputs using **-vf** option for video filters and **-af** option for audio filters. For example, the next command produces a test pattern rotated by 90° clockwise using a transpose filter (described in 7. chapter):

```
ffplay -f lavfi -i testsrc -vf transpose=1
```

The next example slows down the tempo of input audio to 80% using an **atempo** audio filter:

```
ffmpeg -i input.mp3 -af atempo=0.8 output.mp3
```

Filter, filterchain and filtergraph

Filter syntax

in blue - required
in green - optional

[input_link_label1][input_link_label2]...

filter_name=parameters

[output_link_label1][output_link_label2]...

Filterchain = sequence of comma-separated filter descriptions

"filter1,filter2,filter3, ... filterN-2,filterN-1,filterN"

Filtergraph = sequence of semicolon-separated filterchain descriptions

"filterchain1;filterchain2; ... filterchainN-1;filterchainN"

Diagram of simple and complex filtergraph

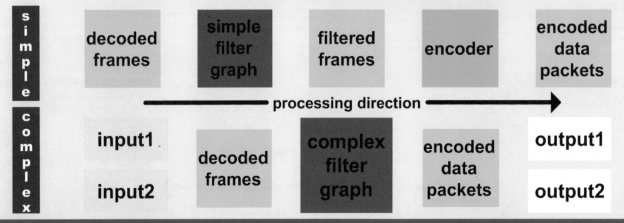

Example: ffmpeg -i video.avi -i logo.png -filter_complex overlay=iw-50:ih-30 out.mp4

Filters are often used in filterchains (sequences of comma-separated filters) and filtergraphs (semicolon-separated sequences of filterchains). If any spaces are used, the filterchain must be enclosed in quotes. In the filtergraphs can be used link labels that represent the output of a selected filterchain and can be used anywhere in the following filtergraphs. For instance we want to compare the input video with an output denoised by a hqdn3d filter. Without the filtergraphs we must use at least 2 commands, for example:

```
ffmpeg -i input.mpg -vf hqdn3d,pad=2*iw output.mp4
ffmpeg -i output.mp4 -i input.mpg -filter_complex overlay=w compare.mp4
```

Using a filtergraph with the link labels, sufficient is only 1 command:

```
ffplay -i i.mpg -vf split[a][b];[a]pad=2*iw[A];[b]hqdn3d[B];[A][B]overlay=w
```

The split filter divided the input to 2 outputs labeled [a] and [b], then [a] link is used as an input in the second filterchain that creates a pad for the comparison labeled [A]. [b] link is used as an input in the 3rd filterchain that creates a denoised output labeled [B]. The last filterchain uses [A] and [B] labels as inputs to the overlay filter that produces the final comparison. Another example is in the next diagram.

Link labels in filterchains and filtergraphs

Filter syntax

[*in_link1*]...[*in_linkN*]*filter_name=parameters*[*out_link1*]...[*out_linkM*]

input link labels   output link labels

Link label is a name of the link associated with the input or output pad of the filter.

Example of a complex filtergraph

split[a][b];[a]pad=2*iw[1];[b]vflip[2];[1][2]overlay=w

filterchain 1   filterchain 2   filterchain 3   filterchain 4

[a]	[a]pad=2*iw[1]	[1]	
split			overlay=w
[b]	[b]vflip[2]	[2]	

F1: The split filter creates 2 copies of the input with link labels [a] and [b].
F2: Link [a] forms the input for the pad filter that outputs double width to a link [1].
F3: Link [b] forms the input for the vflip filter that flips its content to the link [2].
F4: Links [1] and [2] are inputs to the overlay filter that
places the [2] link content beside the [1] link content.

Complete command and displayed result:

ffplay -f lavfi -i rgbtestsrc -vf split[a][b];[a]pad=2*iw[1];[b]vflip[2];[1][2]overlay=w

Selection of media streams

Some media containers like AVI, Matroska, MP4, etc. can contain multiple streams of various type, FFmpeg recognizes 5 stream types: audio (a), attachment (t), data (d), subtitle (s) and video (v).

Stream are selected with **-map** option followed by a stream specifier with the syntax:

```
file_number:stream_type[:stream_number]
```

File_number and stream_number are denoted also file_index and stream_index and are counted from 0, it means that the first one is 0, the second one is 1, etc. There are some special stream specifiers:

- -map 0 selects all streams from all types
- -map i:v selects all video streams from the file with a number i (index), -map i:a selects all audio streams, -map i:s selects all subtitle streams, etc.
- special options **-an**, **-vn**, **-sn** exclude all audio, video or subtitle streams respectively

If the input file(s) contains more streams of the same type and -map option is not used, then selected is only 1 stream of each type. For example, if the file contains 2 video streams, selected is the one with a higher resolution, for audio is selected the stream with more channels, etc., details are in the following diagram:

Selection of streams from input(s) to output

1. Default: selected is 1 stream only of each type

audio - stream with the most channels
subtitle - first subtitle stream
video - stream with the highest resolution

If more audio or video streams have the same parameters, the first one is selected.

2. Manual: with -map option

-map [-]inputfile_id[:stream_specifier][,syncfile_id[:stream_specifier]]

file1 streams	specifier
1st video	0:v:0
2nd video	0:v:1
1st audio	0:a:0
2nd audio	0:a:1
1st subtitle	0:s:0
2nd subtitle	0:s:1
3rd subtitle	0:s:2

file2 streams	specifier
1st video	1:v:0
1st audio	1:a:0
1st subtitle	1:s:0

Example of the command

ffmpeg -i file1 -i file2 *selected_streams* output

Examples of *selected streams*

a) all streams from both files
  -map 0 -map 1

b) file1: 3rd subtitle, file2: 1st video, 1st audio
  -map 0:s:2 -map 1:v:0 -map 1:a:0

c) file1: 2nd video, file2: 1st subtitle, no audio
  -map 0:v:1 -map 1:s:0 -an

d) all streams except 1st video and 2nd audio in file1
  -map 0 -map 1 -map -0:v:0 -map -0:a:1

Complete example, selected is 1. video from A.mov, 1. audio from B.mov and 1. subtitles from C.mov.

ffmpeg -i A.mov -i B.mov -i C.mov -map 0:v:0 -map 1:a:0 -map 2:s:0 clip.mov

Stream types: a - audio, d - data, s - subtitles, t - attachment, v - video

Beside the specific **-map** option, stream specifiers are used with many other options in several forms:

Forms of stream specifiers	
Specifier form	**Description**
stream_index	selects the stream with this index (number)
stream_type[:stream_index]	**stream_type** is 1 of letters **a** (audio), **d** (data),**s** (subtitle), **t** (attachments) or **v** (video); if **stream_index** is added, it selects the stream of this type with given index, otherwise it selects all streams of this type
p:program_id[:stream_index]	if **stream_index** is added, then selects the stream with **stream_index** in program with given **program_id**, else selects all streams in this program
stream_id	selects the stream by format-specific ID

For example, to set the bit rate using **-b** option for the audio and video, we can use the command:

```
ffmpeg -i input.mpg -b:a 128k -b:v 1500k output.mp4
```

Lavfi virtual device

In the previous sections we used a **-f** option with a **lavfi** value, where **lavfi** is a name of the libavfilter virtual input device described in the table:

Input device: lavfi	
Description	Processes data from opened output pads of the filtergraph, for each output pad creates a corresponding stream that is mapped to the encoding. The filtergraph is specified with a -graph option, currently only video output pads are supported.
Syntax	**-f lavfi [-graph[-graph_file]]**
Description of lavfi options	
-graph	filtergraph to use as input, each video open output must be labeled by a unique string of the form "outN", where N is a number starting from 0 corresponding to the mapped input stream generated by the device. The first unlabeled output is automatically assigned to the "out0" label, but all the others need to be specified explicitly. If not specified, it defaults to the filename specified for the input device.
-graph_file	filename of the filtergraph to be read and sent to the other filters, syntax of the filtergraph is the same as the one specified by the option **-graph**

Lavfi is often used to display the test patterns, for example SMPTE bars with the command:

```
ffplay -f lavfi -i smptebars
```

Other often used source is a **color** source that can be displayed with the command:

```
ffplay -f lavfi -i color=c=blue
```

Color names

Some video filters and sources have a color parameter that require to specify wanted color and there are 4 methods of the color specification (the default value is black):

1. Color is specified as a W3C (World Wide Web Consortium) standard name, alphabetical list of standard names with their hexadecimal values is in the following picture. Please note that there are several synonyms: aqua = cyan, fuchsia = magenta and gray = grey.

2. Color is specified as a hexadecimal number in a form 0xRRGGBB[@AA], where RR is a red channel, GG is a green channel and BB is a blue channel, for example 0x0000ff is blue, 0xffff00 is yellow, etc. [@AA] is an optional alpha channel that specifies how much opaque the color is and is divided from color channels with an at sign character @. Alpha channel value is written either as a hexadecimal number from 0x00 to 0xff or as a decimal number between 0.0 and 1.0, where 0.0 (0x00) is completely transparent and 1.0 (0xff) is completely opaque. For example a green color with a half transparency is 0x00ff00@0.5

3. Same as in previous method, but to denote hexadecimal numeral system is used a # sign instead of 0x prefix, the same as in HTML code, for example #ff0000 is red, #ffffff is white, etc. Please note that # prefix cannot be used with the alpha channel, it means that #0000ff@0x34 is good, but #0000ff@#34 no.

4. Color is specified with a special value **random**, that results in a random color produced by computer.

27

Color name	Hex value	Color name	Hex value	Color name	Hex value
AliceBlue	0xF0F8FF	GhostWhite	0xF8F8FF	Moccasin	0xFFE4B5
AntiqueWhite	0xFAEBD7	Gold	0xFFD700	NavajoWhite	0xFFDEAD
Aqua, Cyan	0x00FFFF	GoldenRod	0xDAA520	Navy	0x000080
Aquamarine	0x7FFFD4	Gray	0x808080	OldLace	0xFDF5E6
Azure	0xF0FFFF	Grey	0x808080	Olive	0x808000
Beige	0xF5F5DC	Green	0x008000	OliveDrab	0x6B8E23
Bisque	0xFFE4C4	GreenYellow	0xADFF2F	Orange	0xFFA500
Black	0x000000	HoneyDew	0xF0FFF0	OrangeRed	0xFF4500
BlanchedAlmond	0xFFEBCD	HotPink	0xFF69B4	Orchid	0xDA70D6
Blue	0x0000FF	IndianRed	0xCD5C5C	PaleGoldenRod	0xEEE8AA
BlueViolet	0x8A2BE2	Indigo	0x4B0082	PaleGreen	0x98FB98
Brown	0xA52A2A	Ivory	0xFFFFF0	PaleTurquoise	0xAFEEEE
BurlyWood	0xDEB887	Khaki	0xF0E68C	PaleVioletRed	0xD87093
CadetBlue	0x5F9EA0	Lavender	0xE6E6FA	PapayaWhip	0xFFEFD5
Chartreuse	0x7FFF00	LavenderBlush	0xFFF0F5	PeachPuff	0xFFDAB9
Chocolate	0xD2691E	LawnGreen	0x7CFC00	Peru	0xCD853F
Coral	0xFF7F50	LemonChiffon	0xFFFACD	Pink	0xFFC0CB
CornflowerBlue	0x6495ED	LightBlue	0xADD8E6	Plum	0xDDA0DD
Cornsilk	0xFFF8DC	LightCoral	0xF08080	PowderBlue	0xB0E0E6
Crimson	0xDC143C	LightCyan	0xE0FFFF	Purple	0x800080
DarkBlue	0x00008B	LightGoldenRodYellow	0xFAFAD2	Red	0xFF0000
DarkCyan	0x008B8B	LightGray	0xD3D3D3	RosyBrown	0xBC8F8F
DarkGoldenRod	0xB8860B	LightGrey	0xD3D3D3	RoyalBlue	0x4169E1
DarkGray	0xA9A9A9	LightGreen	0x90EE90	SaddleBrown	0x8B4513
DarkGrey	0xA9A9A9	LightPink	0xFFB6C1	Salmon	0xFA8072
DarkGreen	0x006400	LightSalmon	0xFFA07A	SandyBrown	0xF4A460
DarkKhaki	0xBDB76B	LightSeaGreen	0x20B2AA	SeaGreen	0x2E8B57
DarkMagenta	0x8B008B	LightSkyBlue	0x87CEFA	SeaShell	0xFFF5EE
DarkOliveGreen	0x556B2F	LightSlateGrey	0x778899	Sienna	0xA0522D
DarkOrange	0xFF8C00	LightSteelBlue	0xB0C4DE	Silver	0xC0C0C0
DarkOrchid	0x9932CC	LightYellow	0xFFFFE0	SkyBlue	0x87CEEB
DarkRed	0x8B0000	Lime	0x00FF00	SlateBlue	0x6A5ACD
DarkSalmon	0xE9967A	LimeGreen	0x32CD32	SlateGray	0x708090
DarkSeaGreen	0x8FBC8F	Linen	0xFAF0E6	SlateGrey	0x708090
DarkSlateBlue	0x483D8B	Magenta	0xFF00FF	Snow	0xFFFAFA
DarkSlateGrey	0x2F4F4F	Maroon	0x800000	SpringGreen	0x00FF7F
DarkTurquoise	0x00CED1	MediumAquaMarine	0x66CDAA	SteelBlue	0x4682B4
DarkViolet	0x9400D3	MediumBlue	0x0000CD	Tan	0xD2B48C
DeepPink	0xFF1493	MediumOrchid	0xBA55D3	Teal	0x008080
DeepSkyBlue	0x00BFFF	MediumPurple	0x9370D8	Thistle	0xD8BFD8
DimGray	0x696969	MediumSeaGreen	0x3CB371	Tomato	0xFF6347
DimGrey	0x696969	MediumSlateBlue	0x7B68EE	Turquoise	0x40E0D0
DodgerBlue	0x1E90FF	MediumSpringGreen	0x00FA9A	Violet	0xEE82EE
FireBrick	0xB22222	MediumTurquoise	0x48D1CC	Wheat	0xF5DEB3
FloralWhite	0xFFFAF0	MediumVioletRed	0xC71585	White	0xFFFFFF
ForestGreen	0x228B22	MidnightBlue	0x191970	WhiteSmoke	0xF5F5F5
Fuchsia	0xFF00FF	MintCream	0xF5FFFA	Yellow	0xFFFF00
Gainsboro	0xDCDCDC	MistyRose	0xFFE4E1	YellowGreen	0x9ACD32

Synonyms: aqua = cyan, fuchsia = magenta and gray = grey
can replace 0x, for example 0x0000ff = #0000ff

2. Displaying Help and Features

Help and other information about FFmpeg programs are displayed with various options entered after a space and hyphen, examples show the usage for ffmpeg tool, but the same options are valid for ffplay, ffprobe and ffserver. The parameters are case-sensitive. The development of FFmpeg components is fast and some lists of available items here will be soon incomplete, the results are from November 2012.

Text help in FFmpeg tools

FFmpeg tools has a large console help, that can be displayed complete or about a particular element - decoder, encoder, etc. The next table describes available options, the text in italics will be replaced with the item to display. Similar options are available also for ffplay and ffprobe.

Basic help	Help for selected item
`ffmpeg -?` or `ffmpeg -h`	`ffmpeg -h decoder=decoder_name`
Extended help	`ffmpeg -h encoder=encoder_name`
`ffmpeg -h long` or `ffmpeg -h full`	`ffmpeg -h demuxer=demuxer_name`
`ffmpeg -? topic` or `ffmpeg -h topic`	`ffmpeg -h muxer=muxer_name`

For example, to display information about a FLV decoder, we can use the command:

`ffmpeg -h decoder=flv`

The console output is:

```
Decoder flv [FLV / Sorenson Spark / Sorenson H.263 (Flash Video)]:
    Threading capabilities: no
    Supported pixel formats: yuv420p
```

The complete help is very long, please see the end of this chapter for the formatting solutions.

Available bitstream filters

The command for displaying the built-in bitstream filters is:

`ffmpeg -bsfs`

```
Bitstream filters:
text2movsub
remove_extra
noise
mov2textsub
mp3decomp
mp3comp
mjpegadump
```

```
mjpeg2jpeg
imxdump
h264_mp4toannexb
dump_extra
chomp
aac_adtstoasc
```

Available codecs

Available codecs are displayed with **-codecs** option, we can use the command:

ffmpeg -codecs

```
Codecs:
 D..... = Decoding supported
 .E.... = Encoding supported
 ..V... = Video codec
 ..A... = Audio codec
 ..S... = Subtitle codec
 ...I.. = Intra frame-only codec
 ....L. = Lossy compression
 .....S = Lossless compression
 -------
 D.V.L. 4xm               4X Movie
 D.VI.S 8bps              QuickTime 8BPS video
 .EVIL. a64_multi         Multicolor charset for Commodore 64 (encoders: a64multi )
 .EVIL. a64_multi5        Multicolor charset for Commodore 64, extended with 5th color
                          (colram) (encoders: a64multi5 )
 D.V..S aasc              Autodesk RLE
 DEVIL. amv               AMV Video
 D.V.L. anm               Deluxe Paint Animation
 D.V.L. ansi              ASCII/ANSI art
 DEVIL. asv1              ASUS V1
 DEVIL. asv2              ASUS V2
 D.VIL. aura              Auravision AURA
 D.VIL. aura2             Auravision Aura 2
 D.V... avrn              Avid AVI Codec
 DEVI.. avrp              Avid 1:1 10-bit RGB Packer
 D.V.L. avs               AVS (Audio Video Standard) video
 DEVI.. avui              Avid Meridien Uncompressed
 DEVI.. ayuv              Uncompressed packed MS 4:4:4:4
 D.V.L. bethsoftvid       Bethesda VID video
 D.V.L. bfi               Brute Force & Ignorance
 D.V.L. binkvideo         Bink video
 D.VI.. bintext           Binary text
 DEVI.S bmp               BMP (Windows and OS/2 bitmap)
 D.V..S bmv_video         Discworld II BMV video
 D.V.L. c93               Interplay C93
 DEV.L. cavs              Chinese AVS (Audio Video Standard) (AVS1-P2, JiZhun profile)
                          (encoders: libxavs )
 D.V.L. cdgraphics        CD Graphics video
 D.VIL. cdxl              Commodore CDXL video
 D.V.L. cinepak           Cinepak
```

```
DEVIL. cljr            Cirrus Logic AccuPak
D.VI.S cllc            Canopus Lossless Codec
D.V.L. cmv             Electronic Arts CMV video (decoders: eacmv )
D.V... cpia            CPiA video format
D.V..S cscd            CamStudio (decoders: camstudio )
D.VIL. cyuv            Creative YUV (CYUV)
D.V.L. dfa             Chronomaster DFA
DEV.LS dirac           Dirac (decoders: dirac libschroedinger) (encoders: libschroedinger)
DEVIL. dnxhd           VC3/DNxHD
DEVIL. dpx             DPX image
D.V.L. dsicinvideo     Delphine Software International CIN video
DEVIL. dvvideo         DV (Digital Video)
D.V..S dxa             Feeble Files/ScummVM DXA
D.VI.S dxtory          Dxtory
D.V.L. escape124       Escape 124
D.V.L. escape130       Escape 130
D.VILS exr             OpenEXR image
DEV..S ffv1            FFmpeg video codec #1
DEVI.S ffvhuff         Huffyuv FFmpeg variant
DEV..S flashsv         Flash Screen Video v1
DEV.L. flashsv2        Flash Screen Video v2
D.V..S flic            Autodesk Animator Flic video
DEV.L. flv1            FLV / Sorenson Spark / Sorenson H.263 (Flash Video) (decoders: flv)
                       (encoders: flv )
D.V..S fraps           Fraps
D.VI.S frwu            Forward Uncompressed
..V... g2m             GoToMeeting
DEV..S gif             GIF (Graphics Interchange Format)
DEV.L. h261            H.261
DEV.L. h263            H.263 / H.263-1996, H.263+ / H.263-1998 / H.263 version 2
D.V.L. h263i           Intel H.263
DEV.L. h263p           H.263+ / H.263-1998 / H.263 version 2
DEV.LS h264            H.264/AVC/MPEG-4 AVC/MPEG-4 part 10 (encoders: libx264 libx264rgb )
DEVI.S huffyuv         HuffYUV
D.V.L. idcin           id Quake II CIN video (decoders: idcinvideo )
D.VI.. idf             iCEDraw text
D.V.L. iff_byterun1    IFF ByteRun1
D.V.L. iff_ilbm        IFF ILBM
D.V.L. indeo2          Intel Indeo 2
D.V.L. indeo3          Intel Indeo 3
D.V.L. indeo4          Intel Indeo Video Interactive 4
D.V.L. indeo5          Intel Indeo Video Interactive 5
D.V.L. interplayvideo  Interplay MVE video
DEVILS jpeg2000        JPEG 2000 (decoders: j2k libopenjpeg ) (encoders: j2k libopenjpeg )
DEVILS jpegls          JPEG-LS
D.VIL. jv              Bitmap Brothers JV video
D.V.L. kgv1            Kega Game Video
D.V.L. kmvc            Karl Morton's video codec
D.VI.S lagarith        Lagarith lossless
.EVI.S ljpeg           Lossless JPEG
D.VI.S loco            LOCO
D.V.L. mad             Electronic Arts Madcow Video (decoders: eamad )
D.VIL. mdec            Sony PlayStation MDEC (Motion DECoder)
D.V.L. mimic           Mimic
DEVIL. mjpeg           Motion JPEG
```

```
D.VIL. mjpegb            Apple MJPEG-B
D.V.L. mmvideo           American Laser Games MM Video
D.V.L. motionpixels      Motion Pixels video
DEV.L. mpeg1video        MPEG-1 video
DEV.L. mpeg2video        MPEG-1 video (decoders: mpeg2video mpegvideo )
DEV.L. mpeg4             MPEG-4 part 2 (encoders: mpeg4 libxvid )
..V.L. mpegvideo_xvmc    MPEG-1/2 video XvMC (X-Video Motion Compensation)
D.V.L. msa1              MS ATC Screen
D.V.L. msmpeg4v1         MPEG-4 part 2 Microsoft variant version 1
DEV.L. msmpeg4v2         MPEG-4 part 2 Microsoft variant version 2
DEV.L. msmpeg4v3         MPEG-4 part 2 Microsoft variant version 3 (decoders: msmpeg4 )
                         (encoders: msmpeg4 )
D.V..S msrle             Microsoft RLE
D.V.L. mss1              MS Screen 1
D.VIL. mss2              MS Windows Media Video V9 Screen
DEV.L. msvideo1          Microsoft Video 1
D.VI.S mszh              LCL (LossLess Codec Library) MSZH
D.V.L. mts2              MS Expression Encoder Screen
D.V.L. mxpeg             Mobotix MxPEG video
D.V.L. nuv               NuppelVideo/RTJPEG
D.V.L. paf_video         Amazing Studio Packed Animation File Video
DEVI.S pam               PAM (Portable AnyMap) image
DEVI.S pbm               PBM (Portable BitMap) image
DEVI.S pcx               PC Paintbrush PCX image
DEVI.S pgm               PGM (Portable GrayMap) image
DEVI.S pgmyuv            PGMYUV (Portable GrayMap YUV) image
D.VIL. pictor            Pictor/PC Paint
DEV..S png               PNG (Portable Network Graphics) image
DEVI.S ppm               PPM (Portable PixelMap) image
DEVIL. prores            Apple ProRes (iCodec Pro) (decoders: prores prores_lgpl )
                         (encoders: prores prores_anatoliy prores_kostya )
D.VIL. ptx               V.Flash PTX image
D.VI.S qdraw             Apple QuickDraw
D.V.L. qpeg              Q-team QPEG
DEV..S qtrle             QuickTime Animation (RLE) video
DEVI.S r10k              AJA Kona 10-bit RGB Codec
DEVI.S r210              Uncompressed RGB 10-bit
DEVI.S rawvideo          raw video
D.VIL. rl2               RL2 video
DEV.L. roq               id RoQ video (decoders: roqvideo ) (encoders: roqvideo )
D.V.L. rpza              QuickTime video (RPZA)
DEV.L. rv10              RealVideo 1.0
DEV.L. rv20              RealVideo 1.0
D.V.L. rv30              RealVideo 3.0
D.V.L. rv40              RealVideo 4.0
D.V.L. sanm              LucasArts SMUSH video
DEVIL. sgi               SGI image
D.V.L. smackvideo        Smacker video (decoders: smackvid )
D.V.L. smc               QuickTime Graphics (SMC)
DEV.LS snow              Snow
D.VIL. sp5x              Sunplus JPEG (SP5X)
DEVI.S sunrast           Sun Rasterfile image
DEV.L. svq1              Sorenson Vector Quantizer 1 / Sorenson Video 1 / SVQ1
D.V.L. svq3              Sorenson Vector Quantizer 3 / Sorenson Video 3 / SVQ3
DEVI.S targa             Truevision Targa image
```

```
D.VI.. targa_y216        Pinnacle TARGA CineWave YUV16
D.V.L. tgq               Electronic Arts TGQ video (decoders: eatgq )
D.V.L. tgv               Electronic Arts TGV video (decoders: eatgv )
DEV.L. theora            Theora (encoders: libtheora )
D.VIL. thp               Nintendo Gamecube THP video
D.V.L. tiertexseqvideo   Tiertex Limited SEQ video
DEVI.S tiff              TIFF image
D.VIL. tmv               8088flex TMV
D.V.L. tqi               Electronic Arts TQI video (decoders: eatqi )
D.V.L. truemotion1       Duck TrueMotion 1.0
D.V.L. truemotion2       Duck TrueMotion 2.0
D.V..S tscc              TechSmith Screen Capture Codec (decoders: camtasia )
D.V.L. tscc2             TechSmith Screen Codec 2
D.VIL. txd               Renderware TXD (TeXture Dictionary) image
D.V.L. ulti              IBM UltiMotion (decoders: ultimotion )
DEVI.S utvideo           Ut Video (decoders: utvideo libutvideo) (encoders: utvideo libutvideo)
DEVI.S v210              Uncompressed 4:2:2 10-bit
D.VI.S v210x
DEVI.. v308              Uncompressed packed 4:4:4
DEVI.. v408              Uncompressed packed QT 4:4:4:4
DEVI.S v410              Uncompressed 4:4:4 10-bit
D.V.L. vb                Beam Software VB
D.VI.S vble              VBLE Lossless Codec
D.V.L. vc1               SMPTE VC-1
D.V.L. vc1image          Windows Media Video 9 Image v2
D.VIL. vcr1              ATI VCR1
D.VIL. vixl              Miro VideoXL (decoders: xl )
D.V.L. vmdvideo          Sierra VMD video
D.V..S vmnc              VMware Screen Codec / VMware Video
D.V.L. vp3               On2 VP3
D.V.L. vp5               On2 VP5
D.V.L. vp6               On2 VP6
D.V.L. vp6a              On2 VP6 (Flash version, with alpha channel)
D.V.L. vp6f              On2 VP6 (Flash version)
DEV.L. vp8               On2 VP8 (decoders: vp8 libvpx ) (encoders: libvpx )
DEV.L. wmv1              Windows Media Video 7
DEV.L. wmv2              Windows Media Video 8
D.V.L. wmv3              Windows Media Video 9
D.V.L. wmv3image         Windows Media Video 9 Image
D.VIL. wnv1              Winnov WNV1
D.V.L. ws_vqa            Westwood Studios VQA (Vector Quantiz. Animation) video (decoders:vqavideo)
D.V.L. xan_wc3           Wing Commander III / Xan
D.V.L. xan_wc4           Wing Commander IV / Xxan
D.VI.. xbin              eXtended BINary text
DEVI.S xbm               XBM (X BitMap) image
DEV... xface             X-face image
DEVI.S xwd               XWD (X Window Dump) image
DEVI.. y41p              Uncompressed YUV 4:1:1 12-bit
D.V.L. yop               Psygnosis YOP Video
DEVI.. yuv4              Uncompressed packed 4:2:0
D.V..S zerocodec         ZeroCodec Lossless Video
DEVI.S zlib              LCL (LossLess Codec Library) ZLIB
DEV..S zmbv              Zip Motion Blocks Video
D.A.L. 8svx_exp          8SVX exponential
D.A.L. 8svx_fib          8SVX fibonacci
```

```
..A...  8svx_raw            8SVX raw
DEA.L.  aac                 AAC (Advanced Audio Coding) (encoders: aac libvo_aacenc )
D.A.L.  aac_latm            AAC LATM (Advanced Audio Coding LATM syntax)
DEA.L.  ac3                 ATSC A/52A (AC-3) (encoders: ac3 ac3_fixed )
D.A.L.  adpcm_4xm           ADPCM 4X Movie
DEA.L.  adpcm_adx           SEGA CRI ADX ADPCM
D.A.L.  adpcm_ct            ADPCM Creative Technology
D.A.L.  adpcm_ea            ADPCM Electronic Arts
D.A.L.  adpcm_ea_maxis_xa   ADPCM Electronic Arts Maxis CDROM XA
D.A.L.  adpcm_ea_r1         ADPCM Electronic Arts R1
D.A.L.  adpcm_ea_r2         ADPCM Electronic Arts R2
D.A.L.  adpcm_ea_r3         ADPCM Electronic Arts R3
D.A.L.  adpcm_ea_xas        ADPCM Electronic Arts XAS
DEA.L.  adpcm_g722          G.722 ADPCM (decoders: g722 ) (encoders: g722 )
DEA.L.  adpcm_g726          G.726 ADPCM (decoders: g726 ) (encoders: g726 )
D.A.L.  adpcm_ima_amv       ADPCM IMA AMV
D.A.L.  adpcm_ima_apc       ADPCM IMA CRYO APC
D.A.L.  adpcm_ima_dk3       ADPCM IMA Duck DK3
D.A.L.  adpcm_ima_dk4       ADPCM IMA Duck DK4
D.A.L.  adpcm_ima_ea_eacs   ADPCM IMA Electronic Arts EACS
D.A.L.  adpcm_ima_ea_sead   ADPCM IMA Electronic Arts SEAD
D.A.L.  adpcm_ima_iss       ADPCM IMA Funcom ISS
DEA.L.  adpcm_ima_qt        ADPCM IMA QuickTime
D.A.L.  adpcm_ima_smjpeg    ADPCM IMA Loki SDL MJPEG
DEA.L.  adpcm_ima_wav       ADPCM IMA WAV
D.A.L.  adpcm_ima_ws        ADPCM IMA Westwood
DEA.L.  adpcm_ms            ADPCM Microsoft
D.A.L.  adpcm_sbpro_2       ADPCM Sound Blaster Pro 2-bit
D.A.L.  adpcm_sbpro_3       ADPCM Sound Blaster Pro 2.6-bit
D.A.L.  adpcm_sbpro_4       ADPCM Sound Blaster Pro 4-bit
DEA.L.  adpcm_swf           ADPCM Shockwave Flash
D.A.L.  adpcm_thp           ADPCM Nintendo Gamecube THP
D.A.L.  adpcm_xa            ADPCM CDROM XA
DEA.L.  adpcm_yamaha        ADPCM Yamaha
DEA..S  alac                ALAC (Apple Lossless Audio Codec)
DEA.L.  amr_nb              AMR-NB (Adaptive Multi-Rate NarrowBand) (decoders: amrnb
                            libopencore_amrnb ) (encoders: libopencore_amrnb )
DEA.L.  amr_wb              AMR-WB (Adaptive Multi-Rate WideBand) (decoders: amrwb
                            libopencore_amrwb ) (encoders: libvo_amrwbenc )
D.A..S  ape                 Monkey's Audio
D.A.L.  atrac1              Atrac 1 (Adaptive TRansform Acoustic Coding)
D.A.L.  atrac3              Atrac 3 (Adaptive TRansform Acoustic Coding 3)
..A.L.  atrac3p             Sony ATRAC3+
D.A.L.  binkaudio_dct       Bink Audio (DCT)
D.A.L.  binkaudio_rdft      Bink Audio (RDFT)
D.A.L.  bmv_audio           Discworld II BMV audio
..A.L.  celt                Constrained Energy Lapped Transform (CELT)
DEA.L.  comfortnoise        RFC 3389 Comfort Noise
D.A.L.  cook                Cook / Cooker / Gecko (RealAudio G2)
D.A.L.  dsicinaudio         Delphine Software International CIN audio
DEA.LS  dts                 DCA (DTS Coherent Acoustics) (decoders: dca ) (encoders: dca )
..A.L.  dvaudio
DEA.L.  eac3                ATSC A/52B (AC-3, E-AC-3)
DEA..S  flac                FLAC (Free Lossless Audio Codec)
DEA.L.  g723_1              G.723.1
```

```
D.A.L. g729            G.729
DEA.L. gsm             GSM (decoders: gsm libgsm ) (encoders: libgsm )
DEA.L. gsm_ms          GSM Microsoft variant (decoders:gsm_ms libgsm_ms) (encoders: libgsm_ms)
D.A.L. iac             IAC (Indeo Audio Coder)
..A.L. ilbc            iLBC (Internet Low Bitrate Codec)
D.A.L. imc             IMC (Intel Music Coder)
D.A.L. interplay_dpcm  DPCM Interplay
D.A.L. mace3           MACE (Macintosh Audio Compression/Expansion) 3:1
D.A.L. mace6           MACE (Macintosh Audio Compression/Expansion) 6:1
D.A..S mlp             MLP (Meridian Lossless Packing)
D.A.L. mp1             MP1 (MPEG audio layer 1) (decoders: mp1 mp1float )
DEA.L. mp2             MP2 (MPEG audio layer 2) (decoders: mp2 mp2float )
DEA.L. mp3             MP3 (MPEG audio layer 3) (decoders:mp3 mp3float) (encoders: libmp3lame)
D.A.L. mp3adu          ADU (Application Data Unit) MP3 (MPEG audio layer 3) (decoders:
                       mp3adu mp3adufloat )
D.A.L. mp3on4          MP3onMP4 (decoders: mp3on4 mp3on4float )
D.A..S mp4als          MPEG-4 Audio Lossless Coding (ALS) (decoders: als )
D.A.L. musepack7       Musepack SV7 (decoders: mpc7 )
D.A.L. musepack8       Musepack SV8 (decoders: mpc8 )
DEA.L. nellymoser      Nellymoser Asao
DEA.L. opus            Opus (Opus Interactive Audio Codec) (decoders:libopus) (encoders: libopus)
D.A.L. paf_audio       Amazing Studio Packed Animation File Audio
DEA... pcm_alaw        PCM A-law
D.A..S pcm_bluray      PCM signed 16|20|24-bit big-endian for Blu-ray media
D.A..S pcm_dvd         PCM signed 20|24-bit big-endian
DEA..S pcm_f32be       PCM 32-bit floating point big-endian
DEA..S pcm_f32le       PCM 32-bit floating point little-endian
DEA..S pcm_f64be       PCM 64-bit floating point big-endian
DEA..S pcm_f64le       PCM 64-bit floating point little-endian
D.A..S pcm_lxf         PCM signed 20-bit little-endian planar
DEA... pcm_mulaw       PCM mu-law
DEA..S pcm_s16be       PCM signed 16-bit big-endian
DEA..S pcm_s16le       PCM signed 16-bit little-endian
D.A..S pcm_s16le_planar PCM 16-bit little-endian planar
DEA..S pcm_s24be       PCM signed 24-bit big-endian
DEA..S pcm_s24daud     PCM D-Cinema audio signed 24-bit
DEA..S pcm_s24le       PCM signed 24-bit little-endian
DEA..S pcm_s32be       PCM signed 32-bit big-endian
DEA..S pcm_s32le       PCM signed 32-bit little-endian
DEA..S pcm_s8          PCM signed 8-bit
D.A..S pcm_s8_planar   PCM signed 8-bit planar
DEA..S pcm_u16be       PCM unsigned 16-bit big-endian
DEA..S pcm_u16le       PCM unsigned 16-bit little-endian
DEA..S pcm_u24be       PCM unsigned 24-bit big-endian
DEA..S pcm_u24le       PCM unsigned 24-bit little-endian
DEA..S pcm_u32be       PCM unsigned 32-bit big-endian
DEA..S pcm_u32le       PCM unsigned 32-bit little-endian
DEA..S pcm_u8          PCM unsigned 8-bit
D.A.L. pcm_zork        PCM Zork
D.A.L. qcelp           QCELP / PureVoice
D.A.L. qdm2            QDesign Music Codec 2
..A.L. qdmc            QDesign Music
DEA.L. ra_144          RealAudio 1.0 (14.4K) (decoders: real_144 ) (encoders: real_144 )
D.A.L. ra_288          RealAudio 2.0 (28.8K) (decoders: real_288 )
D.A..S ralf            RealAudio Lossless
```

```
DEA.L. roq_dpcm              DPCM id RoQ
D.A.L. s302m                 SMPTE 302M
D.A..S shorten               Shorten
D.A.L. sipr                  RealAudio SIPR / ACELP.NET
D.A.L. smackaudio            Smacker audio (decoders: smackaud )
D.A.L. sol_dpcm              DPCM Sol
DEA... sonic                 Sonic
.EA... sonicls               Sonic lossless
DEA.L. speex                 Speex (decoders: libspeex ) (encoders: libspeex )
D.A..S tak                   TAK (Tom's lossless Audio Kompressor)
D.A..S truehd                TrueHD
D.A.L. truespeech            DSP Group TrueSpeech
D.A..S tta                   TTA (True Audio)
D.A.L. twinvq                VQF TwinVQ
D.A.L. vima                  LucasArts VIMA audio
D.A.L. vmdaudio              Sierra VMD audio
DEA.L. vorbis                Vorbis (decoders: vorbis libvorbis ) (encoders: vorbis libvorbis )
..A.L. voxware               Voxware RT29 Metasound
D.A... wavesynth             Wave synthesis pseudo-codec
D.A.LS wavpack               WavPack
D.A.L. westwood_snd1         Westwood Audio (SND1) (decoders: ws_snd1 )
D.A..S wmalossless           Windows Media Audio Lossless
D.A.L. wmapro                Windows Media Audio 9 Professional
DEA.L. wmav1                 Windows Media Audio 1
DEA.L. wmav2                 Windows Media Audio 2
D.A.L. wmavoice              Windows Media Audio Voice
D.A.L. xan_dpcm              DPCM Xan
DES... dvb_subtitle          DVB subtitles (decoders: dvbsub ) (encoders: dvbsub )
..S... dvb_teletext          DVB teletext
DES... dvd_subtitle          DVD subtitles (decoders: dvdsub ) (encoders: dvdsub )
..S... eia_608               EIA-608 closed captions
D.S... hdmv_pgs_subtitle     HDMV Presentation Graphic Stream subtitles (decoders: pgssub )
D.S... jacosub               JACOsub subtitle
D.S... microdvd              MicroDVD subtitle
DES... mov_text              MOV text
D.S... realtext              RealText subtitle
D.S... sami                  SAMI subtitle
DES... srt                   SubRip subtitle with embedded timing
DES... ssa                   SSA (SubStation Alpha)/ ASS (Advanced SSA) subtitle (decoders: ass)
                             (encoders: ass )
DES... subrip                SubRip subtitle
D.S... subviewer             SubViewer subtitle
D.S... text                  raw UTF-8 text
D.S... webvtt                WebVTT subtitle
DES... xsub                  XSUB
```

Available decoders

The list of built-in decoders is displayed with the command:

```
ffmpeg -decoders
```

```
Decoders:
 V..... = Video
 A..... = Audio
 S..... = Subtitle
 .F.... = Frame-level multithreading
 ..S... = Slice-level multithreading
 ...X.. = Codec is experimental
 ....B. = Supports draw_horiz_band
 .....D = Supports direct rendering method 1
 ------
 V....D 4xm                   4X Movie
 V....D 8bps                  QuickTime 8BPS video
 V....D aasc                  Autodesk RLE
 V..... amv                   AMV Video
 V....D anm                   Deluxe Paint Animation
 V....D ansi                  ASCII/ANSI art
 V....D asv1                  ASUS V1
 V....D asv2                  ASUS V2
 V....D aura                  Auravision AURA
 V....D aura2                 Auravision Aura 2
 V....D avrn                  Avid AVI Codec
 V....D avrp                  Avid 1:1 10-bit RGB Packer
 V....D avs                   AVS (Audio Video Standard) video
 V....D avui                  Avid Meridien Uncompressed
 V....D ayuv                  Uncompressed packed MS 4:4:4:4
 V....D bethsoftvid           Bethesda VID video
 V....D bfi                   Brute Force & Ignorance
 V....D binkvideo             Bink video
 V....D bintext               Binary text
 V....D bmp                   BMP (Windows and OS/2 bitmap)
 V....D bmv_video             Discworld II BMV video
 V....D c93                   Interplay C93
 V....D cavs                  Chinese AVS (Audio Video Standard) (AVS1-P2, JiZhun profile)
 V....D cdgraphics            CD Graphics video
 V....D cdxl                  Commodore CDXL video
 V....D cinepak               Cinepak
 V....D cljr                  Cirrus Logic AccuPak
 V....D cllc                  Canopus Lossless Codec
 V....D eacmv                 Electronic Arts CMV video (codec cmv)
 V....D cpia                  CPiA video format
 V....D camstudio             CamStudio (codec cscd)
 V....D cyuv                  Creative YUV (CYUV)
 V....D dfa                   Chronomaster DFA
 V..... dirac                 BBC Dirac VC-2
 V..... libschroedinger       libschroedinger Dirac 2.2 (codec dirac)
 VF...D dnxhd                 VC3/DNxHD
 V....D dpx                   DPX image
 V....D dsicinvideo           Delphine Software International CIN video
 V.S..D dvvideo               DV (Digital Video)
 V....D dxa                   Feeble Files/ScummVM DXA
 V....D dxtory                Dxtory
 V....D escape124             Escape 124
 V....D escape130             Escape 130
 VF...D exr                   OpenEXR image
 V.S..D ffv1                  FFmpeg video codec #1
```

```
VF..BD ffvhuff          Huffyuv FFmpeg variant
V....D flashsv          Flash Screen Video v1
V....D flashsv2         Flash Screen Video v2
V....D flic             Autodesk Animator Flic video
V...BD flv              FLV / Sorenson Spark / Sorenson H.263 (Flash Video) (codec flv1)
VF...D fraps            Fraps
V....D frwu             Forward Uncompressed
V....D gif              GIF (Graphics Interchange Format)
V....D h261             H.261
V...BD h263             H.263 / H.263-1996, H.263+ / H.263-1998 / H.263 version 2
V...BD h263i            Intel H.263
V...BD h263p            H.263 / H.263-1996, H.263+ / H.263-1998 / H.263 version 2
VFS..D h264             H.264 / AVC / MPEG-4 AVC / MPEG-4 part 10
VF..BD huffyuv          Huffyuv / HuffYUV
V....D idcinvideo       id Quake II CIN video (codec idcin)
V....D idf              iCEDraw text
V....D iff_byterun1     IFF ByteRun1
V....D iff_ilbm         IFF ILBM
V....D indeo2           Intel Indeo 2
V....D indeo3           Intel Indeo 3
V....D indeo4           Intel Indeo Video Interactive 4
V....D indeo5           Intel Indeo Video Interactive 5
V....D interplayvideo   Interplay MVE video
V..X.. j2k              JPEG 2000 (codec jpeg2000)
VF...D libopenjpeg      OpenJPEG JPEG 2000 (codec jpeg2000)
V....D jpegls           JPEG-LS
V....D jv               Bitmap Brothers JV video
V....D kgv1             Kega Game Video
V....D kmvc             Karl Morton's video codec
VF...D lagarith         Lagarith lossless
V....D loco             LOCO
V....D eamad            Electronic Arts Madcow Video (codec mad)
VF...D mdec             Sony PlayStation MDEC (Motion DECoder)
VF...D mimic            Mimic
V....D mjpeg            MJPEG (Motion JPEG)
V....D mjpegb           Apple MJPEG-B
V....D mmvideo          American Laser Games MM Video
V....D motionpixels     Motion Pixels video
V.S.BD mpeg1video       MPEG-1 video
V.S.BD mpeg2video       MPEG-2 video
V.S.BD mpegvideo        MPEG-1 video (codec mpeg2video)
VF..BD mpeg4            MPEG-4 part 2
V....D msa1             MS ATC Screen
V...BD msmpeg4v1        MPEG-4 part 2 Microsoft variant version 1
V...BD msmpeg4v2        MPEG-4 part 2 Microsoft variant version 2
V...BD msmpeg4          MPEG-4 part 2 Microsoft variant version 3 (codec msmpeg4v3)
V....D msrle            Microsoft RLE
V....D mss1             MS Screen 1
V....D mss2             MS Windows Media Video V9 Screen
V....D msvideo1         Microsoft Video 1
V....D mszh             LCL (LossLess Codec Library) MSZH
V....D mts2             MS Expression Encoder Screen
V....D mxpeg            Mobotix MxPEG video
V....D nuv              NuppelVideo/RTJPEG
V....D paf_video        Amazing Studio Packed Animation File Video
```

```
V....D pam              PAM (Portable AnyMap) image
V....D pbm              PBM (Portable BitMap) image
V....D pcx              PC Paintbrush PCX image
V....D pgm              PGM (Portable GrayMap) image
V....D pgmyuv           PGMYUV (Portable GrayMap YUV) image
V....D pictor           Pictor/PC Paint
V....D png              PNG (Portable Network Graphics) image
V....D ppm              PPM (Portable PixelMap) image
V.S..D prores           ProRes
V.S..D prores_lgpl      Apple ProRes (iCodec Pro) (codec prores)
V....D ptx              V.Flash PTX image
V....D qdraw            Apple QuickDraw
V....D qpeg             Q-team QPEG
V....D qtrle            QuickTime Animation (RLE) video
V....D r10k             AJA Kona 10-bit RGB Codec
V....D r210             Uncompressed RGB 10-bit
V..... rawvideo         raw video
V....D rl2              RL2 video
V....D roqvideo         id RoQ video (codec roq)
V....D rpza             QuickTime video (RPZA)
V....D rv10             RealVideo 1.0
V....D rv20             RealVideo 2.0
VF...D rv30             RealVideo 3.0
VF...D rv40             RealVideo 4.0
V....D sanm             LucasArts SMUSH video
V....D sgi              SGI image
V....D smackvid         Smacker video (codec smackvideo)
V....D smc              QuickTime Graphics (SMC)
V....D snow             Snow
V....D sp5x             Sunplus JPEG (SP5X)
V....D sunrast          Sun Rasterfile image
V....D svq1             Sorenson Vector Quantizer 1 / Sorenson Video 1 / SVQ1
V...BD svq3             Sorenson Vector Quantizer 3 / Sorenson Video 3 / SVQ3
V....D targa            Truevision Targa image
V....D targa_y216       Pinnacle TARGA CineWave YUV16
V....D eatgq            Electronic Arts TGQ video (codec tgq)
V..... eatgv            Electronic Arts TGV video (codec tgv)
VF..BD theora           Theora
V....D thp              Nintendo Gamecube THP video
V....D tiertexseqvideo  Tiertex Limited SEQ video
V....D tiff             TIFF image
V....D tmv              8088flex TMV
V....D eatqi            Electronic Arts TQI Video (codec tqi)
V....D truemotion1      Duck TrueMotion 1.0
V....D truemotion2      Duck TrueMotion 2.0
V....D camtasia         TechSmith Screen Capture Codec (codec tscc)
V....D tscc2            TechSmith Screen Codec 2
V....D txd              Renderware TXD (TeXture Dictionary) image
V....D ultimotion       IBM UltiMotion (codec ulti)
VF...D utvideo          Ut Video
V..... libutvideo       Ut Video (codec utvideo)
V....D v210             Uncompressed 4:2:2 10-bit
V....D v210x            Uncompressed 4:2:2 10-bit
V....D v308             Uncompressed packed 4:4:4
V....D v408             Uncompressed packed QT 4:4:4:4
```

```
V....D v410                Uncompressed 4:4:4 10-bit
V....D vb                  Beam Software VB
V....D vble                VBLE Lossless Codec
V....D vc1                 SMPTE VC-1
V....D vc1image            Windows Media Video 9 Image v2
V....D vcr1                ATI VCR1
V....D xl                  Miro VideoXL (codec vixl)
V....D vmdvideo            Sierra VMD video
V....D vmnc                VMware Screen Codec / VMware Video
VF..BD vp3                 On2 VP3
V....D vp5                 On2 VP5
V....D vp6                 On2 VP6
V.S..D vp6a                On2 VP6 (Flash version, with alpha channel)
V....D vp6f                On2 VP6 (Flash version)
VFS..D vp8                 On2 VP8
V.....  libvpx             libvpx VP8 (codec vp8)
V...BD wmv1                Windows Media Video 7
V...BD wmv2                Windows Media Video 8
V....D wmv3                Windows Media Video 9
V....D wmv3image           Windows Media Video 9 Image
V....D wnv1                Winnov WNV1
V....D vqavideo            Westwood Studios VQA (Vector Quantiz. Animation) video (codec ws_vqa)
V....D xan_wc3             Wing Commander III / Xan
V....D xan_wc4             Wing Commander IV / Xxan
V....D xbin                eXtended BINary text
V....D xbm                 XBM (X BitMap) image
V.....  xface              X-face image
V....D xwd                 XWD (X Window Dump) image
V....D y41p                Uncompressed YUV 4:1:1 12-bit
V.....  yop                Psygnosis YOP Video
V....D yuv4                Uncompressed packed 4:2:0
V....D zerocodec           ZeroCodec Lossless Video
V....D zlib                LCL (LossLess Codec Library) ZLIB
V....D zmbv                Zip Motion Blocks Video
A....D 8svx_exp            8SVX exponential
A....D 8svx_fib            8SVX fibonacci
A....D aac                 AAC (Advanced Audio Coding)
A....D aac_latm            AAC LATM (Advanced Audio Coding LATM syntax)
A....D ac3                 ATSC A/52A (AC-3)
A....D adpcm_4xm           ADPCM 4X Movie
A....D adpcm_adx           SEGA CRI ADX ADPCM
A....D adpcm_ct            ADPCM Creative Technology
A....D adpcm_ea            ADPCM Electronic Arts
A....D adpcm_ea_maxis_xa   ADPCM Electronic Arts Maxis CDROM XA
A....D adpcm_ea_r1         ADPCM Electronic Arts R1
A....D adpcm_ea_r2         ADPCM Electronic Arts R2
A....D adpcm_ea_r3         ADPCM Electronic Arts R3
A....D adpcm_ea_xas        ADPCM Electronic Arts XAS
A....D g722                G.722 ADPCM (codec adpcm_g722)
A....D g726                G.726 ADPCM (codec adpcm_g726)
A....D adpcm_ima_amv       ADPCM IMA AMV
A....D adpcm_ima_apc       ADPCM IMA CRYO APC
A....D adpcm_ima_dk3       ADPCM IMA Duck DK3
A....D adpcm_ima_dk4       ADPCM IMA Duck DK4
A....D adpcm_ima_ea_eacs   ADPCM IMA Electronic Arts EACS
```

```
A....D adpcm_ima_ea_sead      ADPCM IMA Electronic Arts SEAD
A....D adpcm_ima_iss          ADPCM IMA Funcom ISS
A....D adpcm_ima_qt           ADPCM IMA QuickTime
A....D adpcm_ima_smjpeg       ADPCM IMA Loki SDL MJPEG
A....D adpcm_ima_wav          ADPCM IMA WAV
A....D adpcm_ima_ws           ADPCM IMA Westwood
A....D adpcm_ms               ADPCM Microsoft
A....D adpcm_sbpro_2          ADPCM Sound Blaster Pro 2-bit
A....D adpcm_sbpro_3          ADPCM Sound Blaster Pro 2.6-bit
A....D adpcm_sbpro_4          ADPCM Sound Blaster Pro 4-bit
A....D adpcm_swf              ADPCM Shockwave Flash
A....D adpcm_thp              ADPCM Nintendo Gamecube THP
A....D adpcm_xa               ADPCM CDROM XA
A....D adpcm_yamaha           ADPCM Yamaha
A....D alac                   ALAC (Apple Lossless Audio Codec)
A....D amrnb                  AMR-NB (Adaptive Multi-Rate NarrowBand) (codec amr_nb)
A....D libopencore_amrnb      OpenCORE AMR-NB (Adaptive Multi-Rate Narrow-Band) (codec amr_nb)
A....D amrwb                  AMR-WB (Adaptive Multi-Rate WideBand) (codec amr_wb)
A....D libopencore_amrwb      OpenCORE AMR-WB (Adaptive Multi-Rate Wide-Band) (codec amr_wb)
A....D ape                    Monkey's Audio
A....D atrac1                 Atrac 1 (Adaptive TRansform Acoustic Coding)
A....D atrac3                 Atrac 3 (Adaptive TRansform Acoustic Coding 3)
A....D binkaudio_dct          Bink Audio (DCT)
A....D binkaudio_rdft         Bink Audio (RDFT)
A....D bmv_audio              Discworld II BMV audio
A....D comfortnoise           RFC 3389 comfort noise generator
A....D cook                   Cook / Cooker / Gecko (RealAudio G2)
A....D dsicinaudio            Delphine Software International CIN audio
A....D dca                    DCA (DTS Coherent Acoustics) (codec dts)
A....D eac3                   ATSC A/52B (AC-3, E-AC-3)
A....D flac                   FLAC (Free Lossless Audio Codec)
A....D g723_1                 G.723.1
A....D g729                   G.729
A....D gsm                    GSM
A....D libgsm                 libgsm GSM (codec gsm)
A....D gsm_ms                 GSM Microsoft variant
A....D libgsm_ms              libgsm GSM Microsoft variant (codec gsm_ms)
A....D iac                    IAC (Indeo Audio Coder)
A....D imc                    IMC (Intel Music Coder)
A....D interplay_dpcm         DPCM Interplay
A....D mace3                  MACE (Macintosh Audio Compression/Expansion) 3:1
A....D mace6                  MACE (Macintosh Audio Compression/Expansion) 6:1
A....D mlp                    MLP (Meridian Lossless Packing)
A....D mp1                    MP1 (MPEG audio layer 1)
A....D mp1float               MP1 (MPEG audio layer 1) (codec mp1)
A....D mp2                    MP2 (MPEG audio layer 2)
A....D mp2float               MP2 (MPEG audio layer 2) (codec mp2)
A....D mp3                    MP3 (MPEG audio layer 3)
A....D mp3float               MP3 (MPEG audio layer 3) (codec mp3)
A....D mp3adu                 ADU (Application Data Unit) MP3 (MPEG audio layer 3)
A....D mp3adufloat            ADU (Application Data Unit) MP3 (MPEG audio layer 3) (codec mp3adu)
A....D mp3on4                 MP3onMP4
A....D mp3on4float            MP3onMP4 (codec mp3on4)
A....D als                    MPEG-4 Audio Lossless Coding (ALS) (codec mp4als)
A....D mpc7                   Musepack SV7 (codec musepack7)
```

```
A....D mpc8               Musepack SV8 (codec musepack8)
A....D nellymoser         Nellymoser Asao
A....D libopus            libopus Opus (codec opus)
A....D paf_audio          Amazing Studio Packed Animation File Audio
A....D pcm_alaw           PCM A-law / G.711 A-law
A....D pcm_bluray         PCM signed 16|20|24-bit big-endian for Blu-ray media
A....D pcm_dvd            PCM signed 20|24-bit big-endian
A....D pcm_f32be          PCM 32-bit floating point big-endian
A....D pcm_f32le          PCM 32-bit floating point little-endian
A....D pcm_f64be          PCM 64-bit floating point big-endian
A....D pcm_f64le          PCM 64-bit floating point little-endian
A....D pcm_lxf            PCM signed 20-bit little-endian planar
A....D pcm_mulaw          PCM mu-law / G.711 mu-law
A....D pcm_s16be          PCM signed 16-bit big-endian
A....D pcm_s16le          PCM signed 16-bit little-endian
A....D pcm_s16le_planar   PCM 16-bit little-endian planar
A....D pcm_s24be          PCM signed 24-bit big-endian
A....D pcm_s24daud        PCM D-Cinema audio signed 24-bit
A....D pcm_s24le          PCM signed 24-bit little-endian
A....D pcm_s32be          PCM signed 32-bit big-endian
A....D pcm_s32le          PCM signed 32-bit little-endian
A....D pcm_s8             PCM signed 8-bit
A....D pcm_s8_planar      PCM signed 8-bit planar
A....D pcm_u16be          PCM unsigned 16-bit big-endian
A....D pcm_u16le          PCM unsigned 16-bit little-endian
A....D pcm_u24be          PCM unsigned 24-bit big-endian
A....D pcm_u24le          PCM unsigned 24-bit little-endian
A....D pcm_u32be          PCM unsigned 32-bit big-endian
A....D pcm_u32le          PCM unsigned 32-bit little-endian
A....D pcm_u8             PCM unsigned 8-bit
A....D pcm_zork           PCM Zork
A....D qcelp              QCELP / PureVoice
A....D qdm2               QDesign Music Codec 2
A....D real_144           RealAudio 1.0 (14.4K) (codec ra_144)
A....D real_288           RealAudio 2.0 (28.8K) (codec ra_288)
A....D ralf               RealAudio Lossless
A....D roq_dpcm           DPCM id RoQ
A....D s302m              SMPTE 302M
A....D shorten            Shorten
A....D sipr               RealAudio SIPR / ACELP.NET
A....D smackaud           Smacker audio (codec smackaudio)
A....D sol_dpcm           DPCM Sol
A..X.D sonic              Sonic
A....D libspeex           libspeex Speex (codec speex)
A....D tak                TAK (Tom's lossless Audio Kompressor)
A....D truehd             TrueHD
A....D truespeech         DSP Group TrueSpeech
A....D tta                TTA (True Audio)
A....D twinvq             VQF TwinVQ
A....D vima               LucasArts VIMA audio
A....D vmdaudio           Sierra VMD audio
A....D vorbis             Vorbis
A..... libvorbis          libvorbis (codec vorbis)
A....D wavesynth          Wave synthesis pseudo-codec
A....D wavpack            WavPack
```

```
A....D ws_snd1              Westwood Audio (SND1) (codec westwood_snd1)
A....D wmalossless          Windows Media Audio Lossless
A....D wmapro               Windows Media Audio 9 Professional
A....D wmav1                Windows Media Audio 1
A....D wmav2                Windows Media Audio 2
A....D wmavoice             Windows Media Audio Voice
A....D xan_dpcm             DPCM Xan
S..... dvbsub               DVB subtitles (codec dvb_subtitle)
S..... dvdsub               DVD subtitles (codec dvd_subtitle)
S..... pgssub               HDMV Presentation Graphic Stream subtitles (codec hdmv_pgs_subtitle)
S..... jacosub              JACOsub subtitle
S..... microdvd             MicroDVD subtitle
S..... mov_text             3GPP Timed Text subtitle
S..... realtext             RealText subtitle
S..... sami                 SAMI subtitle
S..... srt                  SubRip subtitle with embedded timing
S..... ass                  SSA (SubStation Alpha) subtitle (codec ssa)
S..... subrip               SubRip subtitle
S..... subviewer            SubViewer subtitle
S..... text                 Raw text subtitle
S..... webvtt               WebVTT subtitle
S..... xsub                 XSUB
```

Available encoders

To display a list of the built-in ffmpeg encoders we can use the command:

ffmpeg -encoders

```
Encoders:
 V..... = Video
 A..... = Audio
 S..... = Subtitle
 .F.... = Frame-level multithreading
 ..S... = Slice-level multithreading
 ...X.. = Codec is experimental
 ....B. = Supports draw_horiz_band
 .....D = Supports direct rendering method 1
 ------
 V..... a64multi            Multicolor charset for Commodore 64 (codec a64_multi)
 V..... a64multi5           Multicolor charset for Commodore 64, extended with 5th color
                            (colram) (codec a64_multi5)
 V..... amv                 AMV Video
 V..... asv1                ASUS V1
 V..... asv2                ASUS V2
 V..... avrp                Avid 1:1 10-bit RGB Packer
 V..X.. avui                Avid Meridien Uncompressed
 V..... ayuv                Uncompressed packed MS 4:4:4:4
 V..... bmp                 BMP (Windows and OS/2 bitmap)
 V..... libxavs             libxavs Chinese AVS (Audio Video Standard) (codec cavs)
 V..... cljr                Cirrus Logic AccuPak
 V..... libschroedinger     libschroedinger Dirac 2.2 (codec dirac)
 V.S... dnxhd               VC3/DNxHD
```

```
V.....  dpx                DPX image
V.S...  dvvideo            DV (Digital Video)
V.S...  ffv1               FFmpeg video codec #1
V.....  ffvhuff            Huffyuv FFmpeg variant
V.....  flashsv            Flash Screen Video
V.....  flashsv2           Flash Screen Video Version 2
V.....  flv                FLV / Sorenson Spark / Sorenson H.263 (Flash Video) (codec flv1)
V.....  gif                GIF (Graphics Interchange Format)
V.....  h261               H.261
V.....  h263               H.263 / H.263-1996
V.S...  h263p              H.263+ / H.263-1998 / H.263 version 2
V.....  libx264            libx264 H.264 / AVC / MPEG-4 AVC / MPEG-4 part 10 (codec h264)
V.....  libx264rgb         libx264 H.264 /AVC / MPEG-4 AVC / MPEG-4 part 10 RGB (codec h264)
V.....  huffyuv            Huffyuv / HuffYUV
V..X..  j2k                JPEG 2000 (codec jpeg2000)
V.....  libopenjpeg        OpenJPEG JPEG 2000 (codec jpeg2000)
V.....  jpegls             JPEG-LS
V.....  ljpeg              Lossless JPEG
VFS...  mjpeg              MJPEG (Motion JPEG)
V.....  mpeg1video         MPEG-1 video
V.S...  mpeg2video         MPEG-2 video
V.S...  mpeg4              MPEG-4 part 2
V.....  libxvid            libxvidcore MPEG-4 part 2 (codec mpeg4)
V.....  msmpeg4v2          MPEG-4 part 2 Microsoft variant version 2
V.....  msmpeg4            MPEG-4 part 2 Microsoft variant version 3 (codec msmpeg4v3)
V.....  msvideo1           Microsoft Video-1
V.....  pam                PAM (Portable AnyMap) image
V.....  pbm                PBM (Portable BitMap) image
V.....  pcx                PC Paintbrush PCX image
V.....  pgm                PGM (Portable GrayMap) image
V.....  pgmyuv             PGMYUV (Portable GrayMap YUV) image
VF....  png                PNG (Portable Network Graphics) image
V.....  ppm                PPM (Portable PixelMap) image
VF....  prores             Apple ProRes
VF....  prores_anatoliy    Apple ProRes (codec prores)
V.S...  prores_kostya      Apple ProRes (iCodec Pro) (codec prores)
V.....  qtrle              QuickTime Animation (RLE) video
V.....  r10k               AJA Kona 10-bit RGB Codec
V.....  r210               Uncompressed RGB 10-bit
V.....  rawvideo           raw video
V.....  roqvideo           id RoQ video (codec roq)
V.....  rv10               RealVideo 1.0
V.....  rv20               RealVideo 2.0
V.....  sgi                SGI image
V.....  snow               Snow
V.....  sunrast            Sun Rasterfile image
V.....  svq1               Sorenson Vector Quantizer 1 / Sorenson Video 1 / SVQ1
V.....  targa              Truevision Targa image
V.....  libtheora          libtheora Theora (codec theora)
V.....  tiff               TIFF image
V.....  utvideo            Ut Video
V.....  libutvideo         Ut Video (codec utvideo)
V.....  v210               Uncompressed 4:2:2 10-bit
V.....  v308               Uncompressed packed 4:4:4
V.....  v408               Uncompressed packed QT 4:4:4:4
```

```
V..... v410             Uncompressed 4:4:4 10-bit
V..... libvpx           libvpx VP8 (codec vp8)
V..... wmv1             Windows Media Video 7
V..... wmv2             Windows Media Video 8
V..... xbm              XBM (X BitMap) image
V..... xface            X-face image
V..... xwd              XWD (X Window Dump) image
V..... y41p             Uncompressed YUV 4:1:1 12-bit
V..... yuv4             Uncompressed packed 4:2:0
V..... zlib             LCL (LossLess Codec Library) ZLIB
V..... zmbv             Zip Motion Blocks Video
A..X.. aac              AAC (Advanced Audio Coding)
A..... libvo_aacenc     Android VisualOn AAC (Advanced Audio Coding) (codec aac)
A..... ac3              ATSC A/52A (AC-3)
A..... ac3_fixed        ATSC A/52A (AC-3) (codec ac3)
A..... adpcm_adx        SEGA CRI ADX ADPCM
A..... g722             G.722 ADPCM (codec adpcm_g722)
A..... g726             G.726 ADPCM (codec adpcm_g726)
A..... adpcm_ima_qt     ADPCM IMA QuickTime
A..... adpcm_ima_wav    ADPCM IMA WAV
A..... adpcm_ms         ADPCM Microsoft
A..... adpcm_swf        ADPCM Shockwave Flash
A..... adpcm_yamaha     ADPCM Yamaha
A..... alac             ALAC (Apple Lossless Audio Codec)
A..... libopencore_amrnb OpenCORE AMR-NB (Adaptive Multi-Rate Narrow-Band) (codec amr_nb)
A..... libvo_amrwbenc   Android VisualOn AMR-WB (Adaptive Multi-Rate WideBand) (codec amr_wb)
A..... comfortnoise     RFC 3389 comfort noise generator
A..X.. dca              DCA (DTS Coherent Acoustics) (codec dts)
A..... eac3             ATSC A/52 E-AC-3
A..... flac             FLAC (Free Lossless Audio Codec)
A..... g723_1           G.723.1
A..... libgsm           libgsm GSM (codec gsm)
A..... libgsm_ms        libgsm GSM Microsoft variant (codec gsm_ms)
A..... mp2              MP2 (MPEG audio layer 2)
A..... libmp3lame       libmp3lame MP3 (MPEG audio layer 3) (codec mp3)
A..... nellymoser       Nellymoser Asao
A..... libopus          libopus Opus (codec opus)
A..... pcm_alaw         PCM A-law / G.711 A-law
A..... pcm_f32be        PCM 32-bit floating point big-endian
A..... pcm_f32le        PCM 32-bit floating point little-endian
A..... pcm_f64be        PCM 64-bit floating point big-endian
A..... pcm_f64le        PCM 64-bit floating point little-endian
A..... pcm_mulaw        PCM mu-law / G.711 mu-law
A..... pcm_s16be        PCM signed 16-bit big-endian
A..... pcm_s16le        PCM signed 16-bit little-endian
A..... pcm_s24be        PCM signed 24-bit big-endian
A..... pcm_s24daud      PCM D-Cinema audio signed 24-bit
A..... pcm_s24le        PCM signed 24-bit little-endian
A..... pcm_s32be        PCM signed 32-bit big-endian
A..... pcm_s32le        PCM signed 32-bit little-endian
A..... pcm_s8           PCM signed 8-bit
A..... pcm_u16be        PCM unsigned 16-bit big-endian
A..... pcm_u16le        PCM unsigned 16-bit little-endian
A..... pcm_u24be        PCM unsigned 24-bit big-endian
A..... pcm_u24le        PCM unsigned 24-bit little-endian
```

```
A..... pcm_u32be        PCM unsigned 32-bit big-endian
A..... pcm_u32le        PCM unsigned 32-bit little-endian
A..... pcm_u8           PCM unsigned 8-bit
A..... real_144         RealAudio 1.0 (14.4K) (codec ra_144)
A..... roq_dpcm         id RoQ DPCM
A..X.. sonic            Sonic
A..X.. sonicls          Sonic lossless
A..... libspeex         libspeex Speex (codec speex)
A..X.. vorbis           Vorbis
A..... libvorbis        libvorbis (codec vorbis)
A..... wmav1            Windows Media Audio 1
A..... wmav2            Windows Media Audio 2
S..... dvbsub           DVB subtitles (codec dvb_subtitle)
S..... dvdsub           DVD subtitles (codec dvd_subtitle)
S..... mov_text         3GPP Timed Text subtitle
S..... srt              SubRip subtitle with embedded timing
S..... ass              SSA (SubStation Alpha) subtitle (codec ssa)
S..... subrip           SubRip subtitle
S..... xsub             DivX subtitles (XSUB)
```

Available filters

To display the list of built-in filters we can use the next command:

ffmpeg -filters

```
Filters:
aconvert       A->A    Convert the input audio to sample_fmt:channel_layout.
afifo          A->A    Buffer input frames and send them when they are requested.
aformat        A->A    Convert the input audio to one of the specified formats.
amerge         |->A    Merge two audio streams into a single multi-channel stream.
amix           |->A    Audio mixing.
anull          A->A    Pass the source unchanged to the output.
aresample      A->A    Resample audio data.
asendcmd       A->A    Send commands to filters.
asetnsamples   A->A    Set the number of samples for each output audio frames.
asetpts        A->A    Set PTS for the output audio frame.
asettb         A->A    Set timebase for the audio output link.
ashowinfo      A->A    Show textual information for each audio frame.
asplit         A->|    Pass on the audio input to N audio outputs.
astreamsync    AA->AA  Copy two streams of audio data in a configurable order.
atempo         A->A    Adjust audio tempo.
channelmap     A->A    Remap audio channels.
channelsplit   A->|    Split audio into per-channel streams
earwax         A->A    Widen the stereo image.
ebur128        A->|    EBU R128 scanner.
join           |->A    Join multiple audio streams into multi-channel output
pan            A->A    Remix channels with coefficients (panning).
silencedetect  A->A    Detect silence.
volume         A->A    Change input volume.
volumedetect   A->A    Detect audio volume.
aevalsrc       |->A    Generate an audio signal generated by an expression.
anullsrc       |->A    Null audio source, return empty audio frames.
```

anullsink	A->|	Do absolutely nothing with the input audio.
alphaextract	V->V	Extract an alpha channel as a grayscale image component.
alphamerge	VV->V	Copy the luma value of the 2nd input to the alpha channel of the 1st input.
ass	V->V	Render subtitles onto input video using the libass library.
bbox	V->V	Compute bounding box for each frame.
blackdetect	V->V	Detect video intervals that are (almost) black.
blackframe	V->V	Detect frames that are (almost) black.
boxblur	V->V	Blur the input.
colormatrix	V->V	Color matrix conversion
copy	V->V	Copy the input video unchanged to the output.
crop	V->V	Crop the input video to width:height:x:y.
cropdetect	V->V	Auto-detect crop size.
decimate	V->V	Remove near-duplicate frames.
delogo	V->V	Remove logo from input video.
deshake	V->V	Stabilize shaky video.
drawbox	V->V	Draw a colored box on the input video.
drawtext	V->V	Draw text on top of video frames using libfreetype library.
edgedetect	V->V	Detect and draw edge.
fade	V->V	Fade in/out input video.
field	V->V	Extract a field from the input video.
fieldorder	V->V	Set the field order.
fifo	V->V	Buffer input images and send them when they are requested.
format	V->V	Convert the input video to one of the specified pixel formats.
fps	V->V	Force constant framerate
framestep	V->V	Select one frame every N frames.
gradfun	V->V	Debands video quickly using gradients.
hflip	V->V	Horizontally flip the input video.
hqdn3d	V->V	Apply a High Quality 3D Denoiser.
hue	V->V	Adjust the hue and saturation of the input video.
idet	V->V	Interlace detect Filter.
lut	V->V	Compute and apply a lookup table to the RGB/YUV input video.
lutrgb	V->V	Compute and apply a lookup table to the RGB input video.
lutyuv	V->V	Compute and apply a lookup table to the YUV input video.
mp	V->V	Apply a libmpcodecs filter to the input video.
negate	V->V	Negate input video.
noformat	V->V	Force libavfilter not to use any of the specified pixel formats for the input to the next filter.
null	V->V	Pass the source unchanged to the output.
overlay	VV->V	Overlay a video source on top of the input.
pad	V->V	Pad input image to width:height[:x:y[:color]] (default x and y: 0, default color: black).
pixdesctest	V->V	Test pixel format definitions.
removelogo	V->V	Remove a TV logo based on a mask image.
scale	V->V	Scale the input video to width:height size and/or convert the image format.
select	V->V	Select frames to pass in output.
sendcmd	V->V	Send commands to filters.
setdar	V->V	Set the frame display aspect ratio.
setfield	V->V	Force field for the output video frame.
setpts	V->V	Set PTS for the output video frame.
setsar	V->V	Set the pixel sample aspect ratio.
settb	V->V	Set timebase for the video output link.
showinfo	V->V	Show textual information for each video frame.
slicify	V->V	Pass the images of input video on to next video filter as multiple slices.
smartblur	V->V	Blur the input video without impacting the outlines.
split	V->|	Pass on the input video to N outputs.

super2xsai	V->V	Scale the input by 2x using the Super2xSaI pixel art algorithm.
swapuv	V->V	Swap U and V components.
thumbnail	V->V	Select the most representative frame in a sequence of consecutive frames
tile	V->V	Tile several successive frames together.
tinterlace	V->V	Perform temporal field interlacing.
transpose	V->V	Transpose input video.
unsharp	V->V	Sharpen or blur the input video.
vflip	V->V	Flip the input video vertically.
yadif	V->V	Deinterlace the input image.
cellauto	|->V	Create pattern generated by an elementary cellular automaton.
color	|->V	Provide an uniformly colored input.
life	|->V	Create life.
mandelbrot	|->V	Render a Mandelbrot fractal.
mptestsrc	|->V	Generate various test pattern.
nullsrc	|->V	Null video source, return unprocessed video frames.
rgbtestsrc	|->V	Generate RGB test pattern.
smptebars	|->V	Generate SMPTE color bars.
testsrc	|->V	Generate test pattern.
nullsink	V->|	Do absolutely nothing with the input video.
concat	|->|	Concatenate audio and video streams.
showspectrum	A->V	Convert input audio to a spectrum video output.
showwaves	A->V	Convert input audio to a video output.
amovie	|->|	Read audio from a movie source.
movie	|->|	Read from a movie source.
ffbuffersink	V->|	Buffer video frames and make them available to the end of the filter graph.
ffabuffersink	A->|	Buffer audio frames and make them available to the end of the filter graph.
buffersink	V->|	Buffer video frames and make them available to the end of the filter graph.
abuffersink	A->|	Buffer audio frames and make them available to the end of the filter graph.
buffer	|->V	Buffer video frames and make them accessible to the filterchain.
abuffer	|->A	Buffer audio frames and make them accessible to the filterchain.
buffersink_old	V->|	Buffer video frames and make them available to the end of the filter graph.
abuffersink_old	A->|	Buffer audio frames and make them available to the end of the filter graph.

Available formats

To display built-in audio and video formats, the next command is used:

ffmpeg -formats

```
File formats:
 D. = Demuxing supported
 .E = Muxing supported
 --
  E 3g2            3GP2 (3GPP2 file format)
  E 3gp            3GP (3GPP file format)
 D  4xm            4X Technologies
  E a64            a64 - video for Commodore 64
 D  aac            raw ADTS AAC (Advanced Audio Coding)
 DE ac3            raw AC-3
 D  act            ACT Voice file format
 D  adf            Artworx Data Format
  E adts           ADTS AAC (Advanced Audio Coding)
 DE adx            CRI ADX
```

```
D   aea              MD STUDIO audio
DE  aiff             Audio IFF
DE  alaw             PCM A-law
DE  amr              3GPP AMR
D   anm              Deluxe Paint Animation
D   apc              CRYO APC
D   ape              Monkey's Audio
DE  asf              ASF (Advanced / Active Streaming Format)
 E  asf_stream       ASF (Advanced / Active Streaming Format)
DE  ass              SSA (SubStation Alpha) subtitle
DE  au               Sun AU
DE  avi              AVI (Audio Video Interleaved)
 E  avm2             SWF (ShockWave Flash) (AVM2)
D   avr              AVR (Audio Visual Resarch)
D   avs              AVISynth
D   bethsoftvid      Bethesda Softworks VID
D   bfi              Brute Force & Ignorance
D   bin              Binary text
D   bink             Bink
DE  bit              G.729 BIT file format
D   bmv              Discworld II BMV
D   c93              Interplay C93
DE  caf              Apple CAF (Core Audio Format)
DE  cavsvideo        raw Chinese AVS (Audio Video Standard) video
D   cdg              CD Graphics
D   cdxl             Commodore CDXL video
 E  crc              CRC testing
DE  daud             D-Cinema audio
D   dfa              Chronomaster DFA
DE  dirac            raw Dirac
DE  dnxhd            raw DNxHD (SMPTE VC-3)
D   dshow            DirectShow capture
D   dsicin           Delphine Software International CIN
DE  dts              raw DTS
D   dtshd            raw DTS-HD
DE  dv               DV (Digital Video)
 E  dvd              MPEG-2 PS (DVD VOB)
D   dxa              DXA
D   ea               Electronic Arts Multimedia
D   ea_cdata         Electronic Arts cdata
DE  eac3             raw E-AC-3
DE  f32be            PCM 32-bit floating-point big-endian
DE  f32le            PCM 32-bit floating-point little-endian
 E  f4v              F4V Adobe Flash Video
DE  f64be            PCM 64-bit floating-point big-endian
DE  f64le            PCM 64-bit floating-point little-endian
DE  ffm              FFM (FFserver live feed)
DE  ffmetadata       FFmpeg metadata in text
D   film_cpk         Sega FILM / CPK
DE  filmstrip        Adobe Filmstrip
DE  flac             raw FLAC
D   flic             FLI/FLC/FLX animation
DE  flv              FLV (Flash Video)
 E  framecrc         framecrc testing
 E  framemd5         Per-frame MD5 testing
```

```
DE g722              raw G.722
DE g723_1            raw G.723.1
D  g729              G.729 raw format demuxer
 E gif               GIF Animation
D  gsm               raw GSM
DE gxf               GXF (General eXchange Format)
DE h261              raw H.261
DE h263              raw H.263
DE h264              raw H.264 video
D  hls,applehttp     Apple HTTP Live Streaming
DE ico               Microsoft Windows ICO
D  idcin             id Cinematic
D  idf               iCE Draw File
D  iff               IFF (Interchange File Format)
DE ilbc              iLBC storage
DE image2            image2 sequence
DE image2pipe        piped image2 sequence
D  ingenient         raw Ingenient MJPEG
D  ipmovie           Interplay MVE
 E ipod              iPod H.264 MP4 (MPEG-4 Part 14)
 E ismv              ISMV/ISMA (Smooth Streaming)
D  iss               Funcom ISS
D  iv8               IndigoVision 8000 video
DE ivf               On2 IVF
DE jacosub           JACOsub subtitle format
D  jv                Bitmap Brothers JV
DE latm              LOAS/LATM
D  lavfi             Libavfilter virtual input device
DE libnut            nut format
D  lmlm4             raw lmlm4
D  loas              LOAS AudioSyncStream
D  lvf               LVF
D  lxf               VR native stream (LXF)
DE m4v               raw MPEG-4 video
 E matroska          Matroska
D  matroska,webm     Matroska / WebM
 E md5               MD5 testing
D  mgsts             Metal Gear Solid: The Twin Snakes
DE microdvd          MicroDVD subtitle format
DE mjpeg             raw MJPEG video
 E mkvtimestamp_v2   extract pts as timecode v2 format, as defined by mkvtoolnix
DE mlp               raw MLP
D  mm                American Laser Games MM
DE mmf               Yamaha SMAF
 E mov               QuickTime / MOV
D  mov,mp4,m4a,3gp,3g2,mj2 QuickTime / MOV
 E mp2               MP2 (MPEG audio layer 2)
DE mp3               MP3 (MPEG audio layer 3)
 E mp4               MP4 (MPEG-4 Part 14)
D  mpc               Musepack
D  mpc8              Musepack SV8
DE mpeg              MPEG-1 Systems / MPEG program stream
 E mpeg1video        raw MPEG-1 video
 E mpeg2video        raw MPEG-2 video
DE mpegts            MPEG-TS (MPEG-2 Transport Stream)
```

```
D  mpegtsraw        raw MPEG-TS (MPEG-2 Transport Stream)
D  mpegvideo        raw MPEG video
 E mpjpeg           MIME multipart JPEG
D  msnwctcp         MSN TCP Webcam stream
D  mtv              MTV
DE mulaw            PCM mu-law
D  mvi              Motion Pixels MVI
DE mxf              MXF (Material eXchange Format)
 E mxf_d10          MXF (Material eXchange Format) D-10 Mapping
D  mxg              MxPEG clip
D  nc               NC camera feed
D  nsv              Nullsoft Streaming Video
 E null             raw null video
DE nut              NUT
D  nuv              NuppelVideo
DE ogg              Ogg
DE oma              Sony OpenMG audio
D  paf              Amazing Studio Packed Animation File
D  pmp              Playstation Portable PMP
 E psp              PSP MP4 (MPEG-4 Part 14)
D  psxstr           Sony Playstation STR
D  pva              TechnoTrend PVA
D  qcp              QCP
D  r3d              REDCODE R3D
DE rawvideo         raw video
 E rcv              VC-1 test bitstream
D  realtext         RealText subtitle format
D  rl2              RL2
DE rm               RealMedia
DE roq              raw id RoQ
D  rpl              RPL / ARMovie
DE rso              Lego Mindstorms RSO
DE rtp              RTP output
DE rtsp             RTSP output
DE s16be            PCM signed 16-bit big-endian
DE s16le            PCM signed 16-bit little-endian
DE s24be            PCM signed 24-bit big-endian
DE s24le            PCM signed 24-bit little-endian
DE s32be            PCM signed 32-bit big-endian
DE s32le            PCM signed 32-bit little-endian
DE s8               PCM signed 8-bit
D  sami             SAMI subtitle format
DE sap              SAP output
D  sbg              SBaGen binaural beats script
 E sdl              SDL output device
D  sdp              SDP
 E segment          segment
D  shn              raw Shorten
D  siff             Beam Software SIFF
DE smjpeg           Loki SDL MJPEG
D  smk              Smacker
 E smoothstreaming  Smooth Streaming Muxer
D  smush            LucasArts Smush
D  sol              Sierra SOL
DE sox              SoX native
```

```
DE spdif            IEC 61937 (used on S/PDIF - IEC958)
DE srt              SubRip subtitle
 E stream_segment,ssegment streaming segment muxer
D  subviewer        SubViewer subtitle format
 E svcd             MPEG-2 PS (SVCD)
DE swf              SWF (ShockWave Flash)
D  tak              raw TAK
D  thp              THP
D  tiertexseq       Tiertex Limited SEQ
D  tmv              8088flex TMV
DE truehd           raw TrueHD
D  tta              TTA (True Audio)
D  tty              Tele-typewriter
D  txd              Renderware TeXture Dictionary
DE u16be            PCM unsigned 16-bit big-endian
DE u16le            PCM unsigned 16-bit little-endian
DE u24be            PCM unsigned 24-bit big-endian
DE u24le            PCM unsigned 24-bit little-endian
DE u32be            PCM unsigned 32-bit big-endian
DE u32le            PCM unsigned 32-bit little-endian
DE u8               PCM unsigned 8-bit
D  vc1              raw VC-1
D  vc1test          VC-1 test bitstream
 E vcd              MPEG-1 Systems / MPEG program stream (VCD)
D  vfwcap           VfW video capture
D  vmd              Sierra VMD
 E vob              MPEG-2 PS (VOB)
DE voc              Creative Voice
D  vqf              Nippon Telegraph and Telephone Corporation (NTT) TwinVQ
D  w64              Sony Wave64
DE wav              WAV / WAVE (Waveform Audio)
D  wc3movie         Wing Commander III movie
 E webm             WebM
D  webvtt           WebVTT subtitle
D  wsaud            Westwood Studios audio
D  wsvqa            Westwood Studios VQA
DE wtv              Windows Television (WTV)
DE wv               WavPack
D  xa               Maxis XA
D  xbin             eXtended BINary text (XBIN)
D  xmv              Microsoft XMV
D  xwma             Microsoft xWMA
D  yop              Psygnosis YOP
DE yuv4mpegpipe     YUV4MPEG pipe
```

Available layouts of audio channels

To display a list of available audio channel layouts we can use the command:

ffmpeg -layouts

```
Individual channels:
```

```
NAME            DESCRIPTION
FL              front left
FR              front right
FC              front center
LFE             low frequency
BL              back left
BR              back right
FLC             front left-of-center
FRC             front right-of-center
BC              back center
SL              side left
SR              side right
TC              top center
TFL             top front left
TFC             top front center
TFR             top front right
TBL             top back left
TBC             top back center
TBR             top back right
DL              downmix left
DR              downmix right
WL              wide left
WR              wide right
SDL             surround direct left
SDR             surround direct right
LFE2            low frequency 2

Standard channel layouts:
NAME            DECOMPOSITION
mono            FC
stereo          FL+FR
2.1             FL+FR+LFE
3.0             FL+FR+FC
3.0(back)       FL+FR+BC
4.0             FL+FR+FC+BC
quad            FL+FR+BL+BR
quad(side)      FL+FR+SL+SR
3.1             FL+FR+FC+LFE
5.0             FL+FR+FC+BL+BR
5.0(side)       FL+FR+FC+SL+SR
4.1             FL+FR+FC+LFE+BC
5.1             FL+FR+FC+LFE+BL+BR
5.1(side)       FL+FR+FC+LFE+SL+SR
6.0             FL+FR+FC+BC+SL+SR
6.0(front)      FL+FR+FLC+FRC+SL+SR
hexagonal       FL+FR+FC+BL+BR+BC
6.1             FL+FR+FC+LFE+BC+SL+SR
6.1             FL+FR+FC+LFE+BL+BR+BC
6.1(front)      FL+FR+LFE+FLC+FRC+SL+SR
7.0             FL+FR+FC+BL+BR+SL+SR
7.0(front)      FL+FR+FC+FLC+FRC+SL+SR
7.1             FL+FR+FC+LFE+BL+BR+SL+SR
7.1(wide)       FL+FR+FC+LFE+FLC+FRC+SL+SR
octagonal       FL+FR+FC+BL+BR+BC+SL+SR
downmix         DL+DR
```

FFmpeg license

The information about FFmpeg license can be displayed with uppercase L as the parameter:

```
ffmpeg -L
```

```
ffmpeg is free software; you can redistribute it and/or modify it under the terms of
the GNU General Public License as published by
the Free Software Foundation; either version 3 of the License, or
(at your option) any later version.

ffmpeg is distributed in the hope that it will be useful, but WITHOUT ANY WARRANTY;
without even the implied warranty of MERCHANTABILITY or FITNESS FOR A PARTICULAR
PURPOSE.  See the GNU General Public License for more details.
You should have received a copy of the GNU General Public License
along with ffmpeg.  If not, see http://www.gnu.org/licenses
```

Available pixel formats

The list of built-in formats of pixels can be displayed by the command:

```
ffmpeg -pix_fmts
```

```
Pixel formats:
I.... = Supported Input  format for conversion
.O... = Supported Output format for conversion
..H.. = Hardware accelerated format
...P. = Paletted format
....B = Bitstream format
FLAGS NAME            NB_COMPONENTS BITS_PER_PIXEL
-----
IO... yuv420p              3            12
IO... yuyv422              3            16
IO... rgb24                3            24
IO... bgr24                3            24
IO... yuv422p              3            16
IO... yuv444p              3            24
IO... yuv410p              3             9
IO... yuv411p              3            12
IO... gray                 1             8
IO..B monow                1             1
IO..B monob                1             1
I..P. pal8                 1             8
IO... yuvj420p             3            12
IO... yuvj422p             3            16
IO... yuvj444p             3            24
..H.. xvmcmc               0             0
..H.. xvmcidct             0             0
IO... uyvy422              3            16
..... uyyvyy411            3            12
```

```
IO... bgr8            3         8
.O..B bgr4            3         4
IO... bgr4_byte       3         4
IO... rgb8            3         8
.O..B rgb4            3         4
IO... rgb4_byte       3         4
IO... nv12            3        12
IO... nv21            3        12
IO... argb            4        32
IO... rgba            4        32
IO... abgr            4        32
IO... bgra            4        32
IO... gray16be        1        16
IO... gray16le        1        16
IO... yuv440p         3        16
IO... yuvj440p        3        16
IO... yuva420p        4        20
..H.. vdpau_h264      0         0
..H.. vdpau_mpeg1     0         0
..H.. vdpau_mpeg2     0         0
..H.. vdpau_wmv3      0         0
..H.. vdpau_vc1       0         0
IO... rgb48be         3        48
IO... rgb48le         3        48
IO... rgb565be        3        16
IO... rgb565le        3        16
IO... rgb555be        3        15
IO... rgb555le        3        15
IO... bgr565be        3        16
IO... bgr565le        3        16
IO... bgr555be        3        15
IO... bgr555le        3        15
..H.. vaapi_moco      0         0
..H.. vaapi_idct      0         0
..H.. vaapi_vld       0         0
IO... yuv420p16le     3        24
IO... yuv420p16be     3        24
IO... yuv422p16le     3        32
IO... yuv422p16be     3        32
IO... yuv444p16le     3        48
IO... yuv444p16be     3        48
..H.. vdpau_mpeg4     0         0
..H.. dxva2_vld       0         0
IO... rgb444le        3        12
IO... rgb444be        3        12
IO... bgr444le        3        12
IO... bgr444be        3        12
I.... gray8a          2        16
IO... bgr48be         3        48
IO... bgr48le         3        48
IO... yuv420p9be      3        13
IO... yuv420p9le      3        13
IO... yuv420p10be     3        15
IO... yuv420p10le     3        15
IO... yuv422p10be     3        20
```

```
IO... yuv422p10le        3          20
IO... yuv444p9be         3          27
IO... yuv444p9le         3          27
IO... yuv444p10be        3          30
IO... yuv444p10le        3          30
IO... yuv422p9be         3          18
IO... yuv422p9le         3          18
..H.. vda_vld            0           0
I.... gbrp               3          24
I.... gbrp9be            3          27
I.... gbrp9le            3          27
I.... gbrp10be           3          30
I.... gbrp10le           3          30
I.... gbrp16be           3          48
I.... gbrp16le           3          48
IO... yuva420p9be        4          22
IO... yuva420p9le        4          22
IO... yuva422p9be        4          27
IO... yuva422p9le        4          27
IO... yuva444p9be        4          36
IO... yuva444p9le        4          36
IO... yuva420p10be       4          25
IO... yuva420p10le       4          40
IO... yuva422p10be       4          48
IO... yuva422p10le       4          48
IO... yuva444p10be       4          64
IO... yuva444p10le       4          64
IO... yuva420p16be       4          40
IO... yuva420p16le       4          40
IO... yuva422p16be       4          48
IO... yuva422p16le       4          48
IO... yuva444p16be       4          64
IO... yuva444p16le       4          64
I.... rgba64be           4          64
I.... rgba64le           4          64
..... bgra64be           4          64
..... bgra64le           4          64
IO... 0rgb               3          24
IO... rgb0               3          24
IO... 0bgr               3          24
IO... bgr0               3          24
IO... yuva444p           4          32
IO... yuva422p           4          24
IO... yuv420p12be        3          18
IO... yuv420p12le        3          18
IO... yuv420p14be        3          21
IO... yuv420p14le        3          21
IO... yuv422p12be        3          24
IO... yuv422p12le        3          24
IO... yuv422p14be        3          28
IO... yuv422p14le        3          28
IO... yuv444p12be        3          36
IO... yuv444p12le        3          36
IO... yuv444p14be        3          42
IO... yuv444p14le        3          42
```

```
I.... gbrp12be          3            36
I.... gbrp12le          3            36
I.... gbrp14be          3            42
I.... gbrp14le          3            42
```

Available protocols

For displaying available file protocols is the next command:

ffmpeg -protocols

```
Supported file protocols:
Input:
applehttp
cache
concat
crypto
file
gopher
hls
http
httpproxy
mmsh
mmst
pipe
rtp
tcp
udp
rtmp
rtmpe
rtmps
rtmpt
rtmpte
Output:
file
gopher
http
httpproxy
md5
pipe
rtp
tcp
udp
rtmp
rtmpe
rtmps
rtmpt
rtmpte
```

Available audio sample formats

Audio sample formats included in FFmpeg can be displayed with the command:

```
ffmpeg -sample_fmts
```

```
name    depth
u8         8
s16       16
s32       32
flt       32
dbl       64
u8p        8
s16p      16
s32p      32
fltp      32
dblp      64
```

FFmpeg version

Version of ffmpeg can be displayed with **-version** option, the next result is from the official Windows build created on 25th November 2012.

```
ffmpeg -version
```

```
ffmpeg version N-47062-g26c531c
built on Nov 25 2012 12:21:26 with gcc 4.7.2 (GCC)
configuration: --enable-gpl --enable-version3 --disable-pthreads --enable-
runtime-cpudetect --enable-avisynth --enable-bzlib --enable-frei0r --enable-
libass --enable-libopencore-amrnb --enable-libopencore-amrwb --enable-
libfreetype --enable-libgsm --enable-libmp3lame --enable-libnut --enable-
libopenjpeg --enable-libopus --enable-librtmp --enable-libschroedinger
--enable-libspeex --enable-libtheora --enable-libutvideo --enable-libvo-aacenc
--enable-libvo-amrwbenc --enable-libvorbis --enable-libvpx --enable-libx264
--enable-libxavs --enable-libxvid --enable-zlib
libavutil      52.  9.100 / 52.  9.100
libavcodec     54. 77.100 / 54. 77.100
libavformat    54. 37.100 / 54. 37.100
libavdevice    54.  3.100 / 54.  3.100
libavfilter     3. 23.102 /  3. 23.102
libswscale      2.  1.102 /  2.  1.102
libswresample   0. 17.101 /  0. 17.101
libpostproc    52.  2.100 / 52.  2.100
```

Please see Glossary for details about ffmpeg configuration.

Using MORE command for output formatting

Because the output of the help, available filters, formats, etc. is long and usually does not fit to one screen, the **more** command can be used to display the output text formatted sequentially one screen from the start, the next screen is displayed by pressing the Spacebar, the next line will show after pressing the Enter key and pressing the Q or q will quit the preview. The syntax is

```
ffmpeg -help | more
```

or a shorter form

```
ffmpeg -h|more
```

The **more** command can be used also for displaying text files, the content is again divided to fit one screen, the syntax is:

```
more filename.txt
```

Additional parameters of the **more** command can be displayed by typing:

```
help more
```

Redirecting output to file

Sometimes it is needed to study help, available filters, formats, etc. precisely, so to save this information to the text file, the next command can be used:

```
ffmpeg -help > help.txt
```

This command will create a new file named help.txt in the current directory and will save to it the content of ffmpeg help. If the file with the same name already exists, it will be overwritten. To append output text to existing file without overwriting its content, the greater than signs > should be doubled:

```
ffmpeg -help > data.txt
ffmpeg -filters >> data.txt
```

Now the file data.txt contains ffmpeg help followed by the list of available filters.

3. Bit Rate, Frame Rate and File Size

The bit rate and frame rate are the fundamental characteristics of the video and their proper setting is very important for the overall video quality. If we know the bit rate and duration of all included media streams, we can calculate the final size of the output file. Because a good understanding of the frame rate and bit rate is important in the work with FFmpeg tools, included is a short description for each term.

Frame (frequency) rate introduction

The frame rate is a number of frames per second (FPS or fps) encoded into a video file, the human eye needs at least about 15 fps to see a continuous motion. Frame rate is also called a frame frequency and its unit is the Hertz (Hz), LCD displays have usually 60 Hz frequency.

There are 2 types of frame rates - interlaced (denoted as **i** after FPS number) and progressive (denoted as **p** after FPS number).

Interlaced frame rate is used in the television:
 - NTSC standard uses 60i fps, what means 60 interlaced fields (30 frames) per second
 - PAL and SECAM standards use 50i fps, what means 50 interlaced fields, equals to 25 frames per second

Progressive frame rates of 24p, 25p and 30p are used in the film industry. Newer frame frequency 50p/60p is used in the high-end HDTV products.

Common video frame rates	
FPS **i=interlaced** **p=progressive**	**Description**
24p or 23.976	Standard frame rate for the cinema industry from 1920s, all motion pictures were filmed in this frequency. When the films were adopted to NTSC television broadcast, the frame rate was decreased to 24*1000/1001=23.976 value, but for PAL/SECAM television the frame rate of films was increased to 25 fps.
25p	Standard frame rate for the film and television in countries with 50 Hz electric frequency (PAL and SECAM standard), because 25 progressive video can be easily converted to 50 interlaced television fields.
30p	Common video frame rate, often used on digital cameras and camcorders. It can be adopted to 60 Hz (NTSC) interlaced fields for TV broadcast.
50i	Standard field rate (interlaced frame rate) for the PAL and SECAM television.
60i or 59.94	Standard field rate for NTSC television, after color TV invention, the frame rate was decreased to 60*1000/1001=59.94 value to prevent interference between the chroma subcarrier and the sound carrier.
50p/60p	Common frame rate for HDTV (High Definition TV).
48p	proposed frame rate, currently tested
72p	proposed frame rate, currently tested
120p	progressive format standardized for UHDTV (Ultra High Definition TV), planned to be the single global "double-precision" frame rate for UHDTV (instead of using 100 Hz for PAL standard and 119.88 Hz for NTSC standard)

Frame rate setting
Using -r option
To set the video frame rate we use the **-r** option before the output file, the syntax is:

```
ffmpeg -i input -r fps output
```

For example to change the frame rate of the film.avi file from 25 to 30 fps value, we use the command:

```
ffmpeg -i input.avi -r 30 output.mp4
```

When using a raw input format, the **-r** option can be used also before the input.
Using fps filter
Another way to set a frame rate is to use an **fps** filter, what is useful especially in the filterchains.

Video filter: fps	
Description	Changes video frame rate to the specified value.
Syntax	**fps=fps=number_of_frames**
Description of parameters	
fps	a number or a predefined abbreviation specifying the output frame rate

For example, to change the input frame rate of the clip.mpg file to the value 25, we use the command

```
ffmpeg -i clip.mpg -vf fps=fps=25 clip.webm
```

Predefined values for frame rate
Beside numeric values, both methods for setting the frame rate accept also the next predefined text values:

Predefined abbreviations for the frame rate		
Abbreviation	**Exact value**	**Corresponding FPS**
ntsc-film	24000/1001	23.97
film	24/1	24
pal, qpal, spal	25/1	25
ntsc, qntsc, sntsc	30000/1001	29.97

For example to set the frame rate 29.97 fps, the next 3 commands give the same result:

```
ffmpeg -i input.avi -r 29.97 output.mpg
ffmpeg -i input.avi -r 30000/1001 output.mpg
ffmpeg -i input.avi -r ntsc output.mpg
```

Bit (data) rate introduction

Bit rate (also bitrate or data rate) is a parameter that determines overall audio or video quality. It specifies the number of bits processed per time unit, in FFmpeg the bit rate is expressed in bits per second.

Types of bit rate		
Type	**Abbreviation**	**Description**
Average bit rate	ABR	average number of bits processed per second, this value is used also in encoding with VBR, when needed is certain file size of the output
Constant bit rate	CBR	number of bits processed per second is constant, this is not practical for the storage because parts with a fast motion require more bits than static ones, CBR is used mainly for the multimedia streaming
Variable bit rate	VBR	number of bits processed per second is variable, complex scenes or sounds are encoded with more data and compared to CBR, the files of the same size have a better quality with VBR than CBR (Encoding with VBR needs more time and CPU power than with CBR, but recent media players can decode VBR adequately.)

Setting bit rate

Bit rate determines how many bits are used to store 1 second of encoded streams, it is set with **-b** option, to differentiate audio and video stream it is recommended to use **-b:a** or **-b:v** forms. For example to set an overall 1.5 Mbit per second bit rate, we can use the command:

```
ffmpeg -i film.avi -b 1.5M film.mp4
```

If possible, ffmpeg uses a variable bit rate (VBR) and encode static parts with less bits than the parts with a fast motion. ffmpeg is often used to decrease the bit rate and corresponding file size of the output file utilizing an advanced codec that keeps very good quality, for example:

```
ffmpeg -i input.avi -b:v 1500k output.mp4
```

This command changes the input bitrate to 1500 kilobits per second.

Constant bit rate (CBR) setting

The constant bit rate is used for instance for live video streams like videoconferences, where the transferred data cannot be buffered. To set the constant bit rate for the output, three parameters must have the same value: bitrate (**-b** option), minimal rate (**-minrate**) and maximal rate (**-maxrate**). To **minrate** and **maxrate** options can be added a stream specifier, the **maxrate** option requires a setting of a **-bufsize** option (rate control buffer size in bits). For example to set the CBR of 0.5 Mbit/s, we can use the command:

```
ffmpeg -i in.avi -b 0.5M -minrate 0.5M -maxrate 0.5M -bufsize 1M out.mkv
```

Setting maximum size of output file

To keep the size of the output file under certain value, we use **-fs** option (abbreviation of file size), expected value is in bytes. For example, to specify the maximum output file size of 10 megabytes we can use the command:

```
ffmpeg -i input.avi -fs 10MB output.mp4
```

File size calculation

The final file size of encoded output is the sum of audio and video stream sizes. The equation for video stream size in bytes is (the division by 8 is for the conversion from bits to bytes):

$$video\_size = video\_bitrate * time\_in\_seconds / 8$$

If audio is uncompressed, its size is calculated by the equation:

$$audio\_size = sampling\_rate * bit\_depth * channels * time\_in\_seconds / 8$$

To calculate the file size of a compressed audio stream, we need to know its bitrate and the equation is

$$audio\_size = bitrate * time\_in\_seconds / 8$$

For example to calculate the final size of 10-minutes video clip with the 1500 kbits/s video bit rate and 128 kbits/s audio bitrate, we can use the equations:

```
file_size = video_size + audio_size
file_size = (video_bitrate + audio_bitrate) * time_in_seconds / 8
file_size = (1500 kbit/s + 128 kbits/s) * 600 s
file_size = 1628 kbit/s * 600 s
file_size = 976800 kb = 976800000 b / 8 = 122100000 B / 1024 = 119238.28125 KB
file_size = 119238.28125 KB / 1024 = 116.443634033203125 MB ≈ 116.44 MB
```

- 1 byte (B) = 8 bits (b)
- 1 kilobyte (kB or KB) = 1024 B
- 1 megabyte (MB) = 1024 KB, etc.

The final file size is a little bigger than computed, because included is a muxing overhead and the file metadata.

4. Resizing and Scaling Video

Resizing video in FFmpeg means to change its width and height with an option, while scaling means to change the frame size with a scale filter, which provides advanced features.

Resizing video

The width and height of the output video can be set with **-s** option preceding the output filename. The video resolution is entered in the form **wxh**, where **w** is the width in pixels and **h** is the height in pixels. For example, to resize the input from initial resolution to 320x240 value, we can use the command:

```
ffmpeg -i input_file -s 320x240 output_file
```

Predefined video frame sizes

Instead of entering exact numbers for a video width and height, FFmpeg tools provide predefined video sizes that are listed in the table on the next page. The next 2 commands have the same result:

```
ffmpeg -i input.avi -s 640x480 output.avi
ffmpeg -i input.avi -s vga output.avi
```

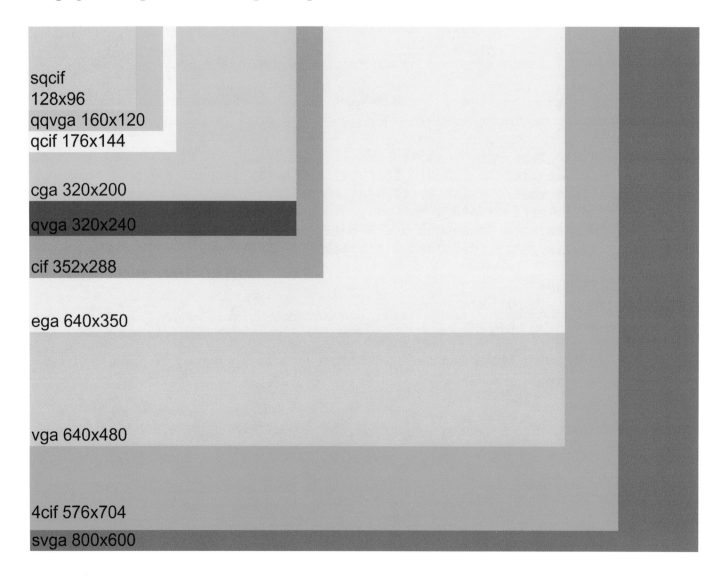

sqcif
128x96
qqvga 160x120
qcif 176x144

cga 320x200

qvga 320x240

cif 352x288

ega 640x350

vga 640x480

4cif 576x704
svga 800x600

Abbreviations for video sizes in FFmpeg		
Frame size	Abbreviation	Typical usage
128x96	sqcif	mobile phones
160x120	qqvga	mobile phones
176x144	qcif	mobile phones
320x200	cga	old CRT displays
320x240	qvga	mobile phones, webcams
352x288	cif	mobile phones
640x350	ega	old CRT displays
640x480	vga	displays, webcams
704x576	4cif	official digital video size for TV
800x600	svga	displays
852x480	hd480, wvga	camcorders
1024x768	xga	displays, cameras
1280x720	hd720	HDTV, camcorders
1280x1024	sxga	displays
1366x768	wxga	displays
1408x1152	16cif	devices using CIF
1600x1024	wsxga	displays
1600x1200	uxga	displays, cameras
1920x1080	hd1080	HDTV, camcorders
1920x1200	wuxga	widescreen displays
2048x1536	qxga	displays
2560x1600	woxga	displays
2560x2048	qsxga	displays
3200x2048	wqsxga	displays
3840x2400	wquxga	displays
5120x4096	hsxga	displays, microscope cameras
6400x4096	whsxga	displays
7680x4800	whuxga	displays

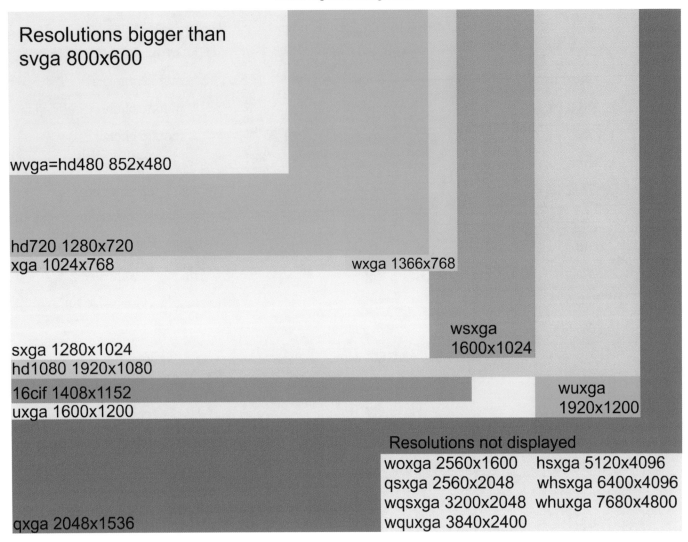

Considerations when resizing - Nyquist sampling theorem

Video is usually resized to a smaller resolution than the source, which is called downsampling, mainly for portable devices, streaming via internet, etc. It is important to consider, that in a smaller size some details will be lost, this fact explains the Nyquist-Shannon sampling theorem. Its general form is related to any signals and informs that for the complete reconstruction of a sampled signal, we must use at least 2 times higher frequency than is the frequency of the source. It means that to keep the small details in a down-scaled video, their original size must be higher than the scaling ratio divided by 2.

For example, video in 800x600 (SVGA) resolution contains a 2 pixels wide detail. When scaled to 640x480 (VGA) resolution, the scaling ratio is 0.8 and 2 pixels are scaled again to 2 pixels:

$$\textbf{640 pixels / 800 pixels = 0.8}$$
$$\textbf{2 pixels * 0.8 = 1.6} \approx \textbf{2 pixels}$$

But when this video is scaled to 160x120 (QQVGA) resolution, the detail is lost:

$$\textbf{160 pixels / 800 pixels = 0.2}$$
$$\textbf{2 pixels * 0.2 = 0.4} \approx \textbf{0 pixels}$$

This means that after downsampling, visible are only details with an input size at least 3 pixels.

Special enlarging filter

Resizing the video to a bigger frame size is relatively rare, because this function provide almost all media players, but the resulting image is sometimes not clear, especially when the source resolution is very small. The special filter for smoothing the upscaled source is a **super2xsai** filter:

Video filter: super2xsai	
Description	Enlarges the source frame size 2 times using a pixel art scaling algorithm without reducing sharpness. "2xSaI" means "2 times scale and interpolate".
Syntax	**-vf super2xsai**

For example to enlarge 128x96 video from a mobile phone to the resolution 256x192 pixels, the next command can be used:

```
ffmpeg -i phone_video.3gp -vf super2xsai output.mp4
```

Advanced scaling

When **-s** option is used to change the video frame size, a **scale** video filter is inserted at the end of related filtergraph. To manage position, where the scaling process begins, the **scale** filter can be used directly.

Video filter: scale	
Description	The source is scaled by changing the output sample aspect ratio, the display aspect ratio remains the same.
Syntax	**scale=*width*:*height*[:interl={1|-1}]**
Variables in expressions of the width and height parameters	
iw or in_w	input width
ih or in_h	input height
ow or out_w	output width
oh or out_h	output height
a	aspect ratio, same as iw/ih
sar	input sample aspect ratio, same as dar/a
dar	input display aspect ratio, it is the same as a*sar
hsub	horizontal chroma subsample value, for yuv422p pixel format is 2
vsub	vertical chroma subsample value, for yuv422p pixel format is 1
Available values for an optional *interl* parameter	
1	interlaced aware scaling is applied
-1	if the source is flagged as interlaced, applied is interlaced aware scaling

For example, the following 2 commands have the same result:

```
ffmpeg -i input.mpg -s 320x240 output.mp4
ffmpeg -i input.mpg -vf scale=320:240 output.mp4
```

The advantage of the scale filter is that for the frame setting can be used additional parameters described in the table above.

Scaling video proportionately to input

Without knowing the size of the input frame, its resolution can be changed proportionately using the **ih** and **iw** parameters of the **scale** filter, for example to create a half sized video, we can use the next command:

```
ffmpeg -i input.mpg -vf scale=iw/2:ih/2 output.mp4
```

Command for 90% sized video:

```
ffmpeg -i input.mpg -vf scale=iw*0.9:ih*0.9 output.mp4
```

Scaling the input with a golden ratio PHI = 1.61803398874989484820...:

```
ffmpeg -i input.mpg -vf scale=iw/PHI:ih/PHI output.mp4
```

Scaling to predefined width or height

When the output video should have a certain width or certain height and the input video size and aspect ratio is unknown, the second dimension can be specified by an **aspect** parameter, like in following examples. To set the output width to 400 pixels and the height proportionately, we can use the command:

```
ffmpeg -i input.avi -vf scale=400:400/a
```

To change the output height to 300 pixels and the width proportionately, the command can be:

```
ffmpeg -i input.avi -vf scale=300*a:300
```

5. Cropping Video

To crop the video means to select wanted rectangular area from the input to the output without a remainder. Cropping is often used with resizing, padding and other editing.

Cropping basics

Older FFmpeg versions had cropbottom, cropleft, cropright and croptop options, but these are now deprecated and for cropping operations is used the **crop** filter described in the following table.

Video filter: crop	
Description	Crops the frames of input video to the specified width and height from the position indicated by **x** and **y** values; **x** and **y** that are the top-left corner coordinates of the output, where the center of coordination system is a top-left corner of the input video frame. If optional **keep_aspect** parameter is used, the output SAR (sample aspect ratio) will be changed to compensate the new DAR (display aspect ratio).
Syntax	`crop=ow[:oh[:x[:y[:keep_aspect]]]]`
Available variables in expressions for <u>ow</u> and <u>oh</u> parameters	
x, y	computed values for x (number of pixels from top left corner horizontally) and y (number of pixels vertically), they are evaluated for every frame, default value of **x** is (iw - ow)/2, default value of **y** is (ih - oh)/2
in_w, iw	input width
in_h, ih	input height
out_w, ow	output (cropped) width, default value = iw
out_h, oh	output (cropped) height, default value = ih
a	aspect ratio, same as iw/ih
sar	input sample aspect ratio
dar	input display aspect ratio, equal to the expression a*sar
hsub, vsub	horizontal and vertical chroma subsample values, for the pixel format yuv422p the value of hsub is 2 and vsub is 1
n	number of input frame, starting from 0
pos	position in the file of the input frame, NAN if unknown
t	timestamp expressed in seconds, NAN if the input timestamp is unknown

The value of **ow** can be derived from **oh** and vice versa, but cannot be derived from **x** and **y**, because these values are evaluated after **ow** and **oh**. The value of **x** can be derived from the value of **y** and vice versa. For example to crop the left third, middle third and right third of the input frame we can use the commands:

```
ffmpeg -i input -vf crop=iw/3:ih:0:0 output
ffmpeg -i input -vf crop=iw/3:ih:iw/3:0 output
ffmpeg -i input -vf crop=iw/3:ih:iw/3*2:0 output
```

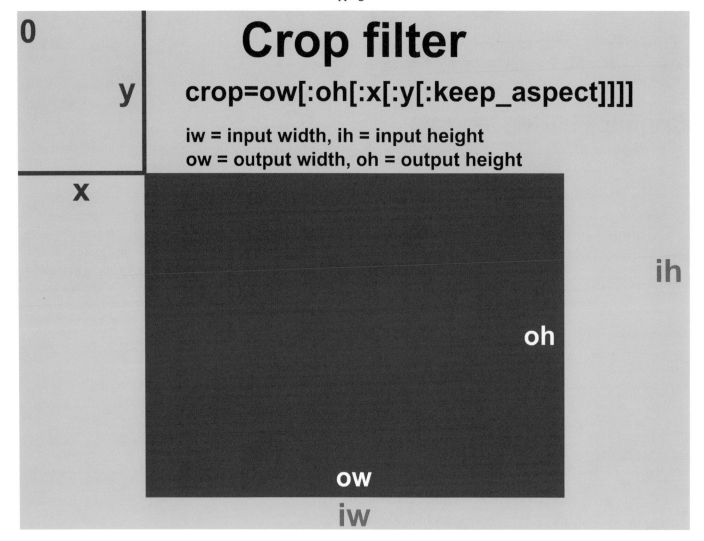

Cropping frame center

The design of the crop filter enables to skip the entering of **x** and **y** parameters when we want to crop the area in the frame center. The default value of x and y is

$$x_{default} = (\text{ input width - output width})/2$$
$$y_{default} = (\text{ input height - output height})/2$$

It means that default values are set to automatically crop the area in the center of the input. The command syntax to crop the rectangular central area of *w* width and *h* height is

```
ffmpeg -i input_file -vf crop=w:h output_file
```

To crop the central half frame, we can use the command:

```
ffmpeg -i input.avi -vf crop=iw/2:ih/2 output.avi
```

Automatic detection of cropping area

To detect a non-black area for the cropping automatically, we can use a **cropdetect** filter, that is described in the following table. This automatic cropping is useful when the input video contains some black bars, usually after the conversion from resolution 4:3 to 16:9 and vice versa.

Video filter: cropdetect	
Description	Detects the crop size for the crop filter, the result is a non-black area of input frame determined by parameters.
Syntax	**cropdetect[=limit[:round[:reset]]]** all parameters are optional
Description of parameters	
limit	threshold, range from 0 (nothing) to 255 (all), default value = 24
round	- even integer, by which the width and height must be divisible - 4:2:2 video needs a value of 2, that gives only even dimensions - offset is changed automatically to center the frames - default value is 16, it is the best for many codecs
reset	Counter that determines after how many frames cropdetect will reset the previously detected largest video area and start over to detect the current optimal crop area. Defaults to 0. This can be useful when channel logos distort the video area. 0 indicates never reset and return the largest area encountered during playback.

The limit parameter specifies how much dark color is selected to the output, the zero value means that only complete black is cropped. For example to crop the non-black output, we can use the command:

```
ffmpeg -i input.mpg -vf cropdetect=limit=0 output.mp4
```

Cropping of timer

Media players usually have a progress bar, that shows the number of elapsed seconds, but most of them displays it only when the mouse pointer is over and hide after a specific duration. FFmpeg contains a **testsrc** video source that contains a timer, we can display it with the command:

```
ffplay -f lavfi -i testsrc
```

The default size of the **testsrc** is 320x240 pixels and the digit 0 of the initial timer has a 29x52 pixels size and its position from the top-left corner is 256 pixels horizontally and 94 pixels vertically. To crop the area of one digit, we can use the command:

```
ffmpeg -f lavfi -i testsrc -vf crop=29:52:256:94 -t 10 timer1.mpg
```

We want to create timers with 1, 2, 3 and 4 digits with this command, the specifications for the crop filter and time durations for each number of digits are in the table:

Number of digits	Crop filter specification	Duration	Picture
1	crop=29:52:256:94	9 seconds 0 min : 9 sec 00:00:09	
2	crop=61:52:224:94	99 seconds 1 min : 39 sec 00:01:39	
3	crop=93:52:192:94	999 seconds 16 min : 39 sec 00:16:39	
4	crop=125:52:160:94	9999 seconds 2 hours : 46 min : 39 sec 02:46:39	

If we want bigger digits than 52 pixels tall, we can specify a bigger size of the **testsrc** output with a **size** parameter (for example: **-i testsrc=size=vga**) and then adjust the crop area accordingly.

To change the color of the digits and the background we can use a **lut** filter that is described in the chapter Color Corrections. Created timers will be used in examples for the video overlay.

6. Padding Video

To pad the video means to add an extra area to the video frame to include additional content. Padding video is often needed, when the input should be played on a display with a different aspect ratio.

Padding basics

For a video padding we use a **pad** filter that is described in the table.

Video filter: pad	
Description	Adds colored padding to the input video frame, which is located to the point [x, y] in the coordination system, where the beginning [0,0] is the top-left corner of the output frame. The size of the output is set by the width and height parameters.
Syntax	`pad=width[:height[:x[:y[:color]]]]` parameters in [] are optional
Description of parameters	
color	RGB color value in hexadecimal form: 0xRRGGBB[@AA], where AA is decimal value from the range (0, 1) or any valid color name like white, blue, yellow etc., the default value is black, please see the *Color names* section in the FFmpeg Fundamentals chapter for details
width, height	width and height of output frame with padding, value of the width can be derived from the height and vice versa, default value of both parameters is 0
x, y	coordinates (offset) of the input top-left corner regarding to the top-left corner of the output frame, default value of both parameters is 0
Available variables in expressions for the parameters height, width, x, y	
a	aspect ratio, same as iw/ih
dar	input display aspect ratio, same as a*sar
hsub, vsub	horizontal and vertical chroma subsample values, for the pixel format yuv422p the value of hsub is 2 and vsub is 1
in_h, ih	input height
in_w, iw	input width
n	number of input frame, starting from 0
out_h, oh	output height, default value = *height*
out_w, ow	output width, default value = *width*
pos	position in the file of the input frame, NAN if unknown
sar	input sample aspect ratio
t	timestamp expressed in seconds, NAN if the input timestamp is unknown
x, y	x and y offsets as specified by *x* and *y* expressions, or NAN if not specified yet

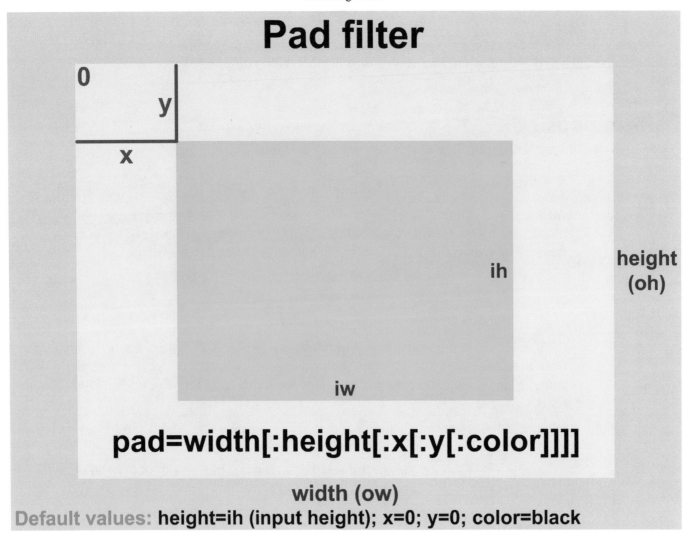

Pad filter

pad=width[:height[:x[:y[:color]]]]

Default values: height=ih (input height); x=0; y=0; color=black

For example, to create a 30-pixel wide pink frame around an SVGA-sized photo, we can use the command:

```
ffmpeg -i photo.jpg -vf pad=860:660:30:30:pink framed_photo.jpg
```

Padding videos from 4:3 to 16:9

Some devices can play videos only in 16:9 aspect ratio and the videos with 4:3 aspect ratio must be padded on both sizes horizontally. In this case the height remains the same and the width equals to the height value multiplied by 16/9. The **x** value (input video frame horizontal offset) is counted from an expression (output_width - input_width)/2, so the syntax for the padding is:

```
ffmpeg -i input -vf pad=ih*16/9:ih:(ow-iw)/2:0:color output
```

For example, without knowing the exact resolution of the film.mpg file with 4:3 aspect ratio, we can add so-called pillarboxes in a default black color with the command:

```
ffmpeg -i film.mpg -vf pad=ih*16/9:ih:(ow-iw)/2:0 film_wide.avi
```

Padding videos from 16:9 to 4:3

To display videos created in 16:9 aspect ratio on the displays with 4:3 aspect ratio, we should pad the input on both sizes vertically. Thus the width remains the same and the height is width * 3/4. The **y** value (input video frame vertical offset) is counted from an expression (output_height - input_height)/2 and the syntax for the padding is:

```
ffmpeg -i input -vf pad=iw:iw*3/4:0:(oh-ih)/2:color output
```

For instance, without knowing the exact resolution of the input file, we can add so-called letterboxes with a default black color to the hd_video.avi file in 16/9 aspect ratio with the command:

```
ffmpeg -i hd_video.avi -vf pad=iw:iw*3/4:0:(oh-ih)/2 video.avi
```

Padding from and to various aspect ratios

Described padding with 4:3 and 16:9 aspect ratio are the most common, but for instance TV ads are created in 14:9 aspect ratio and some films were recorded in a wider ratio than 16/9.

Pillarboxing - adding boxes horizontally

To adjust a smaller width-to-height aspect ratio to the bigger, we need to increase the output width, which value will be the height value multiplied by a new aspect ratio (ar). The generic formula is:

```
ffmpeg -i input -vf pad=ih*ar:ih:(ow-iw)/2:0:color output
```

Letterboxing - adding boxes vertically

To adjust a bigger width-to-height aspect ratio to the smaller, we need to increase the output height, which value will be the width value divided by a new aspect ratio (ar). The generic formula is:

```
ffmpeg -i input -vf pad=iw:iw*ar:0:(oh-ih)/2:color output
```

7. Flipping and Rotating Video

Flipping and rotating of the video frame are common visual operations, that can be used to create various interesting effects like mirrored versions of the input.

Horizontal flip

A horizontally mirrored video version - horizontal flip is created with a **hflip** filter described in the table.

Video filter: hflip	
Description	Horizontally flips the input video, so the output looks like mirrored from the side. The filter has no parameters.
Syntax	**-vf hflip**

To test the horizontal flip on a **testsrc** video source, we can use the command:

```
ffplay -f lavfi -i testsrc -vf hflip
```

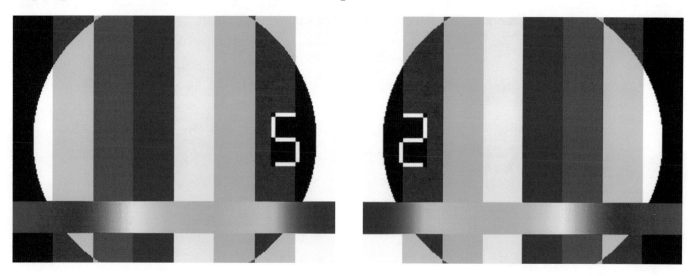

Vertical flip

For flipping the input frames in a vertical direction, we can use a **vflip** filter, described in the table.

Video filter: vflip	
Description	Vertically flips the input video, so the output looks like mirrored from the top or bottom.
Syntax	**-vf vflip**

The image below on the left is an rgbrestsrc pattern described in the 25th chapter. To get its vertical flipped version, we can use the next command:

```
ffplay -f lavfi -i rgbtestsrc -vf vflip
```

Introduction to rotating

Previous FFmpeg versions contained the special filter **rotate**, that enabled video rotating by entering the angle value. This filter is now deprecated and was replaced by a **transpose** filter that enables to rotate and optionally to flip the input at once. The transpose filter is described in the table.

Video filter: transpose	
Description	Transposes the rows with columns of the input and if selected, also flips the result.
Syntax	**transpose={0, 1, 2, 3}** one from the values 0 - 3 is used
Description of available values	
0	input is rotated by 90° counterclockwise and flipped vertically
1	input is rotated by 90° clockwise
2	input is rotated by 90° counterclockwise
3	input is rotated by 90° clockwise and flipped vertically

Please note that the value 0 and 3 of the **transpose** filter provide two operations on the video frames simultaneously - rotating and flipping vertically. This means that usage of the value 0 includes the effect of two filters and the next two commands have the same result:

```
ffplay -f lavfi -i smptebars -vf transpose=0
ffplay -f lavfi -i smptebars -vf transpose=2,vflip
```

Similarly, the value 3 usage can be substituted with two filters like in the next two commands:

```
ffplay -f lavfi -i smptebars -vf transpose=3
ffplay -f lavfi -i smptebars -vf transpose=1,vflip
```

Each value usage of the **transpose** filter with illustrations is described in the following sections.

Rotation by 90 degrees counterclockwise and flip vertically

The next command rotates the input by 90 degrees clockwise with a vertical flip:

```
ffmpeg -i CMYK.avi -vf transpose=0 CMYK_transposed.avi
```

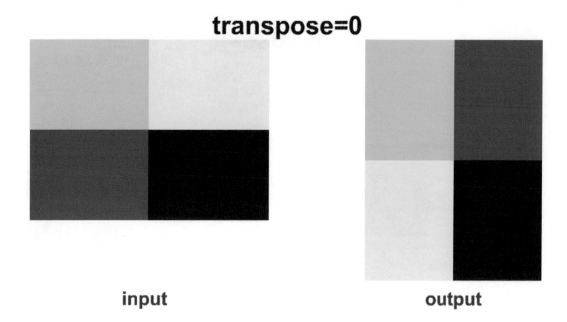

transpose=0

input   output

Rotation by 90 degrees clockwise

The next command rotates the input by 90° clockwise:

```
ffmpeg -i CMYK.avi -vf transpose=1 CMYK_transposed.avi
```

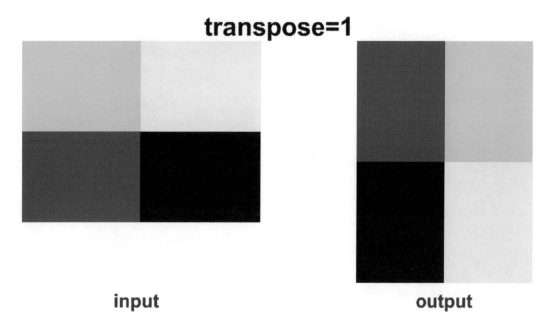

transpose=1

input   output

Rotation by 90 degrees counterclockwise

The next command rotates the input by 90° counterclockwise:

```
ffmpeg -i CMYK.avi -vf transpose=2 CMYK_transposed.avi
```

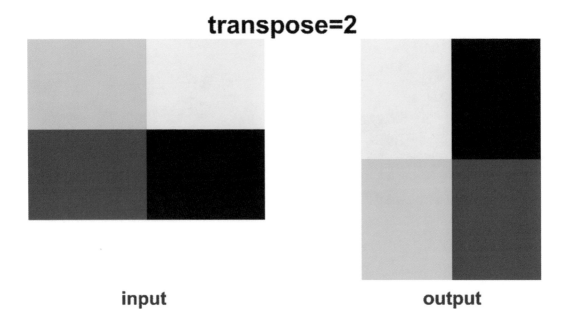

input   **output**

Rotation by 90 degrees clockwise and flip vertically

The next command rotates the input by 90° clockwise and flips it vertically:

```
ffmpeg -i CMYK.avi -vf transpose=3 CMYK_transposed.avi
```

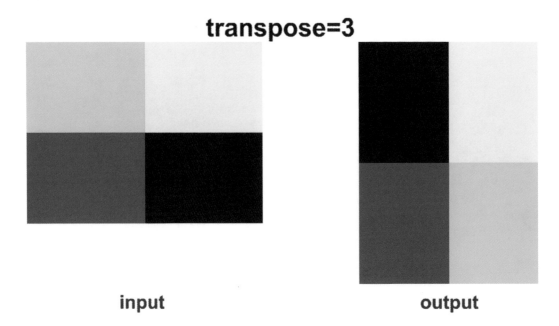

input   **output**

8. Blur, Sharpen and Other Denoising

Video input containing various noise can be enhanced with the denoising filters and options. Denoising is a part of the video preprocessing, before the video is encoded.

Blur video effect

A blur effect is used to increase the quality of certain type of noise in images (video frames), where each output pixel value is calculated from the neighboring pixel values. For instance, the blur effect can improve images scanned from a printed half-tone pictures. To blur an input video we can use a **boxblur** filter described in the table:

Video filter: boxblur	
Description	Creates a blur effect on the input using a boxblur algorithm.
Syntax	**boxblur=luma_r:luma_p[:chroma_r:chroma_p[:alpha_r:alpha_p]]** filter expects 2 or 4 or 6 parameters, r = radius, p = power
Parameters	
alpha_r	- alpha radius of the box used for blurring the related input plane, in pixels - value is an expression with variables described below - default value is derived from luma_radius and luma_power
alpha_p	- alpha power, determines how many times the filter is applied to the related plane - default value is derived from luma_radius and luma_power
chroma_r	- chroma radius of the box used for blurring the related input plane, in pixels - value is an expression with variables described below - default value is derived from luma_radius and luma_power
chroma_p	- chroma power, determines how many times the filter is applied to the related plane - default value is derived from luma_radius and luma_power
luma_r	- luma radius of the box used for blurring the related input plane, in pixels - value is an expression with variables described below
luma_p	- luma power, determines how many times the filter is applied to the related plane
Variables in expressions for alpha, chroma and luma radius	
w,h	input width and height in pixels
cw, ch	width and height in pixels of the input chroma image
hsub	horizontal chroma subsample value, for yuv422p pixel format is 2
vsub	vertical chroma subsample value, for yuv422p pixel format is 1
The radius is a non-negative number, and must not be greater than the value of the expression min(w,h)/2 for luma and alpha planes, and of min(cw,ch)/2 for chroma planes.	

For example to create a blur effect on the input video where luma radius value is 1.5 and luma power value is 1, we can use the next command:

```
ffmpeg -i input.mpg -vf boxblur=1.5:1 output.mp4
```

Another FFmpeg filter with the blur effect is a **smartblur** filter described in the table:

Video filter: smartblur	
Description	Blurs the input without an impact on the outlines.
Syntax	**smartblur=luma_r:luma_s:luma_t[:chroma_r:chroma_s:chroma_t]** parameters in [] are optional, r = radius, p = power, t = threshold
Description of parameters	
chroma_r	chrominance (color) radius, a float number in the range from 0.1 to 5.0 that specifies the variance of the Gaussian filter used to blur the image (slower if larger)
chroma_s	chrominance strength, a float number in the range -1.0 to 1.0 that configures the blurring; a value from 0.0 to 1.0 will blur the image, a value from -1.0 to 0.0 will sharpen the image
chroma_t	chrominance treshold, an integer in the range from -30 to 30 that is used as a coefficient to determine whether a pixel should be blurred or not; a value of 0 will filter all the image, a value from 0 to 30 will filter flat areas and a value from -30 to 0 will filter edges
luma_r	luminance (brightness) radius, a float number in the range from 0.1 to 5.0 that specifies the variance of the Gaussian filter used to blur the image (slower if larger)
luma_s	luminance strength, a float number in the range from -1.0 to 1.0 that configures the blurring; a value from 0.0 to 1.0 will blur the image, a value from -1.0 to 0.0 will sharpen the image
luma_t	luminance treshold, an integer in the range from -30 to 30 that is used as a coefficient to determine whether a pixel should be blurred or not; a value of 0 will filter all the image, a value from 0 to 30 will filter flat areas and a value from -30 to 0 will filter edges
If chroma parameters are not set, luma parameters are used also for the chrominance of the pixels.	

For example, to improve a halftone picture we set the luma radius to maximum value 5, luminance strength to 0.8 and luminance threshold to 0, so the whole image is blurred:

```
ffmpeg -i halftone.jpg -vf smartblur=5:0.8:0 blurred_halftone.png
```

Sharpen video

To sharpen or blur the video frames we can use an **unsharp** filter described in the table.

Video filter: unsharp	
Description	Sharpens or blurs the input video according to the specified parameters.
Syntax	**l_msize_x:l_msize_y:l_amount:c_msize_x:c_msize_y:c_amount** all parameters are optional, if not set, the default is 5:5:1.0:5:5:0.0
Description of parameters	
l_msize_x, luma_msize_x	luma matrix horizontal size, integer between 3 and 13, default value is 5
l_msize_y, luma_msize_y	luma matrix vertical size, integer between 3 and 13, default value is 5
l_amount, luma_amount	luma effect strength, float number between -2.0 and 5.0, negative values create a blur effect, the default value is 1.0
c_msize_x, chroma_msize_x	chroma matrix horizontal size, integer between 3 and 13, default value is 5
c_msize_y, chroma_msize_y	chroma matrix vertical size, integer between 3 and 13, default value is 5
c_amount, chroma_amount	chroma effect strength, float number between -2.0 and 5.0, negative values create a blur effect, the default value is 0.0

The sharpen filter can be used as a common unsharp mask and a Gaussian blur. For example to sharpen the input with default values we can use the command

```
ffmpeg -i input -vf unsharp output.mp4
```

The output will be sharpen with a luma matrix of the size 5x5 and the luma effect strength of 1.0. To create a Gaussian blur effect, we can use a negative number for the luma and/or chroma value, for example

```
ffmpeg -i input -vf unsharp=6:6:-2 output.mp4
```

The next complex image illustrates the usage of the **unsharp** filter with the values:
- image 1: input, the transit of the planet Venus over the Sun on 5th June 2012 recorded by NASA, the video can be downloaded from the NASA website
- image 2: **-vf unsharp** (no parameters, the default values are used)
  Black dots are more evident, no visible artifacts.
- image 3: **-vf unsharp=6:6:3** (relatively strong sharpen effect)
  Black dots evident even more, but visible is a slight distortion.
- image 4: **-vf unsharp=6:6:-2** (relatively strong blur effect)
  Negative value -2 of the luma amount parameter blurs the result and around Venus was created a fictive ring.

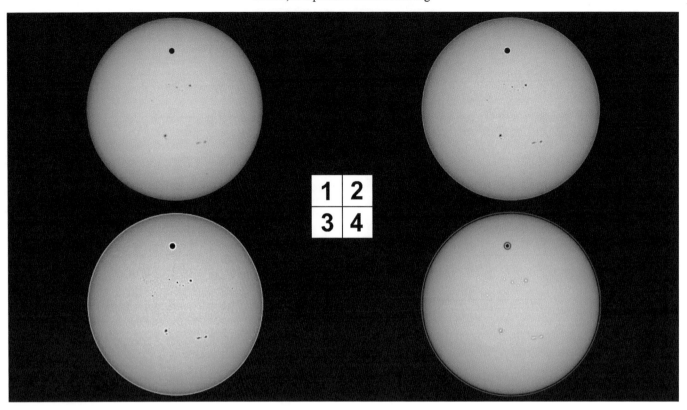

Noise reduction with denoise3d

Video filter **denoise3d** reduces the noise, it is a part of the **mp** filter (from MPlayer project).

Video filter: denoise3d (part of mp filter)	
Description	Produces better quality smooth video frames and also tries to enhance compressibility.
Syntax	`mp=denoise3d[=luma_spatial[:chroma_spatial[:luma_tmp[:chroma_tmp]]]]` (all parameters are optional)
Description of parameters	
luma_spatial	spatial luma strength, a non-negative float number, default value is 4.0
chroma_spatial	spatial chroma strength, a non-negative float number, the default value is 3.0
luma_tmp	temporal luma strength, a non-negative float number, the default value is 6.0
chroma_tmp	temporal chroma strength, a non-negative float number, the default value is luma_tmp*chroma_spatial/luma_spatial

For example to enhance the input with the default values of the denoise3d filter we can use the command

```
ffmpeg -i input.mpg -vf mp=denoise3d output.webm
```

The image illustrates an enhanced archived video from the NASA Apollo project using **denoise3d** filter default values.

Noise reduction with hqdn3d

Advanced version of the denoise3d filter is a **hqdn3d** filter, which is already in the libavfilter library and is a native FFmpeg filter. The name of the filter is an abbreviation of **h**igh **q**uality **den**oise **3-d**imensional filter and it is described in the table:

Video filter: hqdn3d	
Description	Produces high quality smooth video frames and also tries to enhance compressibility, it is an enhanced version of the denoise3d filter.
Syntax	`hqdn3d=[luma_spatial[:chroma_spatial[:luma_tmp[:chroma_tmp]]]]`
Description of parameters	
luma_spatial	spatial luma strength, a non-negative float number, default value is 4.0
chroma_spatial	spatial chroma strength, a non-negative float number, the default value is 3.0*luma_spatial/4.0
luma_tmp	temporal luma strength, a non-negative float number, the default value is 6.0*luma_spatial/4.0
chroma_tmp	temporal chroma strength, a non-negative float number, the default value is luma_tmp*chroma_spatial/luma_spatial

For example, to reduce a noise in the video input with the default hqdn3d values, we can use the command:

```
ffmpeg -i input.avi -vf hqdn3d output.mp4
```

The next image illustrates the usage of hqdn3d filter with various values.

12 FFmpeg hqdn3d filter: 1 is input, 2 is hqdn3d default
34 window 3 uses hqdn3d=6 and window 4 uses hqdn3d=10:8

Noise reduction with nr option

Additional way how to reduce the noise in the video input is a **-nr** (**n**oise **r**eduction) option. Its value is an integer from 0 to 100000, where 0 is the default value and the range 1 - 600 is useful for the common content. If the video contains intensive noise, try to use higher values. Because this option uses much less computer resources than the denoise3d and hqdn3d filters, it is a preferred way of denoising when the speed is important. For example on an older computer we can improve the watching of a slightly noised video with the command:

```
ffplay -i input.avi -nr 500
```

9. Overlay - Picture in Picture

The overlay video technique is used very often, common example are logos of TV channels placed on TV screen, usually in the top-right corner, to identify particular channel. Another example is a Picture-in-picture feature, that enables to display a small window usually in one of the corners of the main screen. Small window contains selected TV channel or other content, while watching the program on the main screen - this is useful when waiting for a certain content, to skip an advertisement, etc.

This chapter contains only simple overlay instances, more complex examples are in the chapters Color Corrections, Advanced Techniques, etc.

Introduction to overlay

Video overlay is a technique that displays a foreground video or image on the (usually bigger) background video or image. We can use an **overlay** video filter that is described in the table:

Video filter: overlay	
Description	Overlays the second input on the first one in a specified location.
Syntax	**overlay[=x:y[[:rgb={0, 1}]]** parameters x and y are optional, their default value is 0 rgb parameter is optional, its value is 0 or 1
Description of parameters	
x	horizontal coordinate from a top-left corner, default value is 0
y	vertical coordinate from a top-left corner, default value is 0
rgb	rgb=0 ... color spaces of inputs do not change, the default value rgb=1 ... color spaces of inputs are set to RGB
Variables, that can be used in expressions for x and y	
main_w or W	main input width
main_h or H	main input height
overlay_w or w	overlay input width
overlay_h or h	overlay input height

Command structure for overlay

The structure of the command for video overlay is below, input1 is the video background and input2 is the foreground:

```
ffmpeg -i input1 -i input2 -filter_complex overlay=x:y output
```

Please note that instead of **-vf** options is used **-filter_complex** option, because now there are 2 input sources (usually video files or images). But using a filtergraph with the link labels, we can utilize a **movie** video source, that will include the second input and used is again only **-vf** option:

```
ffmpeg -i input1 -vf movie=input2[logo];[in][logo]overlay=x:y output
```

Another options is to split one input to the several outputs and using the pad filter to create a background with bigger size. This background is used in the filterchain as the first input for overlay filter, this method was described already in the first chapter, section Filters, filterchains and filtergraphs.

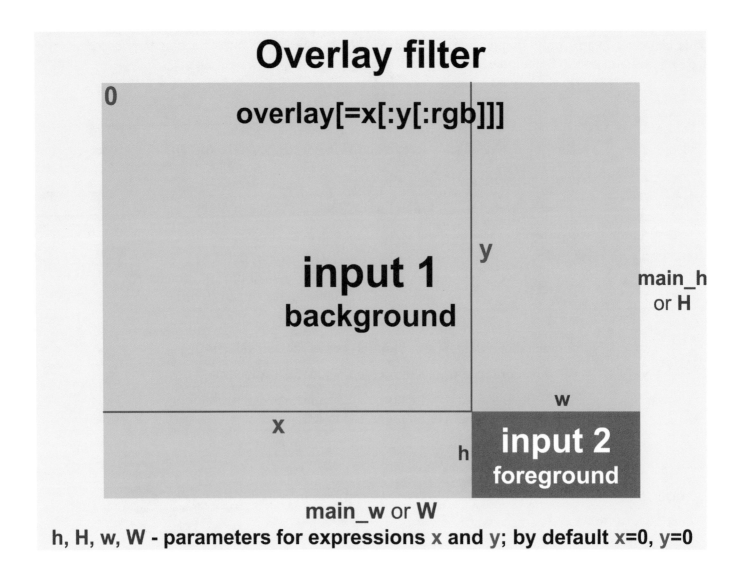

Logo in one of corners

To keep the content visible, logo is often placed in one of four corners on the screen. The next 4 examples use the pair.mp4 video as the first input that contains a wedding pair and the second input is a red heart containing the text M+P (for example, Mary and Peter). The video resolution is 1280x720 pixels and the logo size is 150x140 pixels, but we do not need this sizes to calculate the logo position. The proper location of the logo's top-left corner (x and y coordinate) is derived from the width and height values of the background and foreground:

W, H - width and height of background (video)
w, h - width and height of foreground (logo)

Logo in top-left corner

```
ffmpeg -i pair.mp4 -i logo.png -filter_complex overlay pair1.mp4
```

Logo in top-right corner

```
ffmpeg -i pair.mp4 -i logo.png -filter_complex overlay=W-w pair2.mp4
```

Logo in bottom-right corner

```
ffmpeg -i pair.mp4 -i logo.png -filter_complex overlay=W-w:H-h pair3.mp4
```

Logo in bottom-left corner

```
ffmpeg -i pair.mp4 -i logo.png -filter_complex overlay=0:H-h pair4.mp4
```

Logo shows in specified moment

In some cases, for example when video includes a special introduction, the logo (or other source to overlay) can be added after a time interval with an **-itsoffset** option. For example, to include a red logo on the blue background after 5 seconds from the start, we can use the command:

```
ffmpeg -i video_with_timer.mp4 -itsoffset 5 -i logo.png ^
-filter_complex overlay timer_with_logo.mp4
```

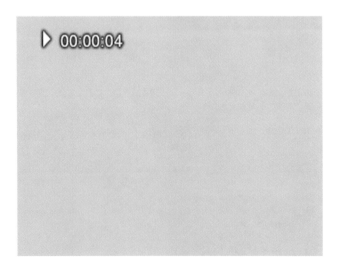
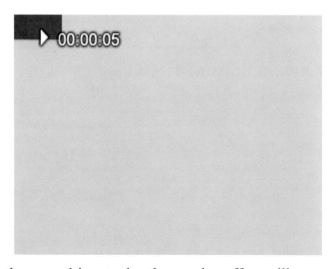

It is important to enter **-itsoffset** option directly before the second input, else the overlay effect will start from the beginning of the output. More examples for **-itsoffset** option are in the chapter Time Operations. Other method to delay the logo is to use the **movie** filter described in the chapter Advanced Techniques.

Video with timer

This example uses a public domain NASA video from 1973, where Apollo 17 starts from the Moon surface to its orbit. Video duration is 29.93 seconds and has 512x384 pixels resolution. We utilize the 2-digit timer like in the chapter Cropping Video using the next command to crop the digits from the **testsrc** source:

```
ffmpeg -f lavfi -i testsrc -vf crop=61:52:224:94 -t 30 timer.ogg
```

Now we have a small video of 61x52 pixels size showing the timer from 0 to 30 seconds. This video will be overlaid on the Apollo 17 Moon Start video in the top-right corner with the command:

```
ffmpeg -i start.mp4 -i timer.ogg -filter_complex overlay=451 start1.mp4
```

The x-coordinate of the timer is 512 - 61 = 451 and the y-coordinate is 0.

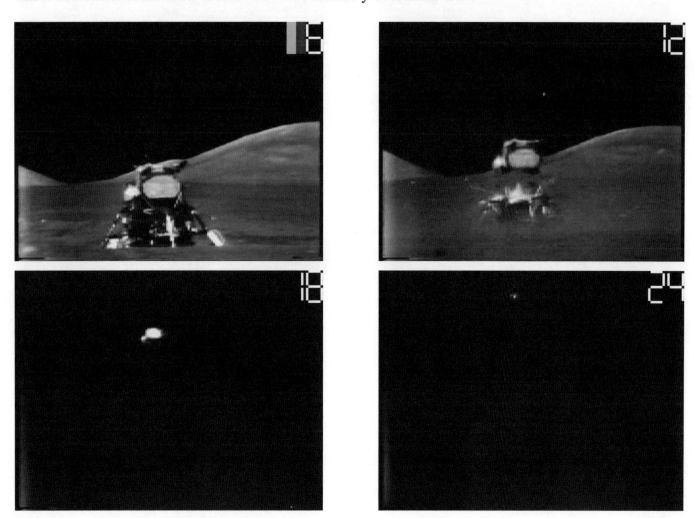

The next command scales the timer to one half and places it bottom-center:

```
ffmpeg -i start.mp4 -vf movie=timer.ogg,scale=15:14[tm];^
[in][tm]overlay=248:371 overlay.mp4
```

Now the timer is almost invisible. We used a named label **[tm]** for the **scale** filter output pad in order to put the resized timer as the second input to the **overlay** filter, the first input was the file start.mp4 denoted by the default **[in]** named label.

Other overlay examples

Overlay technique is used in additional examples:

- chapter FFmpeg Fundamentals, section Filters, filterchains and filtergraphs
- chapter Image Processing, section Flipping, rotating and overlaying images
- chapter Microphone and Webcam, section Using two webcams
- chapter Color Corrections:
- section Comparison in 2 windows
- section Comparison in 3 windows
- section Brightness correction in 2 and 3 windows
- section Comparison in 4 windows
- chapter Advanced Techniques, section Additional media input to filtergraph

10. Adding Text on Video

The textual data included on the video can significantly improve its information quality.

Introduction to adding text on video

Two common methods how to include some text to the video output is to use subtitles or the overlay technique from the previous chapter. The most advanced option with many possibilities is to use a **drawtext** filter described in the table:

Video filter: drawtext	
Description	Adds text on the video from a textfile or string, modified with various parameters. Text is loaded from a file specified by the *textfile* parameter or entered directly with the *text* parameter. Other mandatory parameter is a *fontfile* that specifies selected font. Text position is set by **x** and **y** parameters.
Syntax	**drawtext=fontfile=font_f:text=text1[:p3=v3[:p4=v4[...]]]** p3, p4 ... means parameter #3, parameter #4, etc.
Description of parameters	
box	if box=1, draws a box around the text, color is set by boxcolor parameter, default is 0
boxcolor	color for the box parameter, color name or 0xRRGGBB[AA] format (see the section *Color names* in the Chapter 1 for details), default value is *white*
draw	expression which specifies if the text should be drawn If the expression evaluates to 0, the text is not drawn, default is "1". It is used to specify that the text will be drawn only in specific conditions. Accepted variables and functions are described on the next page and in the chapter Built-in Mathematical Functions.
fix_bounds	if true, text coordinates are fixed to avoid clipping
fontcolor	color for drawing fonts, color name or 0xRRGGBB[AA] format, default is *black*
fontfile	font file to be used for drawing text with proper path, mandatory parameter
fontsize	font size of the text to draw, the default value is 16
ft_load_flags	flags to be used for loading the fonts, default value is "render"; more information is in the documentation for the FT_LOAD_* libfreetype flags
shadowcolor	color for drawing a shadow behind the drawn text, color name or 0xRRGGBB[AA] format possibly followed by an alpha specifier, the default value is *black*
shadowx, shadowy	**x** and **y** offsets for the text shadow position with respect to the position of the text, they can be either positive or negative values, the default value for both is "0"
tabsize	size in number of spaces to use for rendering the tab, the default value is 4
timecode	initial timecode representation in **hh:mm:ss[:;.]ff** format, it can be used with or without text parameter, but the timecode_rate parameter must be specified
timecode_rate, rate, r	timecode frame rate (timecode only)
text	text string to be drawn, it must be a sequence of UTF-8 encoded characters, this parameter is mandatory if the textfile parameter is not specified

Description of parameters (cont. from previous page)	
textfile	text file with the text to be drawn, the text must be a sequence of UTF-8 encoded characters; this parameter is mandatory if the *text* parameter is not used; if both *text* and *textfile* parameters are specified, an error message is displayed
x, y	**x** and **y** values are expressions which specify the offsets where the text will be drawn within the video frame; they are relative to the top-left corner and the default value of x and y is "0"; accepted variables and functions are described below
Accepted variables and functions in expressions for x and y parameters	
dar	input display aspect ratio, it is the same as (w / h) * sar
hsub, vsub	horizontal and vertical chroma subsample values. For example for the pixel format "yuv422p" hsub is 2 and vsub is 1
line_h, lh	height of each text line
main_h, h, H	input height
main_w, w, W	input width
max_glyph_a, ascent	maximum distance from the baseline to the highest/upper grid coordinate used to place a glyph outline point, for all the rendered glyphs; a positive value, due to the grid
max_glyph_d, descent	maximum distance from the baseline to the lowest grid coordinate used to place a glyph outline point, for all the rendered glyphs; a negative value, due to the grid
max_glyph_h	maximum glyph height, that is the maximum height for all the glyphs contained in the rendered text, it is equivalent to ascent - descent.
max_glyph_w	maximum glyph width, that is the maximum width for all the glyphs contained in the rendered text
n	number of input frame, starting from 0
rand(min, max)	returns a random number included between min and max values
sar	input sample aspect ratio
t	timestamp expressed in seconds, NAN if the input timestamp is unknown
text_h or th	height of the rendered text
text_w or tw	width of the rendered text
x, y	x and y coordinates, where the text is drawn, these parameters allow the x and y expressions to refer each other, so you can for example specify y=x/dar

For example, to draw a Welcome message (located in the top-left corner by default) with an Arial font in a black color on a white background, we can use the command (characters are typed on 1 line):

```
ffplay -f lavfi -i color=c=white ^
-vf drawtext=fontfile=/Windows/Fonts/arial.ttf:text=Welcome
```

On Linux the TTF fonts are located in the folder "/usr/share/fonts/TTF". The result is on the picture.

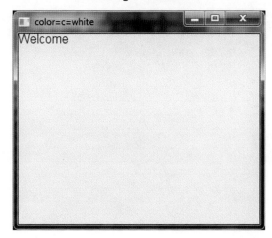

If the path to the font file is difficult to specify, the font file (for example arial.ttf) can be copied to the current directory, so the previous command can be simplified to the form:

```
ffplay -f lavfi -i color=c=white -vf drawtext=fontfile=arial.ttf:text=Welcome
```

To use this example with **ffmpeg**, omit "-f lavfi -i color=c=white" and include an input and output file:

```
ffmpeg -i input -vf drawtext=fontfile=arial.ttf:text=Welcome output
```

To focus on other parameters, the following examples will specify the font file as located in the current directory, you can include the path according to the actual font file location.

Text positioning

The text location is set with **x** and **y** parameters specified to wanted values, which are mathematical expressions that can contain variables and the special rand() function described on the previous page.

Horizontal location setting

The horizontal text placement is managed by setting the **x** coordinate to wanted value, for example to place text 40 pixels from the left we use **x=40**. The expression **x=(w-tw)/2** locates the text to the center, where **tw** is a text width and **w** is a frame width. To align the text to the right, we use the expression **x=w-tw**.

Vertical location setting

The setting of the **y** coordinate determines the horizontal text location, for example to locate the text 50 pixels from the top we use **y=50**. The expression **y=(h-th)/2** positions the text to the center, where **th** is a text height and **h** is a frame height. For alignment to the bottom, we use the expression **x=h-th**.

The next example positions the text in a center of the video frame, please note, that text containing spaces or tabs must be enclosed in quotes and sometimes the ffmpeg engine requires to quote also all **drawtext** parameters, so the next command uses double quotes for all parameters and single quotes for the text parameter (single and double quotes can be exchanged, but cannot be mixed):

```
ffplay -f lavfi -i color=c=white -vf ^
drawtext="fontfile=arial.ttf:text='Good day':x=(w-tw)/2:y=(h-th)/2"
```

Font size and color setting

To make the text more visible and interesting, a colored text with a bigger font than the default 16 pixels is used. With additional parameters **fontcolor** and **fontsize** we can modify the previous example to the centered green text "Happy Holidays" with a 30-pixel font size:

```
ffplay -f lavfi -i color=c=white -vf drawtext=^
"fontfile=arial.ttf:text='Happy Holidays':x=(w-tw)/2:y=(h-th)/2:^
fontcolor=green:fontsize=30"
```

To change a foreground-background colors from green-white to yellow-blue, we replace the white with a blue value and the green with a yellow value, the **fontsize** value is increased to 40:

```
ffplay -f lavfi -i color=c=blue -vf drawtext=^
"fontfile=arial.ttf:text='Happy Holidays':x=(w-tw)/2:y=(h-th)/2:^
fontcolor=yellow:fontsize=40"
```

The color can be specified also in HTML format, for example red=#ff0000, green=#00ff00, etc.

Dynamic text

The **t** (time) variable representing the time in seconds enables to change x and y values according to the current time.

Horizontal text movement

To move the text horizontally across the video frame, we include the **t** variable to the expression for the x parameter, for instance to move provided text every second by **n** pixels in a right-to-left direction, we use an expression **x=w-t*n**. To change the movement to the left-to-right direction, **x=w+t*n** expression is used. For example, to show "Dynamic RTL text" string moving at the top, we use the command

```
ffmpeg -f lavfi -i color=c=#abcdef -vf drawtext=^
"fontfile=arial.ttf:text='Dynamic RTL text':x=w-t*50:^
fontcolor=darkorange:fontsize=30" output
```

More common use is to scroll a line of text near the bottom, where the text is located in a text file that contains only one very long line. The next example uses the textfile parameter with a value **info.txt**:

```
ffmpeg -f lavfi -i color=c=orange -vf drawtext="fontfile=arial.ttf:^
textfile=info.txt:x=w-t*50:y=h-th:fontcolor=blue:fontsize=30" output
```

The content of the info.txt file follows and below it is a picture of scrolling taken at t=5 s.

```
This is a text added to the orange background with a drawtext filter using an
Arial font with a 30 pixels font size.
```

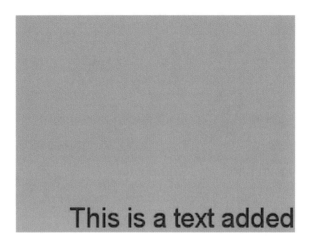

Vertical text movement

Text scrolling vertically from the bottom to the top is often used at the end of the video to show the name of the producer, actors, date, etc. To move the text vertically, the **t** variable is included to the expression for the **y** parameter, for instance to move provided text every second by **n** pixels from top to bottom, we use an expression **y=t*n**. To scroll from bottom to top, **y=h-t*n** expression is used. The next command shows the content of the Credits file moving from bottom up with the speed 100 pixels per second. The content of the Credits file including the spaces at the line beginning is:

```
        Production: FFmpeg User
        Date: December 2012
        Filter: drawtext
```

```
ffmpeg -i palms.avi -vf drawtext="fontfile=arial.ttf:textfile=Credits:^
x=(w-tw)/2:y=h-t*100:fontcolor=white:fontsize=30" clip.mp4
```

11. Conversion Between Formats

The most common usage of ffmpeg tool is related to the conversion from one audio or video format to another. The format parameter is set by **-f** option before the output file or with a raw input also before the input file, available formats are listed in the chapter Displaying Help and Features.

Introduction to media formats

File formats

Media formats are special file types able to store audio or video data. Some of them are able to store more types of data with multiple streams and these are called containers. Available media formats are listed in the second chapter and can be displayed with the command `ffmpeg -formats`.

Video file formats can usually contain both video and audio streams, but there are special formats, that can contain audio only and are described in the chapter Digital Audio.

Media containers

Media containers are a particular type of wrapper files, special file formats for storing multimedia streams and related metadata. Because audio and video can be encoded and decoded by various methods (algorithms), containers provide easy way to store various media streams in one file. Some containers are able to store only audio (AIFF, WAV, XMF...), some only pictures (TIFF...), but most containers store audio, video, subtitles, metadata, etc. All listed video containers support also some subtitle formats, especially SubRip and Advanced SubStation Alpha.

Characteristics of common media containers									
	Support for particular file format								
	Audio					Video			
Container	AAC	AC-3	MP3	PCM	WMA	MPEG1 MPEG2	MPEG4	H.264/ MPEG4 AVC	VC1 WMV	Theora
AVI	Y	Y	Y	Y	Y	Y	Y	partially	Y	Y
Matroska	Y	Y	Y	Y	Y	Y	Y	Y	Y	Y
MP4	Y	Y	Y	N	Y	Y	Y	Y	Y	N
MXF	Y	Y	Y	Y	N	Y	Y	Y	Y	N
Ogg/OGM	N	N	Y	Y	N	Y	Y	Y	Y	Y
QuickTime	Y	Y	Y	Y	Y	Y	Y	Y	Y	Y

If only container changes and the codec remains, we can use **-c copy** or **-c:a copy** or **-c:v copy** options:

```
ffmpeg -i input.avi -q 1 -c copy output.mov
```

Transcoding and conversion

The processing of input files with ffmpeg to the output is called a transcoding and it can include conversion between formats or transcoding only modifies certain data and the output media format remains the same. Data packets can be encoded compressed or uncompressed, the compression includes the use of a specific codec. The transcoding process can be divided to several parts:

- demuxing (demultiplexing) - based on the file extension (.avi, mpg, etc.) is selected the best demux (demultiplexer) from libavformat library that from input file(s) produces encoded data packets
- decoding - data packets are decoded by an appropriate decoder that produces uncompressed frames; if **-c copy** (or **-codec copy**) option is used, no decoding (also no filtering) occurs
- optional filtering - decoded frames can be modified by specified filter(s)
- encoding - uncompressed frames are encoded to the data packets by the selected encoder
- muxing (multiplexing) - data packets are muxed (multiplexed) to the selected media format.

Media formats and codecs in conversion

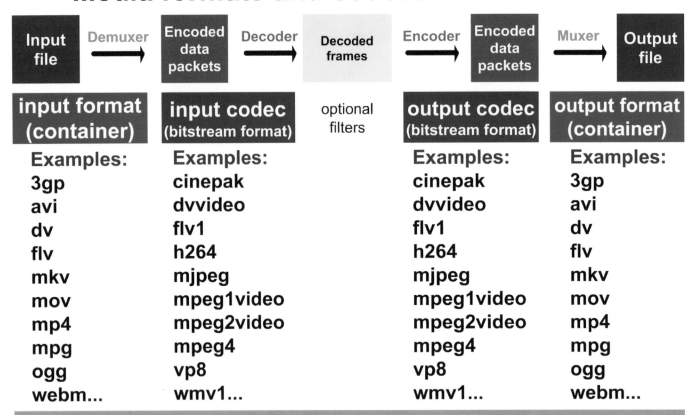

Input file	Demuxer →	Encoded data packets	Decoder →	Decoded frames	Encoder →	Encoded data packets	Muxer →	Output file
input format (container)		**input codec (bitstream format)**		optional filters		**output codec (bitstream format)**		**output format (container)**
Examples:		Examples:				Examples:		Examples:
3gp		cinepak				cinepak		3gp
avi		dvvideo				dvvideo		avi
dv		flv1				flv1		dv
flv		h264				h264		flv
mkv		mjpeg				mjpeg		mkv
mov		mpeg1video				mpeg1video		mov
mp4		mpeg2video				mpeg2video		mp4
mpg		mpeg4				mpeg4		mpg
ogg		vp8				vp8		ogg
webm...		wmv1...				wmv1...		webm...

Demuxer is selected automatically based on the input file extension. If not specified, selected is the default encoder (codec) and the default muxer based on the output file extension.

Available options for the conversion in ffmpeg are divided to generic and private. Generic options can be set for any container, codec or device, private options are specific for selected codec, container or device.

Introduction to codecs

The name codec is derived from words **co**der-**dec**oder (or en**co**der-**dec**oder) and denotes a device or software tool for encoding and decoding a video or audio stream that is compressed with some algorithm. FFmpeg codec definition is a **media bitstream format**. The next commands display available codecs:

- `ffmpeg -codecs` ... displayed are all decoders and encoders
- `ffmpeg -decoders` ... displayed are decoders only
- `ffmpeg -encoders` ... displayed are encoders only

The codec on the command line is specified by **-c** or **-codec** option, the syntax is

```
-codec[:stream_specifier] codec_name
```

Codec can be specified for the input and output files, if the output contains multiple streams, each stream can use a different codec. If we specify the output format without a codec, ffmpeg selects the default one, list of default codecs for the common media formats is in the table:

Default codecs (encoders) for common video file extensions (file formats)		
extension	**codec**	**Additional data**
.avi	mpeg4	mpeg4 (Simple profile), yuv420p; audio: mp3
.flv	flv1	yuv420p; audio: mp3
.mkv	h264	h264 (High), yuvj420p; audio: vorbis codec, fltp sample format
.mov	h264	h264 (High), yuvj420p; audio: aac (mp4a)
.mp4	h264	h264 (High), yuvj420p; audio: aac (mp4a)
.mpg	mpeg1video	yuv420p; audio: mp2
.ogg	theora	yuv422p, bitrate very low; audio excluded during conversion
.ts	mpeg2video	yuv422p; audio: mp2
.webm	vp8	yuv420p; audio: vorbis codec, fltp sample format
Default codecs (encoders) for common audio file extensions (file formats)		
extension	**codec**	**Additional data**
.aac	aac	libvo_aacenc, bitrate 128 kb/s
.flac	flac	FLAC (Free Lossless Audio Codec), bitrate 128 kb/s
.m4a	aac	mp4a, bitrate 128 kb/s
.mp2	mp2	MPEG Audio Layer 2, bitrate 128 kb/s
.mp3	mp3	libmp3lame, bitrate 128 kb/s
.wav	pcm_s16le	PCM (Pulse Code Modulation), uncompressed
.wma	wmav2	Windows Media Audio

Overwriting same named output files

If the file with the specified name in ffmpeg command already exists, the console asks for "y" (yes) or "n" (no) to overwrite the old file. To avoid this question, **-n** option can be used to cancel processing and **-y** option is used to set the overwriting without asking. For example to overwrite the old output file by default we can use the command:

```
ffmpeg -y -i input.avi output.mp4
```

Generic options for conversion

Generic options can be set for any codec, container or device. The most common generic options included in the conversion related to the encoder (codec) specification are described in the table, the **target** column contains 5-letter code that limits the use of particular options. The presence of certain letter means that this option is applicable to encoding (E), decoding (D), video (V), audio (A) or subtitles (S).

Common generic options for trancoding			
option	**type**	**target**	**Description**
-flags	flags	EDVAS	values (details in ffmpeg help): mv4, qpel, loop, gmc, mv0, gray, psnr, naq, ildct, low_delay, global_header, bitexact, aic, cbp, qprd, ilme, cgop
-me_method	int	E..V..	values (please see ffmpeg help for details): zero, full, epzs, esa, tesa, dia, log, phods, x1, hex, umh, iter
-g	int	E..V..	set the group of picture size
-qcomp	float	E..V..	video quantizer scale compression (VBR). Constant of ratecontrol equation. Recommended range for default rc_eq: 0.0-1.0
-qblur	float	E..V..	video quantizer scale blur (VBR)
-qmin	int	E..V..	min video quantizer scale (VBR)
-qmax	int	E..V..	max video quantizer scale (VBR)
-qdiff	int	E..V..	max difference between the quantizer scale (VBR)
-bf	int	E..V..	use 'frames' B frames
-b_qfactor	float	E..V..	qp factor between p and b frames
-rc_strategy	int	E..V..	ratecontrol method
-b_strategy	int	E..V..	strategy to choose between I/P/B-frames
-ps	int	E..V..	rtp payload size in bytes
-lelim	int	E..V..	single coefficient elimination threshold for luminance (negative values also consider dc coefficient)
-celim	int	E..V..	single coefficient elimination threshold for chrominance (negative values also consider dc coefficient)
-strict	int	ED.VA.	how strictly to follow the standards, values (please see ffmpeg help for details): very, strict, normal, unofficial, experimental
-b_qoffset	float	E..V..	qp offset between P and B frames
-err_detect	flags	.D.VA.	set error detection flags, values are (please see ffmpeg help for details): crccheck, bitstream, buffer, explode, careful, compliant, aggressive
-mpeg_quant	int	E..V..	use MPEG quantizers instead of H.263
-qsquish	float	E..V..	how to keep quantizer between qmin - qmax (0=clip, 1=use differentiable function)
-rc_qmod_amp	float	E..V..	experimental quantizer modulation
-rc_qmod_freq	int	E..V..	experimental quantizer modulation

-rc_eq	string	E..V..	Set rate control equation. When computing the expression, besides the standard functions defined in the chapter Mathematical Functions, the following functions are available: bits2qp(bits), qp2bits(qp). Also the following constants are available: iTex pTex tex mv fCode iCount mcVar var isI isP isB avgQP qComp avgIITex avgPITex avgPPTex avgBPTex avgTex.
-i_qfactor	float	E..V..	qp factor between P and I frames
-i_qoffset	float	E..V..	qp offset between P and I frames
-rc_init_cplx	float	E..V..	initial complexity for 1-pass encoding
-dct	int	E..V..	DCT algorithm, values are (please see ffmpeg help for details): auto, fastint, int, mmx, altivec, faan
-lumi_mask	float	E..V..	compresses bright areas stronger than medium ones
-tcplx_mask	float	E..V..	temporal complexity masking
-scplx_mask	float	E..V..	spatial complexity masking
-p_mask	float	E..V..	inter masking
-dark_mask	float	E..V..	compresses dark areas stronger than medium ones
-idct	int	ED.V..	select IDCT implementation, values are (please see ffmpeg help for details): auto, int, simple, simplemmx, libmpeg2mmx, mmi, arm, altivec, sh4, simplearm, simplearmv5te, simplearmv6, simpleneon, simplealpha, h264, vp3, ipp, xvidmmx, faani
-ec	flags	.D.V..	set error concealment strategy, values: guess_mvs (iterative motion vector (MV) search (slow)), deblock (.D.V.. use strong deblock filter for damaged MBs)
-pred	int	E..V..	prediction method, values are (more in ffmpeg help): left, plane, median
-vismv	int	.D.V..	visualize motion vectors (MVs), values are (more in ffmpeg help): pf, bf, bb
-cmp	int	E..V..	full pel me compare function, values (more in ffmpeg help): sad, sse, satd, dct, psnr, bit, rd, zero, vsad, vsse, nsse, w53, w97, dctmax, chroma
-subcmp	int	E..V..	sub pel me compare function, values as in -cmp option (more in ffmpeg help)
-mbcmp	int	E..V..	macroblock compare function, values as in -cmp option (more in ffmpeg help)
-ildctcmp	int	E..V..	interlaced dct compare function, values as in -cmp option (more in ffmpeg help)
-dia_size	int	E..V..	diamond type & size for motion estimation
-last_pred	int	E..V..	amount of motion predictors from the previous frame
-preme	int	E..V..	pre motion estimation
-precmp	int	E..V..	pre motion estimation compare function, values as in -cmp option (more in help)
-pre_dia_size	int	E..V..	diamond type & size for motion estimation pre-pass
-subq	int	E..V..	sub pel motion estimation quality
-me_range	int	E..V..	limit motion vectors range (1023 for DivX player)
-ibias	int	E..V..	intra quant bias
-pbias	int	E..V..	inter quant bias

-coder	int	E..V..	values: vlc (variable length/huffman coder), ac (arithmetic), raw (no encoding), rle (run-length), deflate (deflate-based)
-context	int	E..V..	context model
-mbd	int	E..V..	macroblock decision algorithm (high quality mode), values are (please see ffmpeg help for details): simple, bits, rd
-sc_threshold	int	E..V..	scene change threshold
-lmin	int	E..V..	min lagrange factor (VBR)
-lmax	int	E..V..	max lagrange factor (VBR)
-flags2	flags	ED.VA	values (more in ffmpeg help): fast, sgop, noout, local_header, chunks, showall, skiprd
-threads	int	ED.V..	value auto (detect a good number of threads)
-dc	int	E..V..	intra_dc_precision
-nssew	int	E..V..	nsse weight
-skip_top	int	.D.V..	number of macroblock rows at the top which are skipped
-skip_bottom	int	.D.V..	number of macroblock rows at the bottom which are skipped
-profile	int	E..VA.	values (more in ffmpeg help): unknown, aac_main, aac_low, aac_ssr, aac_ltp, aac_he, aac_he_v2, aac_ld, aac_eld, dts, dts_es, dts_96_24, dts_hd_hra, dts_hd_ma
-level	int	E..VA.	value: unknown
-lowres	int	.D.VA.	decode at 1= 1/2, 2=1/4, 3=1/8 resolutions
-skip_factor	int	E..V..	frame skip factor
-skip_exp	int	E..V..	frame skip exponent
-skipcmp	int	E..V..	frame skip compare function, same values as in -cmp option (more in help)
-border_mask	float	E..V..	increases the quantizer for macroblocks close to borders
-mblmin	int	E..V..	min macroblock lagrange factor (VBR)
-mblmax	int	E..V..	max macroblock lagrange factor (VBR)
-mepc	int	E..V..	motion estimation bitrate penalty compensation (1.0 = 256)
-skip_loop_filter	int	.D.V..	values (more in ffmpeg help): none, default, noref, bidir, nokey, all
-skip_idct	int	.D.V..	the same values as in -skip_loop option (more in ffmpeg help)
-skip_frame	int	.D.V..	the same values as in -skip_loop option (more in ffmpeg help)
-bidir_refine	int	E..V..	refine the two motion vectors used in bidirectional macroblocks
-brd_scale	int	E..V..	downscales frames for dynamic B-frame decision
-keyint_min	int	E..V..	minimum interval between IDR-frames
-refs	int	E..V..	reference frames to consider for motion compensation
-chromaoffset	int	E..V..	chroma qp offset from luma
-trellis	int	E..VA.	rate-distortion optimal quantization

-sc_factor	int	E..V..	multiplied by qscale for each frame and added to scene_change_score
-b_sensitivity	int	E..V..	adjusts sensitivity of b_frame_strategy 1
-colorspace	int	ED.V..	name of color space
-slices	int	E..V..	number of slices, used in parallelized encoding
-thread_type	flags	ED.V..	select multithreading type, values: slice, frame

-rc_init_occupancy	int	E..V..	number of bits to be loaded into the rc buffer before decoding starts
-me_threshold	int	E..V..	motion estimation threshold
-mb_threshold	int	E..V..	macroblock threshold
-skip_threshold	int	E..V..	frame skip threshold
-timecode_frame_start	int64	E..V..	GOP timecode frame start number, in non drop frame format
-request_channels	int	.D..A.	set desired number of audio channels
-channel_layout	int64	ED..A.	available values: ffmpeg -layouts
-audio_service_type	int	E...A.	audio service type, values (more in help): ma, ef, vi, hi, di, co, em, vo, ka
-request_sample_fmt	s_fmt	.D..A.	sample format audio decoders should use (list: `ffmpeg -sample_fmts`)

Examples how to use some options are in the chapter Presets for Codecs. To keep the same quality of the output we use a **-q** or **-qscale**[:stream_specifier] option that sets the fixed quality scale usually from 1 to 31, where the value 1 means the highest quality (some codecs use other scale).

Private options for conversion

While generic options can be set for any codec, container or device, private options are additional options that can be specified only for the selected codec, container or device.

MPEG-1 video encoder

Beside the generic options **mpeg1video** encoder can use the private options described in the table:

option	type	description
-gop_timecode	string	MPEG GOP Timecode in hh:mm:ss[:;.]ff format
-intra_vlc	int	Use MPEG-2 intra VLC table.
-drop_frame_timecode	int	Timecode is in drop frame format.
-scan_offset	int	Reserve space for SVCD scan offset user data.
-mpv_flags	flags	Flags common for all mpegvideo-based encoders, values are (more in ffmpeg help): skip_rd, strict_gop, qp_rd, cbp_rd
-luma_elim_threshold	int	single coefficient elimination threshold for luminance (negative values also consider dc coefficient)
-chroma_elim_threshold	int	single coefficient elimination threshold for chrominance (negative values also consider dc coefficient)
-quantizer_noise_shaping	int	

MPEG-2 video encoder

The **mpeg2video** encoder can use all options of **mpeg1video** encoder and 2 additional options:

option	type	Description
-non_linear_quant	int	Use nonlinear quantizer.
-alternate_scan	int	Enable alternate scan table.

MPEG-4 video encoder

The **mpeg4** encoder includes the next options described in the previous 2 tables:

- data_partioning
- alternate_scan
- mpv_flags
- luma_elim_threshold
- chroma_elim_threshold
- quantizer_noise_shaping

libvpx video encoder

The **libvpx** encoder is used for example by the WEBM format and includes the next options:

option	type	description
-cpu-used	int	Quality/Speed ratio modifier
-auto-alt-ref	int	Enable use of alternate reference frames (2-pass only)
-lag-in-frames	int	Number of frames to look ahead for alternate reference frame selection
-arnr-maxframes	int	altref noise reduction max frame count
-arnr-strength	int	altref noise reduction filter strength
-arnr-type	int	altref noise reduction filter type, values are: backward, forward, centered
-deadline	int	Time to spend encoding, in microseconds, values are: best, good, realtime
-error-resilient	flags	Error resilience configuration: values (more in ffmpeg help): default, partitions
-max-intra-rate	int	Maximum I-frame bitrate (pct) 0=unlimited
-speed	int	
-quality	int	values are: best, good, realtime
-vp8flags	flags	values are (more in ffmpeg help): error_resilient, altref
-arnr_max_frames	int	altref noise reduction max frame count
-arnr_strength	int	altref noise reduction filter strength
-arnr_type	int	altref noise reduction filter type
-rc_lookahead	int	Number of frames to look ahead for alternate reference frame selection
-crf	int	Select the quality for constant quality mode

AC-3 audio encoder

The ac3 audio encoder can use additional options described in the table:

Audio codec: AC-3		
Option	**Value type**	**Description**
per_frame_metadata	integer	allow changing metadata per-frame
center_mixlev	float	center mix level
surround_mixlev	float	surround mix level
mixing_level	integer	mixing level
room_type	integer	room type, values are: notindicated, large, small
copyright	integer	copyright bit
dialnorm	integer	dialogue level (dB)
dsur_mode	integer	Dolby Surround mode, values: notindicated, on, off
original	integer	original bit stream
dmix_mode	integer	preferred stereo downmix mode, values: notindicated
ltrt_cmixlev	float	lt/rt center mix level
ltrt_surmixlev	float	lt/rt surround mix level
loro_cmixlev	float	lo/ro center mix level
loro_surmixlev	float	lo/ro surround mix level
dsurex_mode	integer	Dolby Surround EX mode, values: notindicated, on, off
dheadphone_mode	integer	Dolby Headphone Mode, values: notindicated, on, off
ad_conv_type	integer	A/D Converter type, values: standard (default), hdcd
stereo_rematrixing	integer	stereo rematrixing
channel_coupling	integer	channel coupling, value: auto
cpl_start_band	integer	coupling start band, value: auto

Simplified encoding of VCD, SVCD, DVD, DV and DV50

A special **-target** option enables to use only one option instead of a large set of options needed for certain media types (VCD=Video CD, SVCD=Super Video CD, DV=Digital Video, etc.), available values are:

- vcd, pal-vcd, ntsc-vcd, film-vcd
- svcd, pal-svcd, ntsc-svcd, film-svcd
- dvd, pal-dvd, ntsc-dvd, film-dvd
- dv, pal-dv, ntsc-dv, film-dv
- dv50, pal-dv50, ntsc-dv50, film-dv50

All needed parameters like frame rate, aspect ratio, bitrate etc. are set according to specification of particular media format. For example to encode the video for DVD we can use the command :

```
ffmpeg -i input.avi -target dvd output.mpg
```

12. Time Operations

Multimedia processing includes changing the input duration, setting a delay, selecting only certain parts from the input, etc. These time operations accept the time specification in 2 formats:

- [-]HH:MM:SS[.m...]
- [-]S+[.m...]

where **HH** is number of hours, **MM** is number of minutes, **SS** or **S** is number of seconds and **m** is number of milliseconds.

Duration of audio and video
Setting with -t option
To set the duration of a media file, we can use the **-t** option which value is a time in seconds or in a format HH:MM:SS.milliseconds. For example to set a 3 minutes duration for the music.mp3 file, we can use the command

```
ffmpeg -i music.mp3 -t 180 music_3_minutes.mp3
```

Setting with number of frames
In certain cases it may be useful to set the duration of recording by specifying the number of frames with available options:

- audio: **-aframes** *number* or **-frames:a** *number*
- data: **-dframes** *number* or **-frames:d** *number*
- video: **-vframes** *number* or **-frames:v** *number*

The number of frames is equal to the duration in seconds multiplied by the frame rate. For instance, to set the duration of a video.avi file with a 25 fps frame rate to 10 minutes (600 seconds), we can use the command:

```
ffmpeg -i video.avi -vframes 15000 video_10_minutes.avi
```


Setting delay from start
To start recording of the input from specified time, we can use the **-ss** (seek from start) option, its value is the time in seconds or in HH:MM:SS.milliseconds format. This option can be used both before input file and output file, when used before output file, the encoding is more precise. For example to begin the conversion from the 10th second, we can use the command:

```
ffmpeg -i input.avi -ss 10 output.mp4
```


Extracting specific part from media file
To clip specific part from an audio or video file, we use both **-ss** and **-t** options, ffplay displays current time in the left bottom corner and the playback can be paused on/off with the Spacebar or a P key. For example to save the 5th minute (4x60=240 seconds from the start) from the file video.mpg, we can use the command:

```
ffmpeg -i video.mpg -ss 240 -t 60 clip_5th_minute.mpg
```

Delay between input streams

There are commonly 2 cases, when one of the input streams should be delayed to the output, in both we use the **-itsoffset** (input **t**imestamp **offset**) option to create a delay and **-map** options to select particular streams. Please note that containers like AVI, FLV, MOV, MP4, etc. have different headers and in certain cases the **itsoffset** option does not work, then the slower stream can be saved to the file using -ss option and both files can be merged to one like in the following example, where audio has 1 second delay:

```
ffmpeg -i input.avi -ss 1 audio.mp3
ffmpeg -i input.avi -i audio.mp3 -map 0:v -map 1:a video.mp4
```

One input file

The input file contains audio and video streams that are not synchronized, for example if the audio is 1.5 seconds in advance, we can delay the audio stream with the command:

```
ffmpeg -i input.mov -map 0:v -map 0:a -itsoffset 1.5 -c:a copy ^
-c:v copy output.mov
```

If the video is in advance, for example 5 seconds, we can delay it with the command:

```
ffmpeg -i input.mov -map 0:v -itsoffset 5 -map 0:a -c:a copy -c:v copy ^
output.mov
```

Two or more input files

The output is created from 2 files, and usually audio should start later than the video stream, then we change the mapping parameters, for example to delay audio 3 seconds, we can use the command:

```
ffmpeg -i v.mpg -itsoffset 3 -i a.mp3 -map 0:v:0 -map 1:a:0 output.mp4
```

Limit for processing time

Sometimes it is useful to limit the period during which the ffmpeg command runs and **-timelimit** option can be used to set this limit in seconds. For example to quit encoding after 10 minutes (600 seconds), we can use the next command:

```
ffmpeg -i input.mpg -timelimit 600 output.mkv
```

Shortest stream determines encoding time

To set the overall output duration to the shortest input stream value, an **-shortest** option can be used to finish encoding when processing of the shortest stream is ready. For example to join (to multiplex) files video.avi and audio.mp3, where the audio file duration is less than video, we can use the next command (without -shortest option the remaining audio stream will be substituted with the silence):

```
ffmpeg -i video.avi -i audio.mp3 -shortest output.mp4
```

Timestamp and time bases

To set a recording timestamp in the media container, we can use a **-timestamp** option, which value is a time entered in a form:

- **now** (current time)
- date is specified as **YYYY-MM-DD** or **YYYYMMDD**, if not specified, the current date is used
- time is specified as **HH:MM:SS[.m...]** or **HHMMSS[.m...]**, decimal part of seconds is optional
- before the time value can be an optional letter **T** or **t**
- if **Z** or **z** is appended, the time is UTC, otherwise it is local

Examples of the timestamp: 2010-12-24T12:00:00, 20101224t120000z, 20101224120000

The console output from FFmpeg processing of a video stream contains information about stream timebases that can look like the next example:

```
Stream #0:0, 1, 1/25: Video: mpeg4 (Simple Profile) (FMP4 / 0x34504D46),
yuv420p, 320x240 [SAR 1:1 DAR 4:3], 25 tbr, 25 tbn, 25 tbc
```

The abbreviations **tbr**, **tbn** and **tbc** denotes 3 different time bases for FFmpeg timestamps:

Time bases for timestamps in FFmpeg	
Specification	Console output contains for each video stream 3 time base values, where printed values are reciprocals of real values, it means that printed are values of 1/tbc, 1/tbn and 1/tbr.
Description of time bases	
tbc	time base in AVCodecContext for the codec used for a given stream, it is used for all AVCodecContext and related timestamps
tbn	time base in AVStream coming from the container, it is used for all AVStream timestamps
tbr	time base guessed (computed) from the video stream and equals to the frame rate value, unless the input is interlaced, then it is doubled

Encoder timebase setting

To specify an encoder timebase for the stream copy, we can use the **-copytb** option which value ***mode*** has 3 possible integer values:

- 1 - demuxer timebase is used
  timebase i copied from the corresponding input demuxer to the output encoder, it is sometimes needed when copying video streams with variable frame rate (VBR) to avoid non monotonically increasing timestamps
- 0 - decoder timebase is used
  timestamp is copied from the corresponding input decoder to the output encoder
- -1 - automatic choice for the best output, the default value

For example to select a demuxer timebase for the output, we can use the command:

```
ffmpeg -i input.mp4 -copytb 1 output.webm
```

Audio and video speed modifications

Video speed change

To change the speed of the video file, we can use the **setpts** (**set p**resentation **t**imestamp) filter described in the table:

Video filter: setpts	
Description	Changes presentation timestamp (PTS) of input frames.
Syntax	**setpts=expression**
Available variables in *expression*	
FRAME_RATE	frame rate, only defined for a video with a constant frame
INTERLACED	tell if the current frame is interlaced
N	count of the input frame, starting from 0
NB_CONSUMED_SAMPLES	number of consumed samples, without the current frame (only audio)
NB_SAMPLES	number of samples in the current frame (only audio)
POS	original frame position in the file, or undefined if undefined for the current frame
PREV_INT	previous input time in seconds
PREV_INPTS	previous input PTS
PREV_OUTPTS	previous output PTS
PREV_OUTT	previous output time in seconds
PTS	presentation timestamp in input
SAMPLE_RATE	audio sample rate
STARTPTS	PTS of the first frame
STARTT	time in seconds of the first frame
T	time in seconds of the current frame
TB	time base

Each video frame contains a header with a timestamp value, the difference between 2 frames in sequence is 1/fps, for instance if fps is 25, the difference is 0.04 second. To speed up the video this time difference must be smaller and for a lower speed it must be bigger. For example, to watch the video 3-times faster, the input timestamp is divided by 3 and the command is:

```
ffplay -i input.mpg -vf setpts=PTS/3
```

To watch the video in a 3/4 speed, the input timestamp is divided by 3/4 and we can use the command:

```
ffplay -i input.mpg -vf setpts=PTS/(3/4)
```

Audio speed change

To adjust the tempo of the audio, we can use the special **atempo** filter described in the table.

Audio filter: atempo	
Description	Changes audio tempo - the speed of the audio stream.
Syntax	atempo[=*tempo*]
Description of parameter	
tempo	float number from the range 0.5 - 2.0, values less than 1.0 slows down and values over 1.0 speed up the tempo, the default value is 1.0

For example to hear the input audio with a 2-times faster speed, we can use the command:

```
ffplay -i speech.mp3 -af atempo=2
```

To hear this audio in a half tempo, we can use the **atempo=0.5** setting and if the speed change is not sufficient, the filter can be applied more times.

Synchronizing audio data with timestamps

To synchronize audio data with the timestamps we can use an **asyncts** audio filter described in the table:

Audio filter: asyncts	
Description	Synchronizes audio data with the timestamps by squeezing and dropping samples or by stretching and adding silence when needed.
Syntax	asyncts=parameters
Description of available parameters	
compensate	Enable stretching/squeezing the data to make it match the timestamps. Disabled by default. When disabled, time gaps are covered with silence.
min_delta	Minimum difference between timestamps and audio data (in seconds) to trigger adding/dropping samples. Default value is 0.1. If you get non-perfect sync with this filter, try setting this parameter to 0.
max_comp	max. compensation in samples per second, relevant only if compensate=1, default value 500
first_cts	Assume the first pts should be this value. This allows for padding/trimming at the start of stream. By default, no assumption is made about the first frame's expected pts, so no padding or trimming is done. For example, this could be set to 0 to pad the beginning with silence if an audio stream starts after the video stream.

For example to synchronize with timestamps the data in the file music.mpg we can use the command:

```
ffmpeg -i music.mpg -af asyncts=compensate=1 -f mpegts music.ts
```

13. Mathematical Functions

A big advantage provided by FFmpeg tools are the built-in mathematical functions, that enable various modifications of certain audio and video filters, options and sources.

Expressions that can use mathematical functions

Many FFmpeg options require numeric values as parameters and some of them can be in a form of expression, that can contain arithmetic operators, constants and various mathematical functions. Functions are typically used with audio and video filters and sources, the next table contains their list including where to find their description.

The evaluation of arithmetic expressions in FFmpeg provides an internal formula evaluator implemented via interface located in the file libavutil/eval.h. This evaluator accepts also the International System number prefixes (in FFmpeg documentation are called postfixes, because they are entered immediately after the number). If **i** is appended after the prefix, used are powers of 2 instead of powers of 10. The **B** (byte) prefix multiplies the value by 8, and can be appended after another prefix or used alone. It means that for example **B, KB, MiB** can be used like the prefix. The list of available SI number prefixes is in the chapter FFmpeg Fundamentals. Developers in their C code can extend the list of unary and binary functions, and define additional constants, which will be available in described expressions.

List of expressions which can contain functions		
Filter, option or source		**Described in**
Name	**Type**	
aevalsrc	audio source	chapter Digital Audio
asettb	audio filter	chapter Advanced Techniques
aspect	option	glossary
astreamsync	audio filter	chapter Digital Audio
boxblur	video filter	chapter Blur, Sharpen and Other Denoising
crop	video filter	chapter Cropping Video
drawtext	video filter	chapter Adding Text on Video
hue	video filter	chapter Color Corrections
lut, lutrgb, lutyuv	video filters	chapter Color Corrections
overlay	video filter	chapter Overlay Video
rc_eq	option	this chapter and chapter Conversion Between Formats
pad	video filter	chapter Padding Video
scale	video filter	chapter Resizing and Scaling Video
select	video filter	chapter Advanced Techniques
setdar, setsar	video filters	chapter Advanced Techniques
setpts	video filter	chapter Time Operations
settb	video filter	chapter Advanced Techniques
volume	audio filter	chapter Digital Audio

Built-in arithmetic operators

Users of FFmpeg tools can utilize common unary and binary arithmetic operators, that are described in the following table.

Operator	Type	Description	Example
+	unary	converts a negative value to the positive	+(-3)=3
-	unary	converts a positive value to the negative	-(2+3)=-5
+	binary	provides an operation of addition	4+5=9
-	binary	provides an operation of subtraction	10-6=4
*	binary	provides an operation of multiplication	4*5=20
/	binary	provides an operation of division	9/3=3
^	binary	provides an exponential function	10^2=10*10=100

Built-in constants

Recently FFmpeg contains only 3 constants described in the table below, but developers can define additional constants by modifying the source code.

Symbol	Value	Description
PI	3.14159265358979323846	Ratio of circumference to diameter of a circle
E	2.7182818284590452354	The base of natural logarithm, Euler's number
PHI	1.61803398874989484820	Golden ratio, (1+sqrt(5))/2

PI constant is often used as an argument of trigonometric functions sine, cosine, tangent, etc. For example, to generate a tone of C5 pitch (tenor high C) with the frequency of 523.251 Hz, we can use the command

```
ffplay -f lavfi -i aevalsrc=sin(523.251*2*PI*t)
```

Due to the similar periodicity of the cosine function, the next command gives the same result:

```
ffplay -f lavfi -i aevalsrc=cos(523.251*2*PI*t)
```

Table of built-in mathematical functions

If we work with 2 different expression and want to combine them to form another expression, we can use a notation "expr1;expr2", in which expr1 and expr2 are evaluated in turn, and the new expression evaluates to the value of expr2.

When working with functions that evaluate expressions as "true" if they have a non-zero value, we can utilize the fact that the * sign (asterisk) works like logical AND, and the + sign (plus) works like OR.

The next two pages contains the table of available functions in FFmpeg tools.

114

Functions available in expressions	
Function	**Description**
abs(x)	computes absolute value of x
acos(x)	computes arccosine of x
asin(x)	computes arcsine of x
atan(x)	computes arctangent of x
ceil(expr)	rounds **expr** up to the nearest integer, for example ceil(4.5)=5.0
cos(x)	computes cosine of x
cosh(x)	computes hyperbolic cosine of x
eq(x, y)	test of equality, returns 1 if x=y, otherwise returns 0
exp(x)	computes exponential of x with the base e=2.71828182 (Euler's number)
floor(expr)	rounds **expr** down to the nearest integer, for example floor(4.5)=4, and floor(-4.5)=-5
gauss(x)	computes Gauss function of x, corresponding to exp(-x*x/2) / sqrt(2*PI)
gcd(x, y)	computes greatest common divisor of x and y, if x=y=0 or if x<0 and y<0, the result is undefined
gt(x, y)	greater than comparison, returns 1 if x > y, otherwise returns 0
gte(x, y)	greater than or equal to comparison, returns 1 if x ≥ y, otherwise returns 0
hypot(x, y)	computes hypotenuse (the longest side of a right-angled triangle), sqrt(x*x + y*y)
if(expr1, expr2)	evaluates *expr1*, if the result is non-zero returns the evaluation of *expr1*, else returns 0
ifnot(exp1, exp2)	evaluates *exp1*, if the result is zero returns the evaluation of *exp1*, otherwise returns 0
isinf(x)	returns 1.0 if x is +/-infinity, else returns 0.0
isnan(x)	returns 1.0 if x is NaN (not a number), else returns 0.0
ld(var)	returns a value of internal variable set by st(var, expr) function with a *var* identifier
log(x)	computes natural logarithm of x with the base e=2.71828182 (Euler's number)
lt(x, y)	less than comparison, returns 1 if x < y, otherwise returns 0
lte(x, y)	less than or equal to comparison, returns 1 if x ≤ y, otherwise returns 0
max(x, y)	computes maximum of x and y
min(x, y)	computes minimum of x and y
mod(x, y)	computes modulo, remainder of division x/y
not(expr)	negation, returns 1 if expr is 0, otherwise returns 1
pow(x, y)	computes value of x raised to the power of y, the result is equivalent to (x)^(y)
random(x)	returns a pseudo random number from 0.0 - 1.0, x is the index of the internal variable used to save the seed/state

Function	Description
root(expr, max)	finds x where f(x)=0 in the interval 0..max, function f() must be continuous or the result is undefined
sin(x)	computes sine of x
sinh(x)	computes hyperbolic sine of x
sqrt(expr)	computes square root of **expr**, the result is equivalent to $(expr)^{0.5}$
squish(x)	computes expression $1/(1 + exp(4*x))$
st(var, expr)	stores the value of expression **expr** to internal variable with a number **var** (value 0 to 9), variables are currently not shared between expressions
tan(x)	computes tangent of x
tanh(x)	computes hyperbolic tangent of x
taylor(expr, x) taylor(expr, x, id)	-evaluates a taylor series at x, **expr** represents the LD(**id**)-th derivates of f(x) at 0 -if **id** is not specified then 0 is assumed -if you have the derivatives at y instead of 0, taylor(expr, x-y) can be used -if the series does not converge, the results are undefined
trunc(expr)	rounds **expr** towards zero to the nearest integer, for example floor(-4.5)=-4
while(cond, expr)	evaluates expression **expr** while the expression **cond** is non-zero, and returns the value of the last **expr** evaluation, or NAN if **cond** was always false.
Special functions for -rc_eq option	
bits2qp(bits) qp2bits(qp)	additional functions, that can be used with other functions to define a rate control equation specified by the **-rc_eq** option for the selected codec

Examples of using functions

A large area of application for functions provides the drawtext filter. For instance lt(x, y) and gt(x, y) functions can be used to set the time when the text appears or disappears from the video frame, the next command delays the text 5 seconds from the start:

```
ffplay -f lavfi -i color=c=orange -vf ^
drawtext=fontfile=/Windows/Fonts/arial.ttf:fontcolor=white:fontsize=20:^
text="5 seconds delayed text":x=(w-tw)/2:y=(h-th)/2:draw=gt(t\,5)
```

Additional examples of using functions in the book:
- chapter Adding Text on Video
- chapter Digital Audio, section Sound synthesis
- chapter Batch Jobs

14. Metadata and Subtitles

Metadata in a media file contains additional information like the artist, author, date, genre, publisher, title, etc. and are not displayed in the video frame. Subtitles are textual data usually contained in a separate file and displayed near the bottom of the video frame, though some container file formats like VOB support inclusion of the subtitle file.

Introduction to metadata

Metadata are often used in MP3 files and media players commonly display from them items like the song title, artist, album, etc. For example, to display the metadata from the file Kalimba.mp3, located in a Sample Music folder on Windows 7 (users with other OS can select other media file with metadata that are always present in officially distributed music and video) we can use the command

```
ffplay -i "/Users/Public/Music/Sample Music/Kalimba.mp3"
```

The console output includes metadata in a form:

```
Input #0, mp3, from 'Kalimba.mp3':
  Metadata:
    publisher       : Ninja Tune
    track           : 1
    album           : Ninja Tuna
    artist          : Mr. Scruff
    album_artist    : Mr. Scruff
    title           : Kalimba
    genre           : Electronic
    composer        : A. Carthy and A. Kingslow
    date            : 2008
  Duration: 00:05:50.60, start: 0.000000, bitrate: 191 kb/s
    Stream #0:0, 194, 1/14112000: Audio: mp3, 44100 Hz, stereo, s16, 192 kb/s
     Stream #0:1, 1, 1/90000: Video: mjpeg, yuvj420p, 512x512, 90k tbr, 90k
tbn, 90k tbc
    Metadata:
      title         : thumbnail
      comment       : Cover (front)
```

Creating metadata

Metadata are included to the media files with **-metadata** option followed by a **key=value** pair, where the key or value must be double quoted, if contains spaces. When more keys should be entered, several **-metadata** options can be used, for example:

```
ffmpeg -i input -metadata artist=FFmpeg -metadata title="Test 1" output
```

ASF, FLV, Matroska, WMA and WMV file formats support any metadata keys, while other formats support only certain keys, the details are in the following table (source: FFmpeg Metadata article on MultimediaWiki, wiki.multimedia.cx).

Metadata key support in various media formats (Y = yes, in yellow - any keys)							
Key	**AVI**	**ASF/WMV/ WMA**	**FLV**	**Matroska**	**MP3**	**MPEG TS** transport stream	**Quicktime/ MOV/MP4**
album	Y	Y	Y	Y	Y		Y
album_artist		Y	Y	Y			Y
artist	Y	Y	Y	Y	Y		N
author		Y	Y	Y	Y		Y
comment	Y	Y	Y	Y	Y		Y
composer		Y	Y	Y			Y
copyright	Y	Y	Y	Y			Y
date	Y	Y	Y	Y			
description		Y	Y	Y			Y
encoded_by	Y	Y	Y	Y			
episode_id		Y	Y	Y			Y
genre	Y	Y	Y	Y	Y		Y
grouping		Y	Y	Y			Y
language	Y	Y	Y	Y		Y	
lyrics		Y	Y	Y			Y
network		Y	Y	Y			Y
rating		Y	Y	Y			
show		Y	Y	Y			Y
title	Y	Y	Y	Y	Y	Y	Y
track	Y	Y	Y	Y	Y		Y
year		Y	Y	Y	Y		
user-defined		Y	Y	Y			

User-defined metadata enable to include keys not listed in the table, for example to add information

```
location        : London, United Kingdom
camera type     : SONY DSC
camera mode     : movie
weather         : sunny
```

we can use the command

```
ffmpeg -i video.avi -metadata location="London, United Kingdom" ^
-metadata "camera type"="SONY DSC" -metadata "camera mode"=movie ^
-metadata weather="sunny" video.wmv
```

Saving and loading metadata to/from the file

To save metadata included in the media file, we can use the **ffmetadata** format specified with -f option before the name of the textfile in which the metadata will be stored. For example, to save metadata from the video.wmv file created in the previous example, we can use the command

```
ffmpeg -i video.wmv -f ffmetadata data.txt
```

The output file data.txt contains the following lines (the last line will contain the current encoder version):

```
;FFMETADATA1
weather=sunny
location=London, United Kingdom
camera type=SONY DSC
camera mode=movie
encoder=Lavf54.33.100
```

To load metadata from the file data.txt into other related media file, we can simply include it as a first input file before the media file, for example

```
ffmpeg -i data.txt -i video1.avi video1.wmw
```

Now the file video1.wmv contains the same metadata as the file video.wmv transferred from the data.txt file. Loaded can be not only metadata files saved by ffmpeg, but we can create completely new files with a special formatting. In these files the first line is a header containing the text **;FFMETADATA1**, the next lines are key=value pairs containing required content like in the previous example.

Deletion of metadata

To delete not actual metadata, we can use the **-map_metadata** option set to a negative value, for example to delete all metadata from the file input.avi we can use the command:

```
ffmpeg -i input.avi -map_metadata -1 output.mp4
```

Introduction to subtitles

Subtitles are textual data included near the bottom of the video frame to provide additional information like a translation of the spoken foreign language to the local one, same language subtitles to improve literacy, etc. Subtitles can be divided to 2 main types:
- external that are in a separate file and are included to the video frame during the playback by a media player, advantage is that can be edited and distributed without the video
- internal, that are included in a media file container with the video and audio stream

Other division include the prepared subtitles and live subtitles that are created simultaneously during the live video broadcasting. Other sorting divides subtitles to open and closed - open subtitles cannot be turned off while closed subtitles like teletext and DVD subtitles can be turned on or off.

The list of supported subtitle codecs and file formats is in the table, in the **Support** column **D** means that this format can be decoded and **E** denotes availability of encoding (dvb_teletext and eia_608 are not specified yet). For example to convert the SRT format subtitles to ASS format, we can use the command:

```
ffmpeg -i subtitles.srt subtitles.ass
```

Available codecs for subtitles		
Codec	**Support**	**Description**
dvb_subtitle	DE	DVB subtitles (decoders: dvbsub) (encoders: dvbsub)
dvb_teletext		DVB teletext
dvd_subtitle	DE	DVD subtitles (decoders: dvdsub) (encoders: dvdsub)
eia_608		EIA-608 closed captions
hdmv_pgs_subtitle	D	HDMV Presentation Graphic Stream subtitles (decoders: pgssub)
jacosub	D	JACOsub subtitle
microdvd	D	MicroDVD subtitle
mov_text	DE	MOV text
realtext	D	RealText subtitle
sami	D	SAMI subtitle
srt	DE	SubRip subtitle with embedded timing
ssa	DE	SSA (SubStation Alpha) / ASS (Advanced SSA) subtitle (decoders: ass) (encoders: ass)
subrip	DE	SubRip subtitle
subviewer	D	SubViewer subtitle
text	D	raw UTF-8 text
webvtt	D	WebVTT subtitle
xsub	DE	XSUB
Available file formats for subtitles (Support column: D=demuxing yes, E=muxing yes)		
File format	**Support**	**Description**
ass	DE	SSA (SubStation Alpha) subtitle
jacosub	DE	JACOsub subtitle format
microdvd	DE	MicroDVD subtitle format
realtext	D	RealText subtitle format
sami	D	SAMI subtitle format
srt	DE	SubRip subtitle
subviewer	D	SubViewer subtitle format
vobsub	D	VobSub subtitle format
webvtt	D	WebVTT subtitle

Subtitles encoded directly to video

For example, if we want to include a subtitled video to webpage, we need to encode subtitles to the video stream and 2 filters can do it: **ass** (encodes only ASS format) and **subtitles** filter described in the table:

Video filter: subtitles	
Description	Includes subtitles on the input video using the libass library.
Syntax	**subtitles=*filename*[:*original_size*]**
Description of options	
f, filename	the name of the file containing subtitles
original_size	size of the original video, needed when the input is resized

To prevent error messages on Windows, it is needed to specify a location of the fontconfig configuration file that can be downloaded from **http://ffmpeg.tv/fonts.conf**

Please save the **fonts.conf** file to the same directory where is the file ffmpeg.exe (or f.exe) and add 3 new environment variables by clicking the button **New** under the **System Variables** section in the Environment Variables modal dialog (how to display it is described in the first chapter, section Path setting):

New System Variable modal dialog	
Variable Name	**Variable Value** (*ffmpeg_dir* is location of ffmpeg.exe)
FC_CONFIG_DIR	C:*ffmpeg_dir*
FONTCONFIG_FILE	fonts.conf
FONTCONFIG_PATH	C:*ffmpeg_dir*

Please note that not all subtitle formats are supported by all containers, most containers (AVI, Matroska, MP4, MPG, etc.) support ASS and SRT. For example, to encode subtitles to the video stream from the file titles.srt to the file video.mp4, we can use the command (other example is illustrated on the image):

```
ffmpeg -i video.avi -vf subtitles=titles.srt video.mp4
```

121

15. Image Processing

Though the primary use of FFmpeg tools is related to the audio and video, ffmpeg can decode and encode various image formats and many image related tasks can be done quickly. Using ffmpeg on a webserver enables to create a web image editor, webhosts with FFmpeg support are in the chapter Video on Web.

Supported image formats

Image formats that FFmpeg supports are listed in the table with their characteristic postfix. All these file types except LJPEG (Lossless JPEG) can be decoded, and except EXR, PIC and PTX all can be encoded.

Supported image formats by FFmpeg			
Extension	**Encoding / Decoding**		**Description**
.Y.U.V	X	X	one raw file per component
BMP	X	X	Microsoft BMP image
DPX	X	X	Digital Picture Exchange
EXR		X	OpenEXR
GIF	X	X	animated GIFs are uncompressed
JPG	X	X	Progressive JPEG is not supported.
JP2	X	X	JPEG 2000
JLS	X	X	JPEG-LS
LJPG		X	Lossless JPEG
PAM	X	X	PAM is a PNM extension with alpha support.
PBM	X	X	Portable BitMap image
PCX	X	X	PC Paintbrush
PGM	X	X	Portable GrayMap image
PGMYUV	X	X	PGM with U and V components in YUV 4:2:0
PIC		X	Pictor/PC Paint
PNG	X	X	Portable Network Graphics
PPM	X	X	Portable PixelMap image
PTX		X	V.Flash PTX format
SGI	X	X	SGI RGB image format
RAS	X	X	Sun Rasterfile image format
TIFF	X	X	YUV, JPEG and some extension is not supported yet.
TGA	X	X	Truevision Targa image format
XBM	X	X	X BitMap image format
XFace	X	X	XFace image format
XWD	X	X	X Window Dump image format

Creating images
Screenshots from videos

To save a video frame from a specified moment to the image, an **-ss** (**s**eek from **s**tart) option is used to specify the delay from the start. The syntax for taking a screenshot in the time **t** is

```
ffmpeg -i input -ss t image.type
```

The **-ss** option can be used also before the input file, but the result is less accurate. For example to take a screenshot in the time 1 hour 23 minutes 45 seconds from the file videoclip.avi, we can use the command:

```
ffmpeg -i videoclip.avi -ss 01:23:45 image.jpg
```

Animated GIFs from videos

The video files are created from the frames that can be saved to the frames of an animated GIF, the image type that is frequently used on the web in a form of banners and short animations. Because the frames are saved uncompressed, it is useful only with shorter videos, otherwise the file size of animated GIF can be very large. For example, to convert a short SWF file to the animated GIF to create an alternative for the users without a Flash plugin, we can use the command (the pixel format must be set to **rgb24**):

```
ffmpeg -i promotion.swf -pix_fmt rgb24 promotion.gif
```

Images from FFmpeg video sources

Another option to create images is to use built-in video sources, that are described in the table:

Video sources for creating images		
Name	**Description**	**Picture**
color	Provides any color specified by its name or in hexadecimal format, for example color=c=#87cefa	
mptestsrc	Various tests patterns, detailed description with samples is in the chapter Debugging and Tests.	
rgbtestsrc	Red-Green-Blue color pattern	
smptebars	Color bars pattern from the Society of Motion Picture and Television Engineers, Engineering Guideline EG 1-1990	
testsrc	Video test pattern with a scrolling gradient and a timestamp.	

The default resolution of the **mptestsrc** video source is 512x512 pixels, other listed sources have 320x240 pixels resolution. The most versatile is the color image source that is able to generate the image of any color and any size, for example to create a teal background for a leaderboard banner sized 728x90 pixels, we can use the command

```
ffmpeg -f lavfi -i color=c=#008080:s=728x90 leaderboard.jpg
```

Video source: color	
Description	Provides a colored output in a form of 320x240 sized rectangle with a specified color.
Syntax	**color[=c=*clr*[:d=*time*[:r=*fps*[:sar=*value*[:s=*resolution*]]]]]** all parameters are optional items in italics will be replaced with actual value
Description of parameters	
color, c	color of the source, a name of a color (case insensitive match) or a 0xRRGGBB[AA] sequence, possibly followed by an alpha specifier, the default value is black
duration, d	duration of the source video, accepted syntax is: [-]HH[:MM[:SS[.m...]]] or [-]S+[.m...], if not specified, or if the expressed duration is negative, the video is will be generated forever
rate, r	frame rate of the source video, the number of frames generated per second, it can be a string in the format frame_rate_numerator/frame_rate_denumerator, an integer or a float number or a valid video frame rate abbreviation, the default value is 25
sar	sample aspect ratio of the source video
size, s	size of the source video, a string of the form **widthxheight**, or the corresponding abbreviation, the default value is 320x240

Video conversion to images

The video file is composed of the frames that can be saved into the image files with one command, the number of resulting images is a product of the video frame rate and its duration in seconds. For example, if the clip.avi file have a 1-minute duration and its frame rate is 25 fps, then the following command will produce 60x25=1500 images, 25 for each second:

```
ffmpeg -i clip.avi frame%d.jpg
```

The output directory will contain 1500 files named like frame1.jpg, frame2.jpg, etc. To keep the same length for all file names, we specify the number of appended digits with a number after the **%** sign:

```
ffmpeg -i clip.avi frame%4d.jpg
```

Now the directory contains the files named frame0001.jpg, frame0002.jpg, ..., frame1500.jpg.

Resizing, cropping and padding images

Images can be resized in a similar way as videos, for example the output of the **color** video source has 320x240 pixels resolution and can be enlarged to VGA resolution in 2 ways:

- using the s or size parameter of the color video source
- using the -s option for the output

For example the next two commands have the same result, orange rectangle of a CIF (352x288) size:

```
ffmpeg -f lavfi -i color=c=orange:s=cif orange_rect1.png
ffmpeg -f lavfi -i color=c=orange -s cif orange_rect2.png
```

The size specification with the parameter is useful for the filterchains, when the input should have a certain resolution for the processing inside the filterchain, so the size cannot be specified as an option. A common example is using the **color** source as one of the inputs for the overlay.

Cropping images is the same as with videos using the crop filter, the result of the next example is a 150x150 pixels square from the center of the **rgbtestsrc** video source:

```
ffmpeg -f lavfi -i rgbtestsrc -vf crop=150:150 crop_rgb.png
```

Images can be padded the same way as videos using the pad filter, for example the next command creates an orange frame for the **smptebars** video source:

```
ffmpeg -f lavfi -i smptebars -vf pad=360:280:20:20:orange pad_smpte.jpg
```

Flipping, rotating and overlaying images

Flipping - creation of mirrored versions of images is analogical to flipping videos provided by the **hflip** and **vflip** filters, for example the next two commands flip the input image, the first one horizontally and the second one vertically:

```
ffmpeg -i orange.jpg -vf hflip orange_hflip.jpg
ffmpeg -i orange.jpg -vf vflip orange_vflip.jpg
```

Also rotating images is similar to rotating videos using the **transpose** filter that has four possible values:
- value 0 rotates video by 90 degrees counterclockwise and flips it vertically
- value 1 rotates video by 90 degrees clockwise
- value 2 rotates video by 90 degrees counterclockwise
- value 3 rotates video by 90 degrees clockwise and flips it vertically

For example, to rotate the image clockwise by 90° we can use the command:

```
ffmpeg -i image.png -vf transpose=1 image_rotated.png
```

Similar to video overlay, images can be placed one on the other with the **overlay** filter. For example, to include a smptebars to the rgbtestsrc video source, we can use the commands:

```
ffmpeg -f lavfi -i rgbtestsrc -s 400x300 rgb.png
ffmpeg -f lavfi -i smptebars smpte.png
ffmpeg -i rgb.png -i smpte.png -filter_complex overlay=(W-w)/2:(H-h)/2 ^
rgb_smpte.png
```

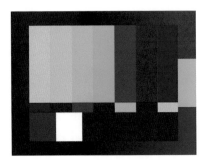

Conversion between image types

Almost all supported image types can be converted one to another, exceptions are EXR, LJPEG, PIC and PTX file types that can be decoded only. The syntax for the conversion is:

```
ffmpeg -i image.type1 image.type2
```

For example, to convert a PNG image to the JPG image format, we can use the command:

```
ffmpeg -i illustration.png illustration.jpg
```

Creating video from images

Video from one image

To convert a still image to a video is easy and can be used to create slideshows, where short videos from images (with added text) are joined together, joining videos is described in the chapter 23. For example to create a 10-second video from the photo.jpg file, we include a **-loop** boolean option with a value **true** or **1** like in the command:

```
ffmpeg -loop 1 -i photo.jpg -t 10 photo.mp4
```

Video from many images

To create a video from multiple images, their filenames must end with a number, where these numbers correspond with the sequence in which the images will be encoded to the video file. In this case the media format is specified before the input and it is an **image2** format. For example, from 100 images named img1.jpg, img2.jpg, ..., img100.jpg can be created a 4-second video with 25 fps frame rate using the command:

```
ffmpeg -f image2 -i img%d.jpg -r 25 video.mp4
```

If the image numbers start with zeros, for example img001.jpg, img002.jpg, etc. to provide the same filename length, then the command is:

```
ffmpeg -f image2 -i img%3d.jpg -r 25 video.mp4
```

The number after the % sign must be the same as the number of digits in the image filenames.

16. Digital Audio

The term digital audio compares to the term digital video, a technology for processing and displaying moving images, while audio works with sounds. Digital audio is a technology for the capturing, recording, editing, encoding and reproducing sounds electronically using bitstreams usually encoded by the pulse-code modulation (PCM). FFmpeg supports many audio formats including AAC, MP3, Vorbis, WAV, WMA, etc. All audio formats available in FFmpeg are listed in the second chapter.

Introduction to digital audio

Sounds perceived by ears can be divided to the tones and noises, tones are created by a regular matter vibrations and noises by irregular vibrations. Mechanical vibrations are transferred to the auditory system in a form of pressure waves that are perceived by an eardrum and converted to the nerve signals.

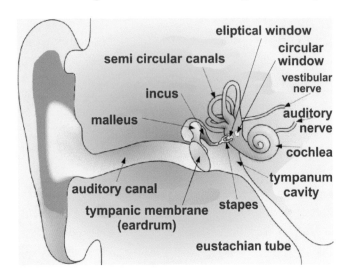

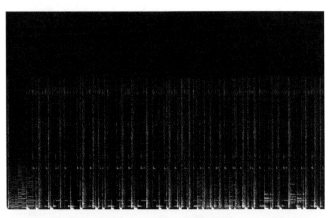

Audio waves displayed by FFmpeg filter
Command: ffplay -i audio.mp3 -vf showwaves

Audio quantization and sampling

Due to physiological limits of the human auditory system, the continuous values of pressure waves can be substituted with a finite series of values that can be stored as numbers in the computer files. Computers use the binary numbers, so the common audio bit depths (audio resolutions) are the powers of two:

Common audio bit depths (quantization levels)		
Bit depth	**Values count**	**Description**
8 bit	2^8=256	used in telephones, older devices
12 bit	2^{12}=4,096	standard for DV (digital video), used in digital cameras, etc.
14 bit	2^{14}=16,384	used in NICAM compression, stereo sound from TV, etc.
16 bit	2^{16}=65,536	standard for Audio CD and DAT (digital audio tape), most common today
20 bit	2^{20}=1,048,576	additional standard for Super Audio CD and DVD Audio
24 bit	2^{24}=16,777,216	standard for Super Audio CD and DVD Audio
32 bit	2^{32}=4,294,967,296	professional equipment, Blu-ray technologies

Audio quantization and sampling

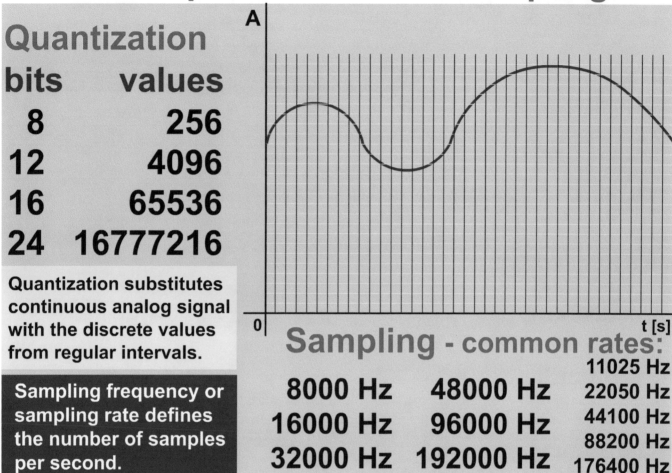

Quantization

bits	values
8	256
12	4096
16	65536
24	16777216

Quantization substitutes continuous analog signal with the discrete values from regular intervals.

Sampling frequency or sampling rate defines the number of samples per second.

Sampling - common rates:

8000 Hz	48000 Hz	11025 Hz
16000 Hz	96000 Hz	22050 Hz
32000 Hz	192000 Hz	44100 Hz
		88200 Hz
		176400 Hz

Analog audio signal (big set of values) is digitized by creating a smaller set of samples per time unit, the common sample frequencies (sample rates) are described in the table:

Common audio sample rates (frequencies)	
8000 Hz	used in telephones, wireless intercoms and microphones, etc.
11025 Hz	used in lower quality PCM and MPEG audio, etc.
16000 Hz	telephone wideband (2 times 8000 Hz), used in VOIP devices, etc.
22050 Hz	used in lower quality PCM and MPEG audio, etc.
32000 Hz	used in DAT, NICAM, mini DV cameras, wireless microphones, etc.
44100 Hz	Audio CD standard, used in MPEG-1, PAL television, etc.
48000 Hz	standard rate for professional use, for consumers in DV, DVD, digital TV, etc.
96000 Hz	standard for DVD-Audio, Blu-ray discs, HD DVD, etc.
192000 Hz	used for DVD-Audio, Blu-ray discs, HD DVD, professional devices
352800 Hz	Digital eXtreme Definition, used for Super Audio CD

Audio file formats

Quantized and sampled audio is saved in various media file formats, the next table describes specific file formats that are only for audio (MP3 format supports also included image):

Common audio formats		
Uncompressed	**Lossless compression**	**Lossy compression**
AIFF (PCM)	ALAC	AAC
AU	ALS	AC-3
BWF	ATRAC	AMR
PCM (raw, without header)	FLAC	MP2, MP3
WAV (PCM)	WavPack	Musepack
	WMA	Speex
		Vorbis (OGG)

More details about audio formats and codecs are in the chapter Conversion Between Formats.

Sound synthesis

Sounds are created from vibrations of objects that oscillate around a fixed position, regular oscillations are called tones and can be represented by the sine and cosine waves of different amplitude and frequency.

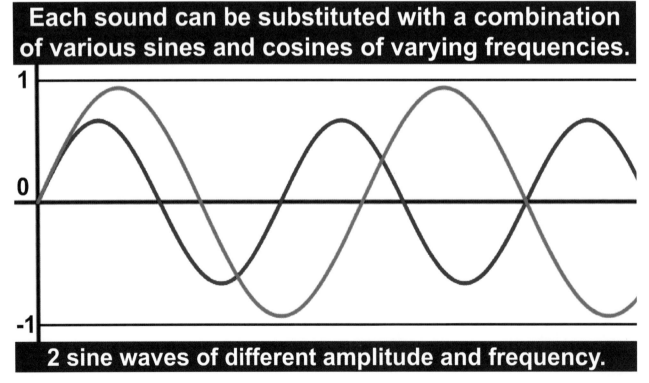

Each sound can be substituted with a combination of various sines and cosines of varying frequencies.

2 sine waves of different amplitude and frequency.

Continuous tone of certain height can be created with an expression $\texttt{sin(}tone\_height\texttt{*2*PI*t)}$ where **tone_height** is the given frequency of the tone in Hz, **PI** is a math constant and **t** is the variable specifying the time in seconds. To create the sound with a mathematical expression, we can use an audio source **aevalsrc**, output of which can be saved as an audio file. The output sound can contain multiple channels, each of them is specified by an expression with 3 possible variables, details are in the table:

Audio source: aevalsrc	
Description	Creates an audio signal specified by one (mono), two (stereo) or more expressions.
Syntax	**aevalsrc=exprs[::options]** *exprs* is a colon-separated list of expressions, every new expression specifies new channel *options* is a colon-separated list of key=value pairs
Description of available variables in expression exprs	
n	number of evaluated sample, starting from 0
t	time of evaluated sample in seconds, starting from 0
s	sample rate
Description of available options	
c or channel_layout	channel layout, number of channels must be equal to number of expressions
d or duration	max. duration, if not specified or if negative, audio is generated until program stops
n or nb_samples	number of samples per channel per each output frame, default is 1024 samples
s or sample_rate	sample rate, default value is 44100 Hz

The next table contains frequencies of the tones from C1 to B8 according to the pitch standard for the note A4 that is 440 Hz. The range of the human voice is from E2 (male bass) to C6 (female soprano).

Frequencies of notes based on A4 = 440 Hz								
Note/Octave	1	2	3	4	5	6	7	8
C	32.703	65.406	130.81	261.63	523.25	1046.5	2093.0	4186.0
C#/Db	34.648	69.296	138.59	277.18	554.37	1108.7	2217.5	4434.9
D	36.708	73.416	146.83	293.66	587.33	1174.7	2349.3	4698.6
Eb/D♯	38.891	77.782	155.56	311.13	622.25	1244.5	2489.0	4978.0
E	41.203	82.407	164.81	329.63	659.26	1318.5	2637.0	5274.0
F	43.654	87.307	174.61	349.23	698.46	1396.9	2793.8	5587.7
F♯/Gb	46.249	92.499	185.00	369.99	739.99	1480.0	2960.0	5919.9
G	48.999	97.999	196.00	392.00	783.99	1568.0	3136.0	6271.9
Ab/G♯	51.913	103.83	207.65	415.30	830.61	1661.2	3322.4	6644.9
A	55.000	110.00	220.00	440.00	880.00	1760.0	3520.0	7040.0
Bb/A♯	58.271	116.54	233.08	466.16	932.33	1864.7	3729.3	7458.6
B	61.735	123.47	246.94	493.88	987.77	1975.5	3951.1	7902.1

To generate the note A4, the tuning standard for musical pitch, we can set the tone_height to 440 Hz:

```
ffmpeg -f lavfi -i aevalsrc=sin(440*2*PI*t) -t 10 noteA4.mp3
```

Stereo and more complex sounds

To create multichannel sounds with the aevalsrc audio source we specify a defining expression for each channel, channels are separated by a colon and their localization is then specified after a double colon. Available channel layouts that can be displayed with the **-layout** option are described in the table:

Abbreviations of available channel layouts							
FL	front left	FLC	front-left-of-center	TFL	top front left	DL	downmix left
FR	front right	FRC	front-right-of-center	TFC	top front center	DR	downmix right
FC	front center	BC	back-center	TFR	top front right	WL	wide left
LFE	low frequency	SL	side-left	TBL	top back left	WR	wide right
BL	back left	SR	side-right	TBC	top back center	SDL	surround direct left
BR	back right	TC	top center	TBR	top back right	SDR	surround direct right
Complex channel layouts (FC is mono and FL+FR is stereo)							
2.1	FL+FR+LFE	5.0 side	FL+FR+FC+SL+SR		6.1	FL+FR+FC+LFE+BL+BR+BC	
3.0	FL+FR+FC	4.1	FL+FR+FC+LFE+BC		6.1 front	FL+FR+LFE+FLC+FRC+SL+SR	
3.0 back	FL+FR+BC	5.1	FL+FR+FC+LFE+BL+BR		7.0	FL+FR+FC+BL+BR+SL+SR	
4.0	FL+FR+FC+BC	5.1 side	FL+FR+FC+LFE+SL+SR		7.0 front	FL+FR+FC+FLC+FRC+SL+SR	
quad	FL+FR+BL+BR	6.0	FL+FR+FC+BC+SL+SR		7.1	FL+FR+FC+LFE+BL+BR+SL+SR	
quad side	FL+FR+SL+SR	6.0 front	FL+FR+FLC+FRC+SL+SR		7.1 front	FL+FR+FC+LFE+FLC+FRC+SL+SR	
3.1	FL+FR+FC+LFE	hexagonal	FL+FR+FC+BL+BR+BC		octagonal	FL+FR+FC+BL+BR+BC+SL+SR	
5.0	FL+FR+FC+BL+BR	6.1	FL+FR+FC+LFE+BC+SL+SR		downmix	DL+DR	

For example to create a C4 tone in the left channel and C5 tone in the right one we can use the command:

```
ffplay -f lavfi -i aevalsrc=sin(261.63*2*PI*t):cos(523.25*2*PI*t)::c=FL+FR
```

Binaural tones for stress reduction

Special type of the stereo sounds are binaural tones (beats) - 2 tones with a small frequency difference about 30 Hz or less, the frequency of both tones must be below 1000 Hz. The listening of binaural tones with stereo headphones provide a positive affect on the listeners like a stress reduction, improved ability to learn and other positive effects on the brain functions, but the results vary with the used frequency base and frequency difference. To create the binaural beat with a 10 Hz difference where the base frequency is 500 Hz we specify a stereo sound with slightly different channels:

```
ffplay -f lavfi -i aevalsrc=sin(495*2*PI*t):sin(505*2*PI*t)::c=FL+FR
```

Sound volume settings

The sound volume should be carefully adjusted to protect our ears and ffmpeg offers 2 methods. The first one uses a **-vol** option that accepts an integer value from 0 to 256, where 256 is maximum, for example:

```
ffmpeg -i sound.wav -vol 180 sound_middle_loud.wav
```

Another method is to use a **volume** filter described in the table:

Audio filter: volume	
Description	Changes an input audio volume to the specified value.
Syntax	**volume=vol**
Description of vol parameter	
vol	Parameter **vol** is an expression and its value can be specified in 2 ways: 1. as a decimal number, then output_volume = vol * input_volume 2. as a decimal number with dB postfix, then output_volume = 10^(vol/20) * input_volume

For example to decrease the sound volume to two thirds, we can use the command:

```
ffmpeg -i music.wav -af volume=2/3 quiet_music.wav
```

To increase the volume by 10 decibels, we can use the command:

```
ffmpeg -i sound.aac -af volume=10dB louder_sound.aac
```

Multiple sounds mixed to one output

To mix several sounds of a different length and to specify a transition interval, we can use an **amix** filter.

Audio filter: amix	
Description	Audio mixer, creates one output of specified duration from several audio inputs with entered dropout duration - a transition time between inputs can be specified.
Syntax	**amix=inputs=*ins*[:duration=*dur*[:dropout_transition=*dt*]]**
Description of parameters	
inputs	number of inputs, default value is 2
duration	specifies how to determine the end of stream, available options are: 1. longest - duration of longest input, default value 2. shortest - duration of shortest input 3. first - duration of first input
dropout_transition	time in seconds for the transition when an input stream ends, intended for a volume renormalization, the default value is 2

For example the next command mixes 4 input audio files to one, which duration is the same as the duration of the longest input and the transition between particular sound inputs is 5 seconds:

```
ffmpeg -i sound1.wav -i sound2.wav -i sound3.wav -i sound4.wav ^
-filter_complex amix=inputs=4:dropout_transition=5 sounds.wav
```

Downmixing stereo to mono, surround to stereo

To downmix a stereo sound to the mono sound, we can use a pan filter described in the table:

Audio filter: pan	
Description	Mixes channels with specific gain levels according to entered channel layout followed by a set of channels definitions. Typical use is to change stereo to mono, change 5+1 channels to stereo, etc. Pan filter can also remap the channels of an audio stream.
Syntax	pan=*layout*:*channel_def*[:*channel_def*[:*channel_def*...]]
Main parameters	
layout	output channel layout or number of channels
channel_def	channel definition in a form: ch_name=[gain*]in_name[+[gain*]in_name...]
Channel definition parameters	
ch_name	channel to define, either a channel name (FL, FR, etc.) or a channel number (c0, c1, etc.)
gain	multiplicative coefficient for the channel, value 1 keeps the volume unchanged
in_name	input channel to use, specified the same way as ch_name, do not mix named and numbered input channels

Several examples of down-mixing stereo to mono sound:
- Both left and right channel are mixed together with the same volume

```
ffmpeg -i stereo.wav -af pan=1:c0=0.5*c0+0.5*c1 mono.wav
```

or simply

```
ffmpeg -i stereo.wav -af pan=mono mono.wav
ffmpeg -i stereo.wav -af pan=1 mono.wav
```

- Left channel is mixed with a bigger volume than the right channel

```
ffmpeg -i stereo.wav -af pan=1:c0=0.6*c0+0.4*c1 mono.wav
```

- Right channel is mixed with a bigger volume than the left channel

```
ffmpeg -i stereo.wav -af pan=1:c0=0.7*c0+0.3*c1 mono.wav
```

A simple method without a filter how to down-mix multichannel audio with more than 2 channels is to use **-ac[:stream_specifier]** option with an integer parameter that specifies the number of output channels:

```
ffmpeg -i 5_1_surround_sound.wav -ac 2 stereo.wav
```

To specify additional parameters for the down-mix like a gain of a particular channel, we use the **pan** filter. The next example automatically reduces to stereo the multichannel audio of 3, 4, 5 or 7 channels:

```
ffmpeg -i surround.wav -af pan=stereo:^
FL<FL+0.5*FC+0.6*BL+0.6*SL:FR<FR+0.5*FC+0.6*BR+0.6*SR stereo.wav
```

Simple audio analyzer

Detailed information about each input audio frame is provided by an **ashowinfo** filter, that outputs 10 various parameters on one line for each audio frame and is described in the table.

Audio filter: ashowinfo	
Description	Shows 1 line for each input audio frame, that contains information in parameters organized to *key=value* pairs.
Syntax	**-af ashowinfo**
Description of generated parameters	
n	sequential number of frame, starts from 0
pts	presentation TimeStamp of input frame, expressed as a number of time base units
pts_time	presentation TimeStamp of input frame, expressed as a number of seconds
pos	frame position in the input stream, value -1 means that this parameter is not available or meaningless (for example with synthetic audio)
fmt	sample format name
chlayout	channel layout (mono, stereo, etc.)
nb_samples	number of samples per each channel in the current frame
rate	audio frame sample rate
checksum	hex value of Adler-32 checksum for all planes in input frame
plane_checksum	hex value of Adler-32 checksum for each input frame plane, expressed in the form [c0 c1 c2 c3 c4 c5 c6 c7]

Because the ashowinfo output can be very long, it should be saved to the file with -report option, for example

```
ffmpeg -report -i audio.wav -af ashowinfo -f null /dev/null
```

The result for a 10 seconds long stereo audio encoded in 44100 Hz, s16 is illustrated in the picture:

```
C:\windows\system32\cmd.exe

:s16 chlayout:stereo nb_samples:1152 rate:44100 checksum:4786A0B7 plane_checksum
[4786A0B7]
[Parsed_ashowinfo_0 @ 01f2fd20] n:379 pts:436608 pts_time:9.90041 pos:158623 fmt
:s16 chlayout:stereo nb_samples:1152 rate:44100 checksum:D447B7BD plane_checksum
[D447B7BD]
[Parsed_ashowinfo_0 @ 01f2fd20] n:380 pts:437760 pts_time:9.92653 pos:159041 fmt
:s16 chlayout:stereo nb_samples:1152 rate:44100 checksum:6DE73DD2 plane_checksum
[6DE73DD2]
[Parsed_ashowinfo_0 @ 01f2fd20] n:381 pts:438912 pts_time:9.95265 pos:159459 fmt
:s16 chlayout:stereo nb_samples:1152 rate:44100 checksum:5C175E86 plane_checksum
[5C175E86]
[Parsed_ashowinfo_0 @ 01f2fd20] n:382 pts:440064 pts_time:9.97878 pos:159877 fmt
:s16 chlayout:stereo nb_samples:1152 rate:44100 checksum:0E7EF48F plane_checksum
[0E7EF48F]
[Parsed_ashowinfo_0 @ 01f2fd20] n:383 pts:441216 pts_time:10.0049 pos:160295 fmt
:s16 chlayout:stereo nb_samples:1152 rate:44100 checksum:6C6E9C21 plane_checksum
[6C6E9C21]
[Parsed_ashowinfo_0 @ 01f2fd20] n:384 pts:442368 pts_time:10.031 pos:160713 fmt:
s16 chlayout:stereo nb_samples:1152 rate:44100 checksum:CD9B2E0D plane_checksum[
CD9B2E0D]
size=      0kB time=00:00:10.05 bitrate=   0.0kbits/s
video:0kB audio:1728kB subtitle:0 global headers:0kB muxing overhead -100.000000
%

c:\media>
```

Adjusting audio for listening with headphones

To increase the stereo effect of the input audio file we can use an **earwax** filter described in the table:

Audio filter: earwax	
Description	Changes the position of the stereo image from inside (a standard for headphones) to the outside and in the front of a listener (like for speakers). It works with CD audio (44,1 kHz frequency), to which it inserts the special cues.
Syntax	**-af earwax**

For example to widen the stereo effect of audio in the file music.mp3, we can use the command:

```
ffmpeg -i music.mp3 -af earwax -q 1 music_headphones.mp3
```

Audio modifications with -map_channel option

The **-map_channel** option enables to change various audio parameters and its syntax is:

```
-map_channel [in_file_id.stream_spec.channel_id|-1][:out_file_id.stream_spec]
```

- if *out_file_id.stream_spec* parameter is not set, the audio channel is mapped on all audio streams
- if "-1" is used instead of *in_file_id.stream_spec.channel_id*, mapped is a muted channel
- order of the **-map_channel** option determines the order of the channels in the output stream, the output channel layout is computed from the number of channels mapped (**mono** if one -map_channel option is used, **stereo** if two -map_channel options are used, etc.).
- an **-ac** option usage in combination with **-map_channel** makes the channel gain levels to be updated if input and output channel layouts do not match (for instance two "-map_channel" options and "-ac 6").

Switching audio channels in stereo input

To exchange the left channel with the right channel in the stereo audio file we can use the command:

```
ffmpeg -i stereo.mp3 -map_channel 0.0.1 -map_channel 0.0.0 ch_switch.mp3
```

Splitting stereo sound to 2 separate streams

To split 2 channels of the stereo input to 2 different streams encoded to 1 output file we use the command (MP3 can contain only 1 audio stream, so the output format must be AAC, OGG, WAV, etc.):

```
ffmpeg -i stereo.mp3 -map 0:0 -map 0:0 -map_channel 0.0.0:0.0 ^
-map_channel 0.0.1:0.1 output.aac
```

Muting one channel from stereo input

To mute a specific channel from the input we can use the **-1** value for the **-map_channel** option. For example to mute the first channel from a stereo sound, we can use the command:

```
ffmpeg -i stereo12.mp3 -map_channel -1 -map_channel 0.0.1 mono2.mp3
```

Merging 2 audio streams to 1 multichannel stream

To join 2 audio streams to 1 multichannel stream we can use an **amerge** filter that has 1 optional parameter **inputs**, which value sets the number of input files, the default value is 2. All input files must be encoded using the same sample rate and file format. For example to merge 2 mono sounds from 2 files to 1 file with a single stereo stream, we can use the command (total duration equals to the duration of the shorter input):

```
ffmpeg -i mono1.mp3 -af amovie=mono2.mp3[2];[in][2]amerge stereo.mp3
```

Audio stream forwarding with buffer order control

Stream synchronization of 2 audio inputs can be controlled by an **astreamsync** filter, that has 1 parameter, which value can be set by an optional expression with several variables. Default value of an expression is $t2-t1$ (described below) that means that always is forwarded the stream with a smaller timestamp.

Audio filter: astreamsync	
Description	Forwards 2 audio streams and controls the order in which the buffers are forwarded.
Syntax	**astreamsync[=expr]** if *expr* < 0, the first stream is forwarded, otherwise is forwarded the second one
Variables available in expression	
b1, b2	number of buffers forwarded till now on stream 1 and 2
s1, s2	number of samples forwarded till now on stream 1 and 2
t1, t2	current timestamps of stream 1 and 2

17. Presets for Codecs

To simplify entering a big number of options used with certain codecs, we can use the preset files, where are the options better formatted and saved for future use.

Introduction to preset files

Preset files are text files used as containers for various options included with specific codecs. They contain *key=value* pair for every option and comments are included on lines that start with a # sign.

Options to specify a preset file		
option	**codec type**	**description**
-apre	audio	for audio only, on Windows is better to use -fpre option
-spre	subtitle	for subtitle only, on Windows is better to use -fpre option
-vpre	video	for video only, on Windows is better to use -fpre option
-fpre	any codec	for any codec type, the value is a filename containing options

A simple preset file named mpeg2.ffpreset can contain only 1 option, for example:

```
vcodec=mpeg2video
```

To encode some input with mpeg2video codec, we can use the command:

ffmpeg -i *input* -fpre mpeg2.ffpreset -q 1 MPEG2_video.mpg

The next command encodes the input with flv (Flash video) codec for the use on the web:

**ffmpeg -i input.avi -vcodec flv -f flv -r 29.97 -vf scale=320:240 ^
-aspect 4:3 -b:v 300k -g 160 -cmp dct -subcmp dct -mbd 2 -flags ^
+aic+mv0+mv4 -trellis 1 -ac 1 -ar 22050 -b:a 56k output.flv**

The command is long and to edit it for various changes on the command line is not easy, so we modify it to the preset file named flv.ffpreset that will contain options related to the flv codec (comments in parentheses are not part of the file):

```
vcodec=flv            (video codec)
b:v=300k              (video bitrate)
g=160                 (group of picture size)
mbd=2                 (macroblock decision algorithm)
flags=+aic+mv0+mv4    (aic - h263 advanced intra coding; always try a mb with
                          mv=<0,0>; mv4 - use 4 motion vector by macroblock)
trellis=1             (rate-distortion optimal quantization)
ac=1                  (number of audio channels)
ar=22050              (audio sampling rate)
b:a=56k               (audio bitrate)
```

Now the command with the same result will be:

```
ffmpeg -i input.avi -f flv -r 29.97 -vf scale=320:240 -aspect 4:3 ^
-cmp dct -subcmp dct -fpre flv.ffpreset output.flv
```

Examples of preset files

Several common presets are provided by FFmpeg documentation and are described below:

Examples of preset files	
libx264-ipod320.ffpreset	**libx264-ipod640.ffpreset**
vcodec=libx264 vprofile=baseline level=13 maxrate=768000 bufsize=3000000	vcodec=libx264 vprofile=baseline level=30 maxrate=10000000 bufsize=10000000

Preset file libvpx-1080p.ffpreset

```
vcodec=libvpx
g=120
lag-in-frames=16
deadline=good
cpu-used=0
vprofile=1
qmax=51
qmin=11
slices=4
b=2M
#ignored unless using -pass 2
maxrate=24M
minrate=100k
auto-alt-ref=1
arnr-maxframes=7
arnr-strength=5
arnr-type=centered
```

Preset file libvpx-1080p50_60.ffpreset

```
vcodec=libvpx
g=120
lag-in-frames=25
deadline=good
cpu-used=0
vprofile=1
```

```
qmax=51
qmin=11
slices=4
b=2M
#ignored unless using -pass 2
maxrate=24M
minrate=100k
auto-alt-ref=1
arnr-maxframes=7
arnr-strength=5
arnr-type=centered
```

Preset file libvpx-360p.ffpreset

```
vcodec=libvpx
g=120
lag-in-frames=16
deadline=good
cpu-used=0
vprofile=0
qmax=63
qmin=0
b=768k
#ignored unless using -pass 2
maxrate=1.5M
minrate=40k
auto-alt-ref=1
arnr-maxframes=7
arnr-strength=5
arnr-type=centered
```

Preset file libvpx-720p.ffpreset

```
vcodec=libvpx
g=120
lag-in-frames=16
deadline=good
cpu-used=0
vprofile=0
qmax=51
qmin=11
slices=4
b=2M
#ignored unless using -pass 2
maxrate=24M
minrate=100k
```

```
auto-alt-ref=1
arnr-maxframes=7
arnr-strength=5
arnr-type=centered
```

Preset file libvpx-720p50_60.ffpreset

```
vcodec=libvpx
g=120
lag-in-frames=25
deadline=good
cpu-used=0
vprofile=0
qmax=51
qmin=11
slices=4
b=2M
#ignored unless using -pass 2
maxrate=24M
minrate=100k
auto-alt-ref=1
arnr-maxframes=7
arnr-strength=5
arnr-type=centered
```

18. Interlaced Video

An interlacing is a technology invented during development of monochrome analog TV to eliminate flicker of old CRT monitors. The video frame is divided horizontally to regular lines and then to 2 fields, where the first field contains odd lines and the second field contains even lines.

NTSC, PAL and SECAM TV standards

In NTSC standard the frame has 525 lines of which 483 are visible, others are used for synchronization, vertical retrace, etc. The frame rate 30 fps means 60 fields per second, which corresponds with 60 Hz frequency of alternating current nominal in U.S.A. and prevents intermodulation, possible source of the rolling bars on the screen. Due to electric power frequency of 50 Hz over 120 countries use PAL or SECAM standard (Africa, Argentina, Asia, Australia, Brazil, Europe, etc.). This standards use 25 fps frame rate with 50 fields and a higher resolution with 625 scan lines. A comparison of NTSC and PAL/SECAM standards is described in the table:

Interlacing of video frames in TV standards		
Feature	NTSC	PAL, SECAM
Number of scan lines	525	625
Visible scan lines	483	576
frames per second	30	25
fields per second	60	50

FFmpeg contains several filters and options enabling to change the frame type and field order, to convert video from interlaced to progressive, etc.

The next diagram illustrates the worldwide usage of NTSC, PAL and SECAM standards, but in recent years they are replaced with the digital TV standards, please see the last section of this chapter for details.

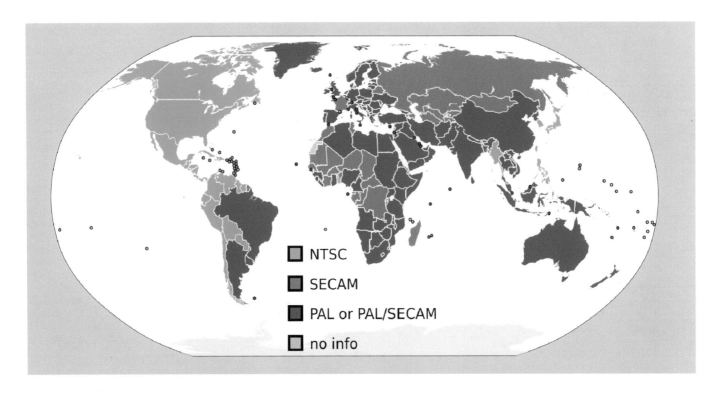

Interlaced frame type setting

When working with fieldorder and yadif filters described in this chapter, in complex transcoding using several filters it can be useful to set the field type for output frames with a **setfield** filter:

Video filter: setfield	
Description	Marks the type of interlaced field in output frames, the content of frame is not changed, only its property is updated. It is useful in a filterchain for the next processing with filters like **fieldorder** and **yadif**.
Syntax	setfield=*type*
Values for the type	
auto	do not mark anything, default value
bff	frame has bottom field first
tff	frame has top field first
prog	frame is progressive

For example to set the field type to the top field first, we can use the command:

```
ffmpeg -i input.vob -vf setfield=tff output.mov
```

Field order change of interlaced video

Videos encoded in PAL DV format are interlaced with bottom field first and the **fieldorder** filter can change it when transcoding from or to other interlaced formats.

Video filter: fieldorder	
Description	Changes the field order of interlaced video input from bottom field first to top field first and vice versa. Transformation shifts the frame content up or down by 1 line, and fills the remaining line with appropriate frame content. The method complies with most broadcast field order converters. If the input is not interlaced, or if its field order is the same as set in the command, then the input is not altered..
Syntax	fieldorder[=*order_type*]
Values for order_type parameter	
0 or bff	bottom field first
1 or tff	top field first, default value

For example to convert an interlaced video from DVD (VOB format) to DV (Digital Video) format, we can use the command:

```
ffmpeg -i dvd.vob -vf fieldorder=0 output.dv
```

Deinterlacing

Interlaced video was developed for analog CRT displays and cannot be reproduced on progressive digital displays like LCDs, plasma displays, etc. Some hardware or software utility must be used to deinterlace it, it means to join corresponding fields into complete video frames, that are encoded to the output video stream.

yadif filter

FFmpeg contains a special filter named **yadif** (**y**et **a**nother **d**e**i**nterlacing **f**ilter) providing deinterlacing of the input, but resulting video has a lower quality than the original, because the interlaced source cannot be completely restored.

Video filter: yadif	
Description	yadif = Yet Another DeInterlacing Filter
Syntax	`yadif[=mode[:parity[:auto]]]`
Parameters	
mode	interlacing mode, 4 integer values are available: 0 - output 1 frame for each frame, default value 1 - output 1 frame for each field 2 - like 0, but spatial interlacing check is skipped 3 - like 1, but spatial interlacing check is skipped
parity	picture field parity of input interlaced video, 3 integer values are available: 0 - top field first, default value if interlacing is unknown 1 - bottom field first -1 - enable automatic detection, default value
auto	sets which frames are deinterlaced, a boolean value: 0 - all frames, default value 1 - only frames marked as interlaced

For example to deinterlace the movie.avi file, we can use the command:

```
ffmpeg -i movie.avi -vf yadif movie-progressive.mov
```

Option -deinterlace

This option has no parameters and provides deinterlacing of video frames, but due to lower quality it is recommended to use the yadif or other deinterlacing filter.

Deinterlacing filters from MPlayer project

MPlayer project contains several filters designed for deinterlacing including detc, divtc, ivtc, mcdeint, pullup, softpulldown, softskip, etc. This filters use an experimental wrapper of **mp** filter and the quality is not always optimal. For example, to deinterlace an input using the ivtc filter, we can use the command:

```
ffmpeg -i input.mpg -vf mp=ivtc output.mp4
```

Pullup filter

The pullup filter from MPlayer project is designed to be much more robust than detc or ivtc filters, by taking advantage of future context in making its decisions. Like ivtc, pullup is stateless in the sense that it does not lock onto a pattern to follow, but instead it looks forward to the following fields in order to identify matches and rebuild progressive frames.

Video filter: pullup	
Description	Third-generation pulldown reversal (inverse telecine) filter, capable of handling mixed hard-telecine, 24000/1001 fps progressive, and 30000/1001 fps progressive content. Required is to follow pullup with the softskip filter when encoding to ensure that pullup is able to see each frame. Failure to do so will lead to incorrect output and will usually crash, due to design limitations in the codec/filter layer.
Syntax	**mp=pullup[=jl:jr:jt:jb:sb:mp]**
Description of parameters	
jt jl jr jb	These options set the amount of "junk" to ignore at the left, right, top, and bottom of the image, respectively. Left/right are in units of 8 pixels, while top/bottom are in units of 2 lines. The default is 8 pixels on each side.
sb	Strick breaks option, setting it to 1 will reduce the chances of pullup generating an occasional mismatched frame, but it may also cause an excessive number of frames to be dropped during high motion sequences. Conversely, setting it to −1 will make pullup match fields more easily. This may help processing of video where there is slight blurring between the fields, but may also cause there to be interlaced frames in the output.
mp	Metric plane option, it may be set to 1 or 2 to use a chroma plane instead of the luma plane for doing pullup's computations. This may improve accuracy on very clean source material, but more likely will decrease accuracy, especially if there is chroma noise (rainbow effect) or any grayscale video. The main purpose of setting mp to a chroma plane is to reduce CPU load and make pullup usable in realtime on slow machines.

The height of the input must be divisible by 4 and recommended is to use also the setpts filter to change the presentation timestamp. For example to deinterlace a telecine video in the film.vob file, we can use the command:

```
ffmpeg -i film.vob -qscale 2 -vf ^
mp=pullup=4:4:20:20:-1:0,mp=softskip,setpts=N/(24000/1001*TB) ^
-r 24001/1001 film.avi
```

Interlaced video and digital television

In recent years the analog TV broadcast using the interlaced video format is replaced with the digital TV standards that use a progressive format. Digital TV offers higher quality and more channels transmitted at the same bandwidth. Though the main transmission format is an MPEG Transport Stream (container specified in MPEG-2 Part 1), interlaced video is still supported in ATSC and DVB standards. The next picture illustrates the worldwide usage of digital TV terrestrial broadcast in 2012:

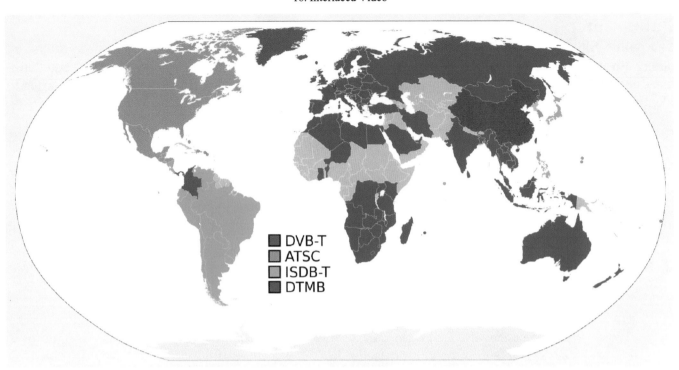

Comparison of digital TV standards for terrestrial broadcast (colored support interlaced video)				
	ATSC	**DTMB**	**DVB-T**	**ISDB-T**
Complete name	Advanced Television Systems Committee	Digital Terrestrial Multimedia Broadcast	Digital Video Broadcasting - Terrestrial	Integrated Services Digital Broadcasting -Terrestrial
Frequency range	various	various	470–862 MHz 174–230 MHz	470 MHz-770 MHz
Video coding	MPEG-2, MPEG-4	MPEG-2, AVS	MPEG-2, MPEG-4	MPEG-2, MPEG-4
Modulation	8VSB	TDS-OFDM	CP-OFDM	COFDM
Bandwidth per channel	6 MHz	8 MHz	6, 7, 8 MHz	6, 7, 8 MHz
Bitrate	max. 19.39 Mbit/s	from 4.813 Mbit/s to 32.486 Mbit/s	5 - 32 Mbit/s	3.65 - 30.98 Mbit/s
Countries	Canada, South Korea, USA, etc.	Cambodia, China, Hong Kong, Laos, Macau, etc.	Africa (north and south), Asia, Australia, Europe	Japan, Philippines, Thailand, South America

MPEG Transport Stream (MPEG-TS) has a **.ts** file extension and its format (muxer) is **mpegts**, so to multiplex output to this format we can use the command:

```
ffmpeg -i input.avi -f mpegts output.ts
```

19. FFmpeg Components and Projects

FFmpeg project consists of 4 command line tools and 9 software libraries, that are utilized by many companies and software projects. The syntax and usage of ffmpeg tool is described in the first chapter.

FFplay introduction

FFplay is a simple media player able to playback all media formats that ffmpeg tool can decode, please see the second chapter for displaying available formats and other lists.

FFmpeg component: ffplay	
Description	Simple media player that uses FFmpeg and SDL libraries, it was designed mainly for the testing and development.
Syntax	**ffplay [options] [input_file]**
Description of parameters	
options	almost all options available for the ffmpeg tool can be used also with ffplay
input_file	input can be a regular file, pipe, network stream, grabbing device, etc.

FFplay is very useful in showing the same output before it will be encoded to the file, please see the **Displaying output preview** section in the first chapter for details. For example to use ffplay to show various testsrc video source on a lightorange background, we can use the command:

```
ffplay -f lavfi -i testsrc -vf pad=400:300:(ow-iw)/2:(oh-ih)/2:orange
```

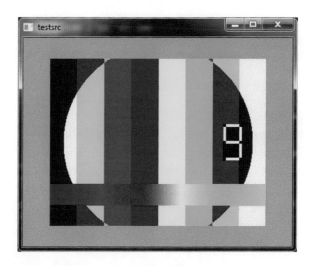

If we want to watch the video from the file document.avi and to listen audio from the file comments.mp3, we can use the command:

```
ffplay -i lavfi "movie=document.avi[out0];amovie=comments.mp3[out1]
```

If FFmpeg was compiled with **--enable-libiec61883** option, an input from a FireWire DV/HDV device connected to the computer can be displayed with the command:

```
ffplay -f iec61883 -i auto
```

Key and mouse controls during playback

While playing, ffplay can be controlled with the keys and mouse, details are in the table:

ffplay controls during playback	
key	**description**
q, ESC	quit
f	toggle fullscreen
p, Spacebar	toggle pause
a	cycle audio channel
v	cycle video channel
t	cycle among available subtitles
w	cycle among available show mode options: video, rdft, audio waves
arrow left / arrow right	seek 10 seconds backward / forward
pageDn / pageUp	seek 10 minutes backward / forward
mouse click	seek the percentage in file corresponding to the part of the width

Like the MPlayer, also ffplay quits on **ESC** key and toggles pause with a **spacebar**. The **f** key toggles the fullscreen mode, but sometimes it halts the Windows computer, at least older versions. If the media file contains multiple video streams, they can be cycled with the **v** key, audio streams can be cycled with the **a** key and subtitle streams with the **t** key. Pressing the **arrow right** key forwards the video by 10 seconds and the **PageUp** key by 10 minutes; **arrow left** key returns video by 10 seconds and the **pageDown** key by 10 minutes. More flexible time seeking offer the mouse clicks, we can move to any part by clicking on the corresponding player window part, for example a click on center will move to the middle of the media file.

FFplay show modes

When playing a video file, ffplay displays the **video**, it is the default value for its **-showmode** option, other values are **rdft** (inverse Real Discrete Fourier Transform) and **waves** (audio waves like from the filter showwaves). We can change between these modes during the playback by pressing the **w** key:

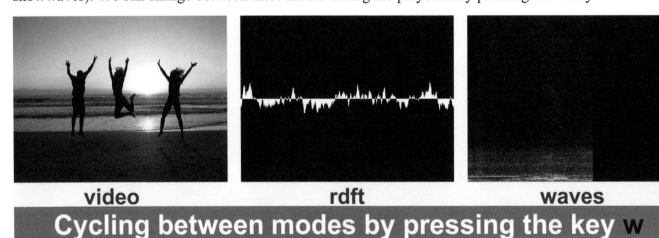

video   rdft   waves
Cycling between modes by pressing the key **w**

FFprobe introduction

The ffprobe is a utility that gathers information from multimedia streams and prints it in human and machine readable fashion. It can be used to check the format of the container used by a multimedia stream and the format and type of each media stream in it. Options are used to list some of the formats supported by ffprobe or to set which information to show, and to set how ffprobe shows it. Its output is easily parsable by a textual filter, and consists of one or more sections of a form defined by the selected writer specified by the **-of** (or -print_format) option. Examples of ffprobe usage are in the Debugging and Tests chapter.

FFmpeg component: ffprobe	
Description	Command line tool that detects various data from multimedia streams for analysis. It can be used standalone or with a textual filter to get sophisticated processing.
Syntax	**ffprobe [options] [input_file]**
Description of parameters	
options	almost all options available for the ffmpeg tool can be used also with ffprobe
input_file	input can be a regular file, pipe, network stream, grabbing device, etc.
Additional ffprobe options	
-bitexact	force bitexact output, useful to produce output not dependent on specific build
-count_frames	count number of frames per stream and report it in corresponding stream section
-count_packets	count number of packets per stream and report it in correspond. stream section
-of *w_name*[=*w_options*]	set printing format, ***w_name*** is writer name, ***w_options*** are writer options
-select_streams *str_spec*	select only streams specified by ***str_spec***, what can be a letter from the next: a=audio, d=data, s=subtitles, t=attachment, v=video
-show_data	show payload data, as hex and ASCII dump, coupled with **-show_packets**, it dumps packets' data, coupled with **-show_streams** it dumps the codec extradata
-show_error	show information about the found errors while probing the input
-show_format	show information about the container format of the input media stream
-show_format_entry *name*	like **-show_format**, but only prints the entry specified by ***name*** of the container format information, not all
-show_frames	show information about each frame contained in the input media stream
-show_library_version	show information related to library versions
-show_packets	how information about each packet contained in the input media stream
-show_private_data -private	show data depending on format of particular shown element, option is enabled by default, but can be set to 0, e.g. when creating XSD-compliant XML output
-show_streams	show information about each media stream contained in the input media stream
-show_versions	show information related to program and library versions, it is the equivalent of setting both **-show_program_version** and **-show_library_versions** options

FFserver introduction

The ffserver is a multimedia streaming server running on Linux, official Windows binaries are not yet available.

FFmpeg component: ffserver	
Description	Utility providing a streaming server for both audio and video. It supports several live feeds, streaming from files and time shifting on live feeds. If a sufficient feed storage is specified in the ffserver.conf configuration file, it is possible to seek to positions in the past on each live feed. ffserver runs on Linux in daemon mode by default, it means that it puts itself to the background and detaches from its console, unless it is started in debug mode or a NoDaemon option is specified in the configuration file.
Syntax	**ffserver [options]**
Description of parameters	
options	almost all options available for the ffmpeg tool can be used also with ffserver
Additional ffserver options	
-d	enable debug mode, this increases log verbosity, directs log messages to stdout and causes ffserver to run in the foreground and not as a daemon
-f *configfile*	use **configfile** instead of **/etc/ffserver.conf**
-n	enable no-launch mode, this disables all the Launch directives in the various <Stream> sections, since ffserver will not launch any ffmpeg instances, you will have to launch them manually

FFmpeg software libraries

libavcodec

The libavcodec is a library of codecs for decoding and encoding multimedia, it is very popular and multiplatform media players like MPlayer and VLC use it for the playback of many audio and video formats. It is able to decode and in certain cases also to encode some proprietary formats, including ones without official specification. These codecs in the standard libavcodec framework offer advantages over using the original codecs, mainly increased portability, and sometimes also better performance, because libavcodec contains a standard library of precisely optimized implementations of common building blocks like DCT and color space conversion.

The list of implemented codecs in libavcodec is in the Displaying Help and Features chapter.

libavdevice

The libavdevice is a special devices muxing/demuxing library and is a complement to libavformat library. It provides various platform-specific muxers and demuxers, for instance for grabbing devices, audio capture and playback. Therefore the (de)muxers in libavdevice are of the AVFMT_NOFILE type (they use their own I/O functions). The filename passed to avformat_open_input() often does not refer to an actually existing file, but has some special device-specific meaning, for example for the x11grab device it is the display name.

Available devices are listed in the second chapter, section Available media formats.

libavfilter

The libavfilter is a library of filters that provides the media filtering layer to FFmpeg and client libraries or applications. It simplifies the design of FFmpeg tools and enhances their flexibility.

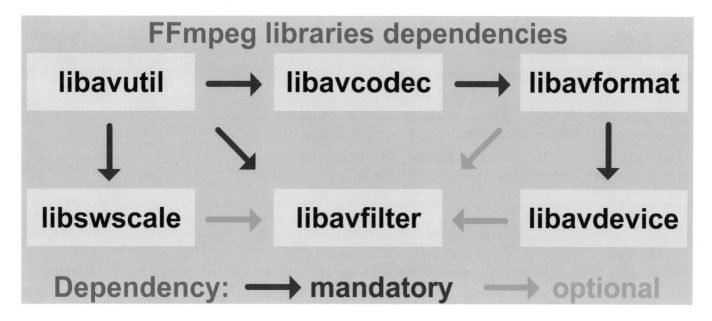

libavfilter contains advanced mechanism of a format negotiation and minimizes pixel/format conversions. A filter processes buffers, where buffer can contain a video frame or audio sources. The properties of each buffer - frame type, timestamp, file position, etc., can be accessed and handled during the processing. The list of available filters is in the second chapter.

libavformat

The libavformat is a library containing demuxers and muxers for audio/video container formats. Among implemented muxers are crc, framecrc, ico, md5, MOV/MP4/ISMV, mpegts, matroska, etc.
Available media formats are listed in the second chapter.

libavutil

The libavutil is a helper library containing routines for different parts of FFmpeg, for example:
- **av_get_token** function in **libavutil/avstring.h** file can be used to parse a token quoted or escaped
- **libavutil/eval.h** file contains an interface for evaluating arithmetic expressions
- **libavutil/samplefmt.h** file contains definitions of available audio sample formats
- **libavutil/audioconvert.h** file contains specification for audio channel layouts

libpostproc

The libpostproc is a library containing video postprocessing routines.

libswresample

The libswresample library is capable of handling different sample formats, sample rates and different number of channels and different channel layout. It supports directly converting sample formats and packed/planar in a single pass.

libswscale

The libswscale is a library containing video image scaling routines and provides a fast and modular scaling interface.

Projects using FFmpeg components

The number of projects using various FFmpeg tools and libraries is big and many of them are listed on **http://ffmpeg.org/projects.html**

HTML5 support in Google Chrome

Probably the most used application utilizing FFmpeg libraries is the Google Chrome web browser, one of the most popular web browsers. FFmpeg libraries were included to the Chrome in 2009 to support HTML5 audio and video elements. Other browsers using FFmpeg include Chromium and Orygin web browser.

Videoprocessing on YouTube and Facebook

The biggest video sharing website YouTube and the largest social network Facebook are the world's largest users of ffmpeg in terms of processed videos, what represents several million videos per week.

Multimedia frameworks utilizing FFmpeg

Multimedia frameworks using FFmpeg libraries are described in the table.

Multimedia frameworks using FFmpeg		
Name	**Website**	**Description**
ffdshow	ffdshow-tryout.sourceforge.net	Media encoder and decoder, implemented as DirectShow and VFW filter, Windows only
GStreamer	gstreamer.freedesktop.org	Library for constructing graphs of media-handling components. The applications it supports range from simple Ogg/Vorbis playback, audio/video streaming to complex audio (mixing) and video (non-linear editing) processing.
MLT	www.mltframework.org	MLT is an open source multimedia framework, designed and developed for television broadcasting. It provides a toolkit for broadcasters, video editors, media players, transcoders, web streamers and other types of applications.
OpenMAX	www.khronos.org/openmax	OpenMAX is a royalty-free, cross-platform API that provides comprehensive streaming media codec and application portability by enabling accelerated multimedia components to be developed, integrated and programmed across multiple operating systems and silicon platforms.

Video editors

- Avidemux
- Blender (3D)
- Cinelerra
- Kdenlive
- Kino

Audio editors

- Audacity
- Sox

Media players using FFmpeg

Media frameworks utilizing FFmpeg libraries are described in the table:

Media players using FFmpeg		
Name	**Website**	**Description**
Audacious	audacious-media-player.org	Audacious is an open source audio player. Drag and drop folders and individual song files, search for artists and albums in your entire music library, or create and edit your own custom playlists. Listen to CD's or stream music from the Internet. Tweak the sound with the graphical equalizer or experiment with LADSPA effects. Enjoy the modern GTK-themed interface or change things up with Winamp classic skins. Use the plugins included with Audacious to fetch lyrics for your music, to set an alarm in the morning, and more.
Gnash	www.gnashdev.org	Gnash is the GNU SWF movie player, which can be run standalone on the desktop or an embedded device, as well as as a plugin for several browsers.
KMPlayer	http://kmplayer.kde.org	Video player plugin for Konqueror and basic MPlayer / Xine / ffmpeg / ffserver / VDR frontend for KDE. The KMPlayer KPart plugin for Konqueror mimics QuickTime, MS Media Player and RealPlayer plugin browser plugins.
MPlayer	www.mplayerhq.hu	Movie player which runs on many systems. It plays most MPEG/VOB, AVI, Ogg/OGM, VIVO, ASF/WMA/WMV, QT/MOV/MP4, RealMedia, Matroska, NUT, NuppelVideo, FLI, YUV4MPEG, FILM, RoQ, PVA files, supported by many native, XAnim, and Win32 DLL codecs. You can watch VideoCD, SVCD, DVD, 3ivx, DivX 3/4/5, WMV and even H.264 movies.
Rockbox	www.rockbox.org	Rockbox is a free replacement firmware for digital music players. It runs on a wide range of players.
VLC	www.videolan.org/vlc	VLC is a free and open source cross-platform multimedia player and framework that plays most multimedia files as well as DVD, Audio CD, VCD, and various streaming protocols.
V-Player	vchannel.sourceforge.net/player.html	Cross-platform media player based on ffmpeg library. Now V-Player supports Windows, Linux and OS X platforms. User interface is written on C++ with Qt 4 on all platforms.
Xine	www.xine-project.org	Free multimedia player. It plays back CDs, DVDs, and VCDs. It also decodes multimedia files like AVI, MOV, WMV, and MP3 from local disk drives, and displays multimedia streamed over the Internet.

20. Microphone and Webcam

Microphone and a webcam (web camera) are the common parts of the computer equipment and FFmpeg contains elements for their usage.

Introduction to input devices

FFmpeg recognizes microphone and webcam like input devices that are defined as elements that enable to access the data from attached multimedia devices. On Windows microphone and webcam are accessed with a **dshow** input device, that is described in the table:

Input device: dshow	
Description	Input device on Windows OS, supported are audio and video devices.
Syntax	*options type=media_type[:type=media_type]* parameter in [] is optional
Description of *type* parameter	
type	value can be video or audio
Available values for *options* parameter	
audio_buffer_size	audio device buffer size in milliseconds (which can directly impact latency, depends on the device), defaults to using the device's default buffer size (usually some multiple of 500ms); setting this value too low can degrade performance
audio_device_number	audio device number for devices with same name (starts at 0, defaults to 0)
channels	number of channels in the captured audio
framerate	framerate in the captured video
list_devices	if set to 1, prints a list of devices and exits
list_options	if set to 1, prints a list of selected device's options and exits
pixel_format	pixel format to use, can be set only when video codec is not set or set to rawvideo
sample_rate	sample rate (in Hz) of the captured audio
sample_size	sample size (in bits) of the captured audio
video_device_number	video device number for devices with same name (starts at 0, defaults to 0)
video_size	video size in the captured video

List of available cameras and microphones

Portable computers have a webcam already built-in or we can connect one to the computer, usually via the USB port. Microphone is also often built in the computer, or we can attach one to the computer's microphone jack, commonly pink, the jack for the earphones is green. To display all available input devices on Windows with DirectShow, we use the **list_devices** option of the **dshow** device like in the command:

```
ffmpeg -list_devices 1 -f dshow -i dummy
```

The output depends on the used computer, an example output illustrates the next image:

Output shows that available is one webcam named "HP Webcam" and one microphone named "Microphone (Realtek High Defini". The complete name of the microphone is 'Microphone (Realtek High Definition)', but displayed are only 31 characters.

Available options for webcam

Webcam has usually several working modes that are displayed with **-list_options** parameter. To display options for the webcam named "HP Webcam" from the previous output we can use the command:

```
ffmpeg -list_options true -f dshow -i video="HP Webcam"
```

The output depends on the camera type and usually shows available resolutions (frame sizes) and frame rates:

```
[dshow @ 021bd040] DirectShow video device options
[dshow @ 021bd040]  Pin "Capture"
[dshow @ 021bd040]   min s=640x480 fps=15 max s=640x480 fps=30
[dshow @ 021bd040]   min s=640x480 fps=15 max s=640x480 fps=30
[dshow @ 021bd040]   min s=160x120 fps=15 max s=160x120 fps=30
[dshow @ 021bd040]   min s=160x120 fps=15 max s=160x120 fps=30
[dshow @ 021bd040]   min s=176x144 fps=15 max s=176x144 fps=30
[dshow @ 021bd040]   min s=176x144 fps=15 max s=176x144 fps=30
[dshow @ 021bd040]   min s=320x240 fps=15 max s=320x240 fps=30
[dshow @ 021bd040]   min s=320x240 fps=15 max s=320x240 fps=30
[dshow @ 021bd040]   min s=352x288 fps=15 max s=352x288 fps=30
[dshow @ 021bd040]   min s=352x288 fps=15 max s=352x288 fps=30
video=HP Webcam: Immediate exit requested
```

Displaying and recording webcam input

When we know the webcam name, we can display its input on the screen or record it to the file. The next commands displays the webcam input with default settings (usually it is the maximal size and maximal frame rate), the first one with ffplay media player and the second one with SDL output device:

```
ffplay -f dshow -i video="HP Webcam"
ffmpeg -f dshow -i video="HP Webcam" -f sdl "webcam via ffmpeg"
```

To record the webcam input to the file we can use the command:

```
ffmpeg -f dshow -i video="HP Webcam" webcam.avi
```

Webcams usually have a default media format like AVI, MOV, etc. to which they save their input with an associated application for working with webcam. Using these default file format sometimes results in a better video quality than using other file format.

Using two webcams

If two webcams are available, we can connect them to the computer via USB port and display their output at once with ffmpeg tool. The next command shows the webcam names including the microphone name(s), the console output follows:

```
ffmpeg -list_devices 1 -f dshow -i dummy

[dshow @ 01f7d000] DirectShow video devices
[dshow @ 01f7d000]  "Sirius USB2.0 Camera"
[dshow @ 01f7d000]  "HP Webcam"
[dshow @ 01f7d000] DirectShow audio devices
[dshow @ 01f7d000]  "Microphone (Realtek High Defini"
dummy: Immediate exit requested
```

The options for HP Webcam and the command how to display them are in the section **Available options for webcam**, below are options for the second webcam named **Sirius USB2.0 Camera**:

```
[dshow @ 003fd080] DirectShow video device options
[dshow @ 003fd080]  Pin "Capture"
[dshow @ 003fd080]   pixel_format=yuyv422  min s=640x480 fps=15 max s=640x480 fps=30
[dshow @ 003fd080]   pixel_format=yuyv422  min s=640x480 fps=15 max s=640x480 fps=30
[dshow @ 003fd080]   pixel_format=yuyv422  min s=352x288 fps=15 max s=352x288 fps=30
[dshow @ 003fd080]   pixel_format=yuyv422  min s=352x288 fps=15 max s=352x288 fps=30
[dshow @ 003fd080]   pixel_format=yuyv422  min s=320x240 fps=15 max s=320x240 fps=30
[dshow @ 003fd080]   pixel_format=yuyv422  min s=320x240 fps=15 max s=320x240 fps=30
[dshow @ 003fd080]   pixel_format=yuyv422  min s=176x144 fps=15 max s=176x144 fps=30
[dshow @ 003fd080]   pixel_format=yuyv422  min s=176x144 fps=15 max s=176x144 fps=30
[dshow @ 003fd080]   pixel_format=yuyv422  min s=160x120 fps=15 max s=160x120 fps=30
[dshow @ 003fd080]   pixel_format=yuyv422  min s=160x120 fps=15 max s=160x120 fps=30
[dshow @ 003fd080]   pixel_format=yuyv422  min s=800x600 fps=10 max s=800x600 fps=20
[dshow @ 003fd080]   pixel_format=yuyv422  min s=800x600 fps=10 max s=800x600 fps=20
[dshow @ 003fd080]   pixel_format=yuyv422  min s=1280x960 fps=5 max s=1280x960 fps=7.5
[dshow @ 003fd080]   pixel_format=yuyv422  min s=1280x960 fps=5 max s=1280x960 fps=7.5
[dshow @ 003fd080]   pixel_format=yuyv422  min s=1280x1024 fps=5 max s=1280x1024 fps=7.5
[dshow @ 003fd080]   pixel_format=yuyv422  min s=1280x1024 fps=5 max s=1280x1024 fps=7.5
[dshow @ 003fd080]   pixel_format=yuyv422  min s=1600x1200 fps=2.5 max s=1600x1200 fps=5
[dshow @ 003fd080]   pixel_format=yuyv422  min s=1600x1200 fps=2.5 max s=1600x1200 fps=5
[dshow @ 003fd080]  vcodec=mjpeg  min s=640x480 fps=7.5 max s=640x480 fps=15
[dshow @ 003fd080]  vcodec=mjpeg  min s=640x480 fps=7.5 max s=640x480 fps=15
[dshow @ 003fd080]  vcodec=mjpeg  min s=352x288 fps=7.5 max s=352x288 fps=15
[dshow @ 003fd080]  vcodec=mjpeg  min s=352x288 fps=7.5 max s=352x288 fps=15
[dshow @ 003fd080]  vcodec=mjpeg  min s=320x240 fps=7.5 max s=320x240 fps=15
[dshow @ 003fd080]  vcodec=mjpeg  min s=320x240 fps=7.5 max s=320x240 fps=15
[dshow @ 003fd080]  vcodec=mjpeg  min s=176x144 fps=7.5 max s=176x144 fps=15
[dshow @ 003fd080]  vcodec=mjpeg  min s=176x144 fps=7.5 max s=176x144 fps=15
[dshow @ 003fd080]  vcodec=mjpeg  min s=160x120 fps=7.5 max s=160x120 fps=15
[dshow @ 003fd080]  vcodec=mjpeg  min s=160x120 fps=7.5 max s=160x120 fps=15
[dshow @ 003fd080]  vcodec=mjpeg  min s=800x600 fps=7.5 max s=800x600 fps=15
[dshow @ 003fd080]  vcodec=mjpeg  min s=800x600 fps=7.5 max s=800x600 fps=15
[dshow @ 003fd080]  vcodec=mjpeg  min s=1280x960 fps=7.5 max s=1280x960 fps=15
[dshow @ 003fd080]  vcodec=mjpeg  min s=1280x960 fps=7.5 max s=1280x960 fps=15
[dshow @ 003fd080]  vcodec=mjpeg  min s=1280x1024 fps=7.5 max s=1280x1024 fps=15
[dshow @ 003fd080]  vcodec=mjpeg  min s=1280x1024 fps=7.5 max s=1280x1024 fps=15
[dshow @ 003fd080]  vcodec=mjpeg  min s=1600x1200 fps=7.5 max s=1600x1200 fps=15
[dshow @ 003fd080]  vcodec=mjpeg  min s=1600x1200 fps=7.5 max s=1600x1200 fps=15
video=Sirius USB2.0 Camera: Immediate exit requested
```

To display the input from both webcams we can use the **overlay** filter and because the default video size of both webcams is 640x480 pixels, we set the size of the second input to 320x240 (qvga) with **-video_size** option, the command is (single quotes return error, only double quotes can be used):

```
ffmpeg -f dshow -i "video=Sirius USB2.0 Camera" -f dshow -video_size qvga ^
-i "video=HP Webcam" -filter_complex overlay -f sdl "2 webcams"
```

The previous command locate the second webcam input to the top left corner, to place it for example to the bottom right corner, we add the width and height parameters to the overlay filter: **overlay=W/2:H/2**

Recording sound and sending it to loudspeakers

Similar to the webcam, also microphone has several working modes that are displayed with **-list_options** parameter set to **true** or **1**. For the input parameter is used an **audio** type instead of **video**, the command for the microphone that was listed with the **-list_devices** option in the previous sections is:

```
ffmpeg -list_options 1 -f dshow -i "audio=Microphone (Realtek High Defini"

[dshow @ 0030d0c0] DirectShow audio device options
[dshow @ 0030d0c0]  Pin "Capture"
[dshow @ 0030d0c0]   min ch=1 bits=8 rate= 11025 max ch=2 bits=16 rate= 44100
audio=Microphone (Realtek High Defini: Immediate exit requested
```

To send the sound from the microphone to the loudspeakers we can use the command:

```
ffplay -f dshow -i audio="Microphone (Realtek High Defini"
```

The command for recording the sound to the audio file is:

```
ffmpeg -f dshow -i audio="Microphone (Realtek High Defini" -t 60 mic.mp3
```

To record both audio and video from the microphone and webcam we can use the command:

```
ffmpeg -f dshow -i audio="Microphone (Realtek High Defini":^
video="HP Webcam" webcam_with_sound.avi
```

21. Batch Files

Advantages of batch files

FFmpeg tools are often used for various tasks and it is not easy to remember all parameters of different codecs, filters, etc. Saving various command combinations to the batch files optimizes the work and brings the development to the next level. Batch files are text files with a **.bat** extension and on Windows OS are used mainly for administrative tasks. They contain commands, which are processed sequentially and can print various messages, ask for input, etc. Example of a simple batch file is a text:

```
@echo off
ffmpeg -i %1
```

This text is saved to a file **test.bat** and called by the next command, where *filename* is the media file the properties of which we want to see (**.bat** extension in the command is optional):

test.bat *filename*   **(or)**   **test** *filename*

Batch file commands

Available Windows console commands can be displayed with the command **help** or **help|more**. Some of them are specific to the batch files. These and additional commands are described in the table:

Basic batch file commands	
@	Used at the beginning of the line, then the command is not echoed. Example: @echo off
%n (n is natural number)	Placeholder for space-separated parameters entered on the command line after the name of the batch file, for example **greeting.bat** with 2 lines: **@echo off** **Good %1, %2** If called with the command: **greeting day friends** displayed result is: Good day, friends
:label	Starting point for GOTO command, changes the processing sequence, example of batch file: **line 1 ... line 10** (lines 1 - 10 contains various commands) **:NewItem** **line 12 ... line 16** (lines 12 - 16 contains various commands) **GOTO NewItem** When the processing flow comes to the line 17, GOTO command sends it back to the NewItem label and the run continues on the line 12.
CALL	Syntax: call [drive][path] filename [batch parameters] Calls another batch file and after all of its commands are ready, processing continues on the next line of the calling file. If the called file does not exist, an error message is displayed.
CHOICE	Stops the processing and let the user to select one of choices, usually yes or no. Syntax: CHOICE [/C[:]choices] [/N] [/S] [/T[:]c,nn] [text] /C[:]choices Specifies allowable keys. Default is YN. /N Does not display choices and ? at end of prompt string. /S Treats choice keys as case sensitive. /T[:]c,nn Defaults choice to c after <nn> seconds. text Prompts string to display.
CLS	Clears the screen and the console output continues from the top.

ECHO	Syntax: ECHO [ON | OFF] or ECHO [message] Command "echo off" stops printing of commands during processing, "echo on", that is default, turns it on again. Command "echo some_text" will print **some_text** during processing.
FOR	Runs a specified command for each file in a set of files. FOR %%variable IN (set) DO command [CommandLineOptions] %variable Specifies a replaceable parameter, which value is used by the command. (set) Specifies a set of one or more files, wildcards may be used, e.g. (*.doc) command Specifies the command to carry out for each file. command-parameters Specifies parameters or switches for the specified command. Example command to display all TXT files (in batch is used **%%f**, on cmd line **%f** form): **FOR %%F IN (*.txt) DO type %%F**
GOTO label	Redirects processing to the specified label, please see :label command above for the example.
IF	IF [NOT] ERRORLEVEL number command IF [NOT] string1==string2 command IF [NOT] EXIST filename command NOT Specifies that DOS should carry out the command only if the condition is false. ERRORLEVEL number Specifies a true condition if the last program run returned an exit code equal to or greater than the number specified. command Specifies the command to carry out if the condition is met. string1==string2 Specifies a true condition if the specified text strings match. EXIST filename Specifies a true condition if the specified filename exists. IF command specifies conditional processing.
PAUSE	Stops processing and displays the message: "Press any key to continue...".
REM	Syntax: REM [comment] Used to add descriptions and other information, that is not used during processing.
SHIFT	Syntax: SHIFT [n] (n is natural number) Used to shift the position of numbered parameters entered via command line and used in the batch file with %1, %2, etc. Example of the batch file name shift.bat: **@ECHO OFF** **ECHO %1** **SHIFT** **ECHO %1** Now when we start this file with **shift First Second**, the result is: First First
START	START ["title"] [/Dpath] [/I] [/MIN] [/MAX] [/SEPARATE | /SHARED] [/LOW | /NORMAL | /HIGH | /REALTIME | /ABOVENORMAL | /BELOWNORMAL] [/WAIT] [/B] [command/program] [parameters] Starts a new window for the specified command. For the description of all options, please type **help start**

Typical usage of batch files

- video conversion for portable devices
- audio conversion from various formats to MP3 files for MP3 players
- decreasing the frame size and bitrate for the usage on the web.

Batch files are used for audio and video processing tasks that are often repeated. For example, we can place a shortcut on the desktop to the file **yt2mp3.bat** located in the directory C:\media, where are saved videos downloaded from YouTube for conversion to MP3 format. The yt2mp3.bat file contains the next lines:

```
@echo off
set /p i=Please enter the name of input file:
set /p o=Please enter the name of output file without MP3 extension:
ffmpeg -i %i% -b:a 128k -ar 44100 %o%.mp3
ffplay %o%.mp3
```

After the successful conversion the ffplay starts to play the created MP3 file.

Tone generator

ToneGenerator.bat is a batch file that generates tones of specified pitch and duration. In order to distinguish 2 tones of the same pitch in a sequence, to each tone is added the file silence.mp3, which duration is 0.2 second, if we plan to speed up the tempo highly, it can be 0.3 or more seconds, the command is:

```
ffmpeg -f lavfi -i aevalsrc=0 -t 0.2 silence.mp3
```

The file ToneGenerator.bat has the following content (the line numbers was added for easier explanation and are not present in the ToneGenerator.bat computer file):

```
1  @echo off
2  set /p n=Please enter the note name:
3  set /p f=Please enter the frequency:
4  set /p d=Please enter the duration in seconds:
5  ffmpeg -f lavfi -i aevalsrc=sin(%f%*2*PI*t) -t %d% tone%n%_%d%.mp3
6  copy /b tone%n%%d%.mp3+silence.mp3 tone%n%_%d%.mp3
```

Explanation of particular lines (if the tone will be used alone, adding the silence can be skipped):

1: Command echo off stops displaying the content of the commands during batch file processing, @ sign excludes also this command from displaying.

2: Command set /p variable_name=text creates a variable and during the job processing displays a line with text and waits for the input ended by the Enter key. Here the string "Please enter the note name: " is displayed and after pressing Enter, a new variable **n** is created and contains the entered value.

3: Similar to Line 2, created is the variable **f** with entered frequency.

4: Similar to Line 2, created variable **d** contains duration of the tone in seconds.

5: ffmpeg uses lavfi (libavfilter virtual input device) and aevalsrc audio input device to generate sound of frequency specified by variable **f** with a duration set by variable **d**. The output file in MP3 format has its name combined from the note name and duration.

6: A short MP3 file with 0.2 second length is added to the generated file for a differentiation between tones by the **copy** command with **/b** option, that specifies a binary mode. The name of the final file has the form "tone+note-name+_duration+.mp3", for example for A4 tone with 1 second duration it is noteA4_1.mp3.

Creating Jingle Bells

Jingle Bells is a popular winter song and its refrain has only 5 notes, though some are in more durations, the image shows the sequence with the text:

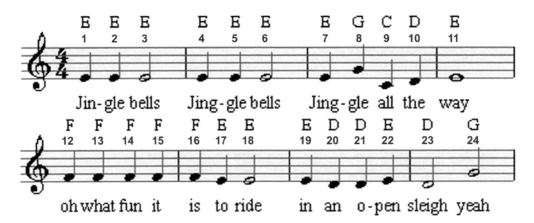

Now we generate 9 different tones with the ToneGenerator.bat from the previous section:

- E4, frequency 329.63 Hz, duration 1 second - file E_1.mp3
- E4, frequency 329.63 Hz, duration 2 seconds - file E_2.mp3
- E4, frequency 329.63 Hz, duration 4 seconds - file E_4.mp3
- G4, frequency 392.00 Hz, duration 1 second - file G_1.mp3
- G4, frequency 392.00 Hz, duration 2 seconds - file G_2.mp3
- C4, frequency 261.63 Hz, duration 1 second - file C_1.mp3
- D4, frequency 293.66 Hz, duration 1 second - file D_1.mp3
- D4, frequency 293.66 Hz, duration 2 seconds - file D_2.mp3
- F4, frequency 349.23 Hz, duration 1 second - file F_1.mp3

The octave number 4 was skipped from the filenames. The tones from the first line and second lines can be joined with the next 2 commands, the third command joins the both lines:

```
copy /b E_1.mp3+E_1.mp3+E_2.mp3+E_1.mp3+E_1.mp3+E_2.mp3+E_1.mp3+^
G_1.mp3D+C_1.mp3+D_1.mp3+E_4.mp3 line1.mp3
copy /b F_1.mp3+F_1.mp3+F_1.mp3+F_1.mp3+F_1.mp3+E_1.mp3+E_2.mp3+^
E_1.mp3D+D_1.mp3+D_1.mp3+E_1.mp3+D_2.mp3+G_2.mp3 line2.mp3
copy /b line1.mp3+line2.mp3 refrain.mp3
```

Another method is to modify the ToneGenerator.bat file to produce numbered filenames and then to join them with a batch file at once. The modified version of ToneGenerator.bat file is below, we can use it to produce 24 MP3 files with the filenames tone01.mp3, tone02.mp3, ..., tone24.mp3:

```
@echo off
echo If the number of notes is over 9, start numbering with 0.
set /p n=Please enter the note number:
set /p f=Please enter the frequency:
set /p d=Please enter the duration in seconds:
ffmpeg -f lavfi -i aevalsrc=sin(%f%*2*PI*t) -t %d% %n%.mp3
copy /b %n%.mp3+silence.mp3 tone%n%.mp3
```

Now we can join all 24 MP3 files by the FileJoiner.bat batch file with the content:

```
@echo off
copy /y nul output >nul
set /p t=Please enter the file type:
for %%f in (*.%t%) do copy /b output+%%f output
ren output output.%t%
```

- Line 2 creates an empty file that is used as an initial file to which is copied the first file from the directory.
- Line 3 asks for the file extension and stores it in the **t** variable, files with this extension will be joined.
- Line 4 uses the **for** loop to copy files sequentially to the file **output**.
- Line 5 adds the extension to the file **output**.

Both methods produces refrains that are very slow compared to the original song and the **atempo** filter can be used to adjust the speed:

```
ffmpeg -i output.mp3 -af atempo=2 refrain.mp3
```

The atempo filter can be applied more times, details are in the chapter Time Operations.

Simplified conversion

Chapter Preset for Codecs explained how to simplify conversion with the preset files. If you often convert media with various presets, the batch file asking for particular preset can be useful, example of a simple batch file called Conversion.bat is below:

```
1  @echo off
2  echo Please enter 0 as the filename if no preset should be used.
3  set /p i=Please enter the name of input file:
4  set /p e=Please enter the output file extension:
5  set /p o=Please enter the name of output file:
6  set /p p=Please enter the name of the preset file:
7  set /p a=Please enter additional parameters:
8  if %p% == 0 goto NOPRESET
9  ffmpeg -i %i% -fpre %p%.ffpreset %a% %o%.%e%
10 exit
11 :NOPRESET
12 ffmpeg -i %i% %a% %o%.%e%
```

Please see previous sections for the description of the lines 1 - 7.
- Line 8 uses the IF construct to select the conversion with or without the preset file, if variable p is 0, then the processing continues after the label NOPRESET due to the GOTO command directive
- Line 9 converts the input if the preset file was specified
- Line 10 terminates the processing so the conversion on line 12 is skipped
- Line 12 converts the input without the preset file using an optional additional parameters.

The file Conversion.bat can be modified in many ways, for example to include filtering, more inputs, etc.

22. Color Corrections

Color corrections usually denote image editions like adjusting brightness, color balance (red, green and blue channels), gamma, hue, saturation, etc. These modifications in FFmpeg are provided by specifying adequate parameters to various filters, therefore included is a theoretical introduction.

Video modifications with lookup table

FFmpeg contains 3 video filters, that can produce a lookup table (LUT), which binds each pixel component input value to an output value. New values are applied to the input video frames and encoded to the output.

<table>
<tr><th colspan="6" align="center">Video filters: lut, lutrgb, lutyuv</th></tr>
<tr>
<td>Description</td>
<td colspan="5">The lut filter creates a look up table for binding each pixel component input value to an output value and applies it to the input video. This filter requires either YUV or RGB pixel format in input. Exact component related to each option depends on the format in input.
The lutrgb filter is the same as lut filter, but requires an RGB pixel format in the input.
The lutyuv filter is the same as lut filter, but requires a YUV pixel format in the input.</td>
</tr>
<tr>
<td>Syntax</td>
<td colspan="5" align="center"><code>lut=[c0=expr[:c1=expr[:c2=expr[:c3=expr]]]]</code>
<code>lutrgb=[r=expr[:g=expr[:b=expr[:a=expr]]]]</code>
<code>lutyuv=[y=expr[:u=expr[:v=expr[:a=expr]]]]</code></td>
</tr>
<tr><th colspan="6" align="center">Description of parameters</th></tr>
<tr><th colspan="2" align="center">lut filter</th><th colspan="2" align="center">lutrgb filter</th><th colspan="2" align="center">lutyuv filter</th></tr>
<tr><td>c0</td><td>first pixel component</td><td>r</td><td>red component</td><td>y</td><td>Y or luminance component</td></tr>
<tr><td>c1</td><td>second pixel component</td><td>g</td><td>green component</td><td>u</td><td>U or Cb component</td></tr>
<tr><td>c2</td><td>third pixel component</td><td>b</td><td>blue component</td><td>v</td><td>V or Cr component</td></tr>
<tr><td>c3</td><td>fourth, same as alpha</td><td>a</td><td>alpha component</td><td>a</td><td>alpha component</td></tr>
<tr><th colspan="6" align="center">Variables and functions available in expression expr</th></tr>
<tr><td colspan="2" align="center">w, h</td><td colspan="4">input width and height</td></tr>
<tr><td colspan="2" align="center">val</td><td colspan="4">input value for the pixel element</td></tr>
<tr><td colspan="2" align="center">clipval</td><td colspan="4">input value clipped in the minval-maxval range</td></tr>
<tr><td colspan="2" align="center">maxval</td><td colspan="4">maximum value for the pixel component</td></tr>
<tr><td colspan="2" align="center">minval</td><td colspan="4">minimum value for the pixel component</td></tr>
<tr><td colspan="2" align="center">negval</td><td colspan="4">negated value for the pixel component value clipped in the minval - maxval range; negval = maxval - clipval + minval</td></tr>
<tr><td colspan="2" align="center">clip(val)</td><td colspan="4">computed value in val clipped in the minval - maxval range</td></tr>
<tr><td colspan="2" align="center">gammaval(gamma)</td><td colspan="4">computed gamma correction value clipped in the minval - maxval range</td></tr>
<tr><td colspan="6">Note: default value of all expressions is val (pixel input value), so by default the output is unchanged.</td></tr>
</table>

Conversion to monochrome (black-and-white) image

Changing color input to the monochrome output that contains only a black and white colors is useful for the playback on monochrome monitors. To show SMPTE bars in B&W, we can use one of the commands:

```
ffplay -f lavfi -i smptebars -vf lut=c1=128:c2=128
ffplay -f lavfi -i smptebars -vf lutyuv=u=128:v=128
```

| **SMPTE bars** | **Monochrome version** |

Introduction to color spaces

To use **lutrgb** and **lutyuv** filters properly, the RGB and YUV color spaces are compared in the table:

Comparison of RGB and YUV color spaces		
	RGB	**YUV (Y'CbCr)**
Description	additive color space in which any color is created by adding red, green and blue light	image is divided to 1 luma and 2 chroma components
Components	R = red channel	Y' = luma (brightness)
	G = green channel	U = Y' - B = Cb (luma - blue)
	B = blue channel	V = Y' - R = Cr (luma - red)
Usage	computers, digital cameras, etc.	television, video, etc.
Illustration		

All colors can be created by the combination of 3 fundamental colors: red, green and blue. To adapt this fact into the digital video, developed were color models and color spaces that specify standards how to present colors as numbers. The basic color space is RGB (red-green-blue), where any color is expressed as a result of mixing these 3 colors with a various intensity, usually expressed on a scale from 0 to 255 ($256=16^2$ values) or hexadecimally from x00 to xff.

YUV color space and its derivatives

When color TV was invented, TV broadcast in color had to be displayed on the black-and-white TV sets. Based on the fact that human eyes are mostly sensitive to the green, less to red and even less to blue color, developed was a new color space YUV and later Y'CbCr, where

- Y' is gamma corrected brightness of a green color
- Cr is a chroma component of red color minus luma
- Cb is a chroma component of blue color minus luma

Luma (luminance) and chroma (chrominance)

Luma and luminance denote a brightness of the image (achromatic part), luma is used in the video engineering and luminance in the color theory (CIE, ICC, etc.), the details are in the next table:

Luma and luminance comparison		
	luma	**luminance**
definition	weighted sum of gamma-corrected R'G'B' video components	weighted sum of linear RGB video components
symbol	Y' (prime symbol means gamma-correction)	Y
formula for CCIR 601	$Y' = 0.299\ R' + 0.587\ G' + 0.114\ B'$	$Y = 0.299\ R + 0.587\ G + 0.114\ B$
formula for Rec. BT 709	$Y' = 0.2126\ R' + 0.7152\ G' + 0.0722\ B'$	$Y = 0.2126\ R + 0.7152\ G + 0.0722\ B$
Coefficients for R, G and B was derived as average values from a color sensitivity test with many persons.		

Chroma and chrominance denote the color part of the image, the term chrominance is used mainly in a color theory and the term chroma is used in video engineering, especially in chroma subsampling. Chroma is usually divided to two components (prime symbol ' denotes a gamma correction):

- $U = B' - Y'$ or $U = C_B$ (blue color - luma)
- $V = R' - Y'$ or $V = C_R$ (red color - luma)

Pixel formats

The theory of color spaces is implemented on the computers in the pixel formats (listed in the 2nd chapter). Common pixel formats include: rgb8, rgb24, rgba (with alpha value for opacity), yuv420p, yuv422p, etc. For example to display **rgbtestsrc** with only blue color, we set the red and green components to zero:

```
ffplay -f lavfi -i rgbtestsrc -vf lutrgb=r=0:g=0
```

RGB test   **Modified version**

RGB pixel format modifications

To change the particular channels of RGB input format we use the **lutrgb** filter. It adjusts the color balance by setting the value of r, g and b parameters from 0 to 255 (any value above 255 is considered 255) and the usage of common combinations illustrate the next two images.

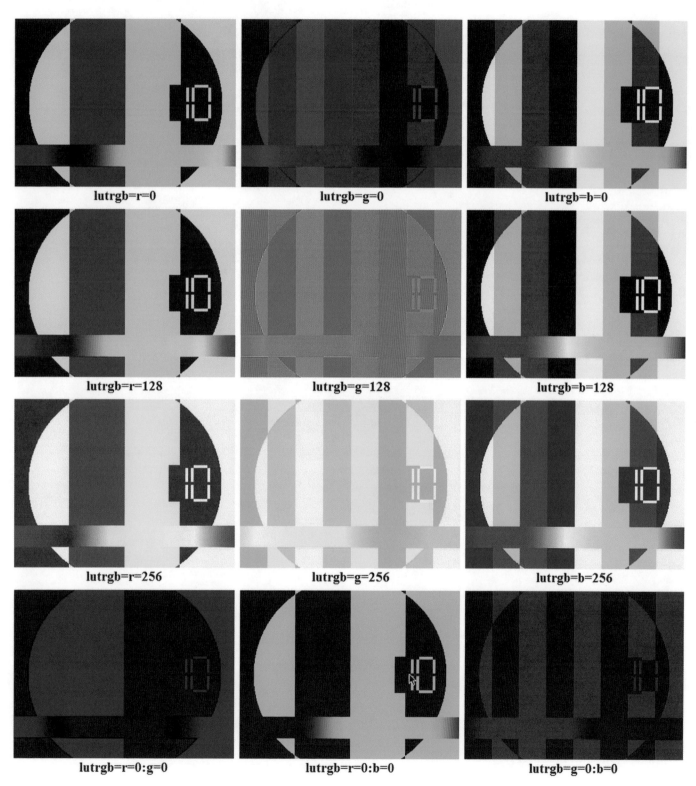

167

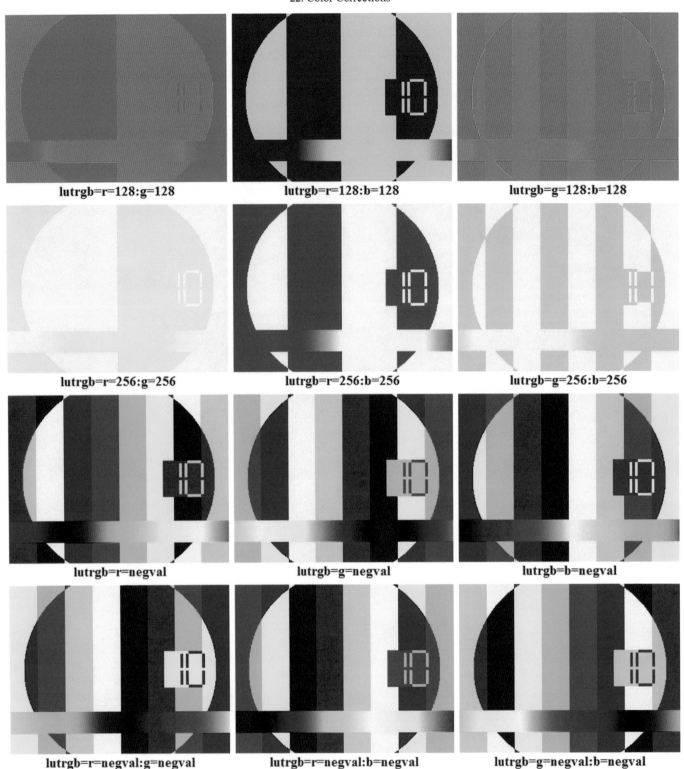

lutrgb=r=128:g=128   lutrgb=r=128:b=128   lutrgb=g=128:b=128

lutrgb=r=256:g=256   lutrgb=r=256:b=256   lutrgb=g=256:b=256

lutrgb=r=negval   lutrgb=g=negval   lutrgb=b=negval

lutrgb=r=negval:g=negval   lutrgb=r=negval:b=negval   lutrgb=g=negval:b=negval

Color balance

To adjust an intensity of red, green or blue color channel we set a number from 0 to 255 and enter it for the r, g or b parameter of lutrgb filter. We can also divide (decrease) or multiply (increase) the input value, for example to double the blue color intensity we can use an expression **lutrgb=b=val*2**.

Modifications of YUV pixel format

To modify components of YUV format we use the **lutyuv** filter. The **y** parameter adjusts the brightness (luma), the **u** parameter adjusts the blue color balance and the **v** parameter adjusts the red color balance. The common combinations of these parameters illustrate the next two images.

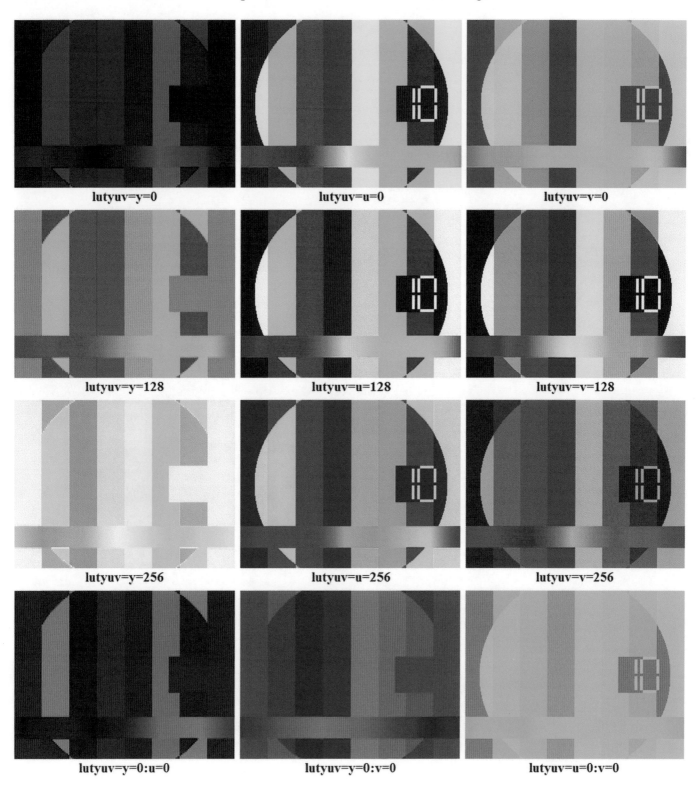

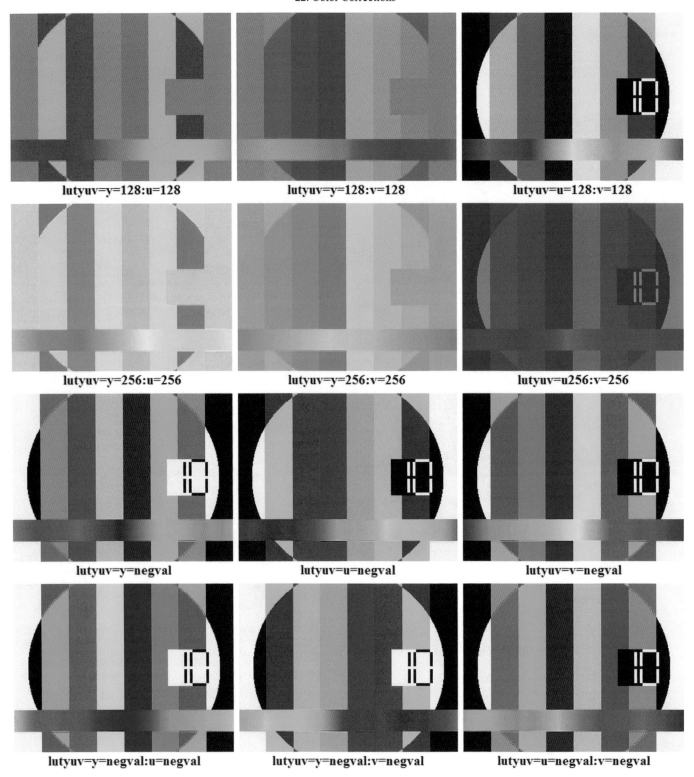

Brightness correction

While in RGB color model the brightness is set by the combination of 3 colors, in YUV (Y'CbCr) model is set directly with y (luma) parameter. For example to adjust brightness to 90% of the input, we can use an expression `lutyuv=y=val*0.9`.

Hue and saturation setting

Another approach to represent an RGB color space is an HSB (HSV), hue-saturation-brightness (hue-saturation-value) color space. Instead of the linear cube it uses a cylindrical coordinate system, where hue is an angle around the central vertical axis and saturation is a distance from this axis. For the hue and saturation adjustment FFmpeg provides a **hue** filter that is described in the table:

Video filter: hue	
Video filter: hue	
Description	Adjusts the hue and saturation of the input frames.
Syntax	**hue[=h=*expr*[:s=*expr*]]**
Description of parameters	
h, H	hue angle in degrees, default value is 0.0
s	float number from the range -10 to 10, the default value is 1.0
Variables available in expressions *expr*	
n	frame number of the input frame, numbers start from 0
pts	presentation timestamp of the input frame, expressed is in time base units
r	frame rate of the input video, NaN if unknown
t	timestamp expressed in seconds, NaN if unknown
tb	time base of the input video
Alternative syntax is **hue=*hue*:*saturation***, where *hue* and *saturation* are numbers, not expressions.	

Hue angles and corresponding colors

| 0 | 60 | 120 | 180 | 240 | 300 | 360 |

Hue is an angle in the range from 0 to 360 degrees and is defined by CIE as "the degree to which a stimulus can be described as similar to or different from stimuli that are described as red, green, blue, and yellow". For example to adjust hue of the input to 60 degrees, we can use the command:

```
ffplay -i coconut.jpg -vf hue=60
```

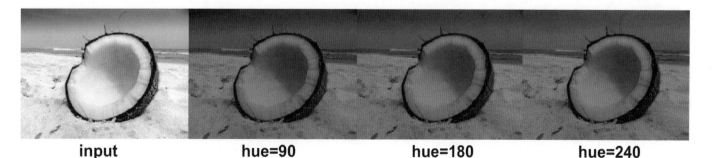

input   hue=90   hue=180   hue=240

To adjust the image saturation we set the **s** parameter to adequate value, for example to increase saturation to the value 5, we can use the command:

```
ffplay -i strawberry.jpg -vf hue=s=5
```

The next picture illustrates the usage of values -10, -5, 0, 5 and 10. Please note that the value 0 results in a monochrome (black-and-white) image.

| input | hue=s=-10 | hue=s=-5 | hue=s=0 | hue=s=5 | hue=s=10 |

Comparison in 2 windows

Many image and video editors in various settings offer a second window to compare how the input will change. To provide similar comparison with FFmpeg we can use the **pad** and **overlay** filters in the filtergraph with 4 filterchains.

2 windows compared horizontally

This type of comparison was explained already the 1st chapter, section Filters, filterchains and filtergraphs. The first filterchain splits the input to two outputs labeled [1] and [2], second filterchain creates a pad for two windows labeled [A] and the third one applies the filter(s) to the output [2] with the result labeled [B]. The fourth filterchain overlays modified input ([B]) on a new pad ([A]). The next example uses a lutrgb filter to illustrate this method:

```
ffplay -f lavfi -i testsrc -vf ^
split[1][2];[1]pad=iw*2[A];[2]lutrgb=g=256[B];[A][B]overlay=w
```

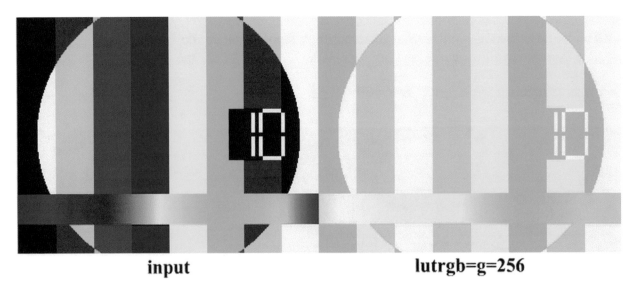

input   lutrgb=g=256

172

2 windows compared vertically

To provide a comparison in the windows located vertically, only the second and fourth filtergraph is changed, other parameters remain the same like in the horizontal comparison. In the second filtergraph we add **ih** (input height) multiplied by 2 for **y** parameter and in the fourth filtergraph we specify a zero for **x** parameter and **h** (input height) for **y** parameter. To demonstrate this method, the next example compares the same images as the previous, only the position of windows is modified (the change is underlined):

```
ffplay -f lavfi -i testsrc -vf ^
split[1][2];[1]pad=iw:ih*2[A];[2]lutrgb=g=256[B];[A][B]overlay=0:h
```

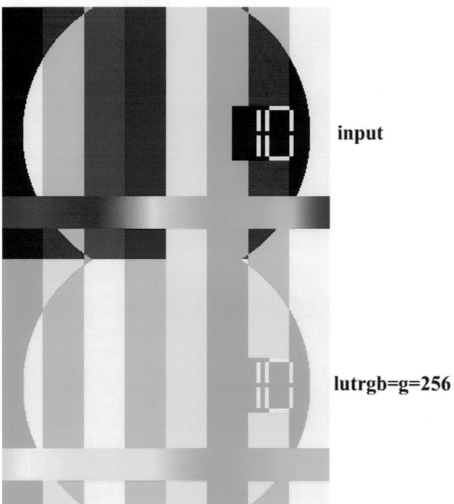

input

lutrgb=g=256

Space between windows

If we need a space between 2 windows, for instance 10 pixels, we specify it:

- in the second filterchain like **pad=iw:ih*2+10**
- in the fourth filterchain like **overlay=0:h+10**

For the 50 pixel space in the horizontal comparison we specify

- in the second filterchain: **pad=iw*2+10**
- in the fourth filterchain: **overlay=w+10**

Modified version first

To put the modified version first and the input beside horizontally, we can use the command:

```
ffplay -f lavfi -i testsrc -vf ^
split[1][2];[1]pad=iw*2:ih:iw[A];[2]lutrgb=g=256[B];[A][B]overlay
```

A vertical comparison with the modified input at the top is created with the command:

```
ffplay -f lavfi -i testsrc -vf
split[1][2];[1]pad=iw:ih*2:0:ih[A];[2]lutrgb=g=256[B];[A][B]overlay
```

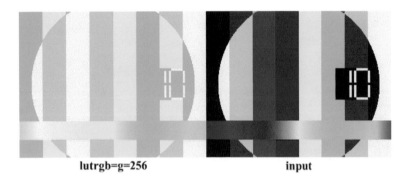

lutrgb=g=256   input

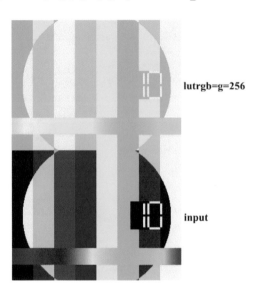

lutrgb=g=256

input

2 modified versions without input

The next command displays 2 modified versions of the input without the input itself, the second filterchain includes a second filter that modifies the content of the first window:

```
ffplay -f lavfi -i testsrc -vf split[1][2]; ^
[1]pad=iw*2,lutrgb=b=256[A];[2]lutrgb=g=256[B];[A][B]overlay=w
```

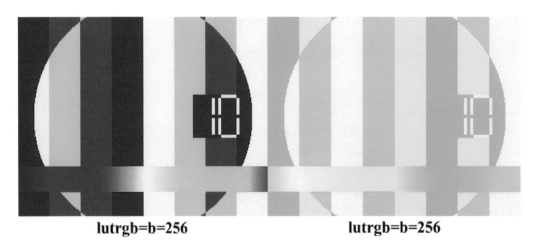

lutrgb=b=256   lutrgb=b=256

Comparison in 3 windows

In a complex video editing it can be useful to compare the input with 2 modifications at once. To display a comparison in 3 windows we use the filtergraph with 6 filterchains.

3 windows compared horizontally

To create a horizontal 3 windows comparison, 6 filterchains can be specified:
- 1. filterchain splits the input with the split filter to 3 identical outputs labeled [1], [2], [3]
- 2. filterchain creates from [1] input a pad with 3 times bigger width, output is labeled [A]
- 3. filterchain modifies [2] input with some filter(s), output is labeled [B]
- 4. filterchain modifies [3] input with some filter(s), output is labeled [C]
- 5. filterchain overlays [B] input on [A] input where **x** coordinate is **w**, output is labeled [D]
- 6. filterchain overlays [C] input on [D] input where **x** coordinate is **w*2** (2 times input width)

For example the next command compares the **testsrc** pattern with modified **u** component (2. window) and with modified **v** component (3. window):

```
ffplay -f lavfi -i testsrc -vf ^
split=3[1][2][3];[1]pad=iw*3[A];[2]lutyuv=u=val*1.5[B];^
[3]lutyuv=v=val*1.5[C];[A][B]overlay=w[D];[D][C]overlay=w*2
```

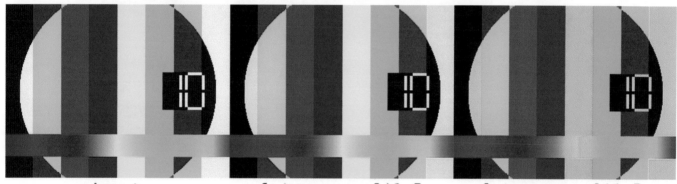

```
      input              lutyuv=u=val*1.5        lutyuv=v=val*1.5
```

3 windows compared vertically

For a vertical comparison we change the next filterchains:
- 2. filterchain - in the pad filter **width** parameter is input width, **height** parameter is input height multiplied by 3: **pad=iw:ih*3**
- 5. filterchain - in the overlay filter **x** parameter is zero and **y** parameter is input height: **overlay=0:h**
- 6. filterchain - in the overlay filter **x** parameter is zero and **y** parameter is input height times 2: overlay=0

The next example compares the same images as the previous, but vertically (changes are underlined):

```
ffplay -f lavfi -i testsrc -vf ^
split=3[1][2][3];[1]pad=iw:ih*3[A];^
[2]lutyuv=u=val*1.5[B];[3]lutyuv=v=val*1.5[C];^
[A][B]overlay=0:h[D];[D][C]overlay=0:h*2
```

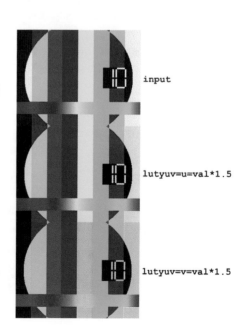

Input in the middle window

The next command places the input to the middle, the modification of filterchains is analogical to the previous examples (**x** coordinate of unchanged input is set to the input width, **iw**):

```
ffplay -f lavfi -i testsrc -vf ^
split=3[1][2][3];[1]pad=iw*3:ih:iw[A];[2]lutyuv=u=val*1.5[B];^
[3]lutyuv=v=val*1.5[C];[A][B]overlay[D];[D][C]overlay=w*2
```

To place the input to the middle vertically, we can use the command:

```
ffplay -f lavfi -i testsrc -vf ^
split=3[1][2][3];[1]pad=iw:ih*3:0:ih[A];[2]lutyuv=u=val*1.5[B];^
[3]lutyuv=v=val*1.5[C];[A][B]overlay[D];[D][C]overlay=0:h*2
```

lutyuv=u=val*1.5   input   lutyuv=v=val*1.5

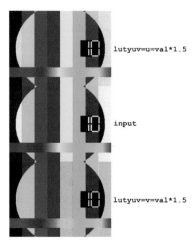

Brightness correction in 2 and 3 windows

The next examples illustrate the adjustment of brightness in 2 and 3 windows preview. To display an image beside the version where brightness is a 1.5 multiple of the input value, we can use the command:

```
ffplay -i apple.avi -vf ^
split[1][2];[1]pad=iw*2[A];[2]lutyuv=y=val*1.5[B];[A][B]overlay=w
```

input   lutyuv=y=val*1.5

The next example is a 3-windows version of the previous, to the middle was added a modified version, where the multiple of the input brightness is 1.2:

```
ffplay -i apple.avi -vf ^
split=3[1][2][3];[1]pad=iw*3[A];[2]lutyuv=y=val*1.2[B];^
[3]lutyuv=y=val*1.5[C];[A][B]overlay=w[D];[D][C]overlay=w*2
```

| input | lutyuv=y=val*1.2 | lutyuv=y=val*1.5 |

To locate the input into the central window, we can use the command:

```
ffplay -i apple.avi -vf ^
split=3[1][2][3];[1]pad=iw*3:ih:iw[A];[2]lutyuv=y=val*1.2[B];^
[3]lutyuv=y=val*1.5[C];[A][B]overlay[D];[D][C]overlay=w*2
```

| lutyuv=y=val*1.2 | input | lutyuv=y=val*1.5 |

If we want the input in the 3. window, only 2 filterchains are modified from the previous example:
- 2. filterchain: x parameter value of the pad filter is set to iw*2
- 6. filterchain: x parameter of the overlay filter is set to w (input width)

The next command displays the input in the third window:

```
ffplay -i apple.avi -vf ^
split=3[1][2][3];[1]pad=iw*3:ih:iw*2[A];[2]lutyuv=y=val*1.2[B];^
[3]lutyuv=y=val*1.5[C];[A][B]overlay[D];[D][C]overlay=w
```

Comparison in 4 windows

For the better results and various experiments we can compare the input with 3 modifications at once. To display a comparison in 4 windows, the filtergraph contains 8 filterchains:

- 1. filterchain splits the input with the split filter to 4 identical outputs labeled [1], [2], [3], [4]
- 2. filterchain creates from [1] input a pad with a double width and double height, output is labeled [A]
- 3. filterchain modifies [2] input with some filter(s), output is labeled [B]
- 4. filterchain modifies [3] input with some filter(s), output is labeled [C]
- 5. filterchain modifies [4] input with some filter(s), output is labeled [D]
- 6. filterchain overlays [B] input on [A] input where **x** coordinate is input width, output label is [E]
- 7. filterchain overlays [C] input on [E] input where **x** is zero and **y** is input height, output label is [F]
- 8. filterchain overlays [D] input on [F] input where **x** coordinate is input width and **y** is input height.

For example the next command compares a tomato with versions where the particular color channels values are doubled. In the top-right window is intensified the red channel, in the bottom-left the green channel and in the bottom-right the blue channel:

```
ffplay -i tomato.mpg -vf split=4[1][2][3][4];[1]pad=iw*2:ih*2[A];^
[2]lutrgb=r=val*2[B];[3]lutrgb=g=val*2[C];[4]lutrgb=b=val*2[D];^
[A][B]overlay=w[E];[E][C]overlay=0:h[F];[F][D]overlay=w:h
```

input   lutrgb=r=val*2

lutrgb=g=val*2   lutrgb=b=val*2

23. Advanced Techniques

Joining audio and video files

There are several kinds of joining media files and they are described in the table:

	Joining audio and video files		
type	**description**	**for audio**	**for video**
concatenation	encoding files one after another; where the 1st ends, the 2nd begins	Yes	Yes
merge	encoding all audio streams to one, for example 2 mono to 1 stereo	Yes	No
mix	encoding 2 or more audio channels to 1, volume can be adjusted	Yes	No
multiplex (mux)	encoding 2 or more files to 1, for example 1 audio and 1 video file, if more streams of the same type are present, the choice is on user	Yes	Yes
overlay (PiP)	2 or more videos are displayed at once beside or one over another	No	Yes

Concatenation with shell command

	Prerequisites for media files concatenation
special file format	Concatenated can be only certain file formats: audio - MP3 (header of 2nd file will disappear), uncompressed like WAV, PCM, etc. video - MPEG-1, MPEG-2 TS, DV
format conformance	all concatenated files are of the same format, it means 2 MP3 files can be joined, but 1 MP3 with 1 WAV cannot
stream conformance	all concatenated files: - contains the same number of streams of each type - audio streams use the same codec, sample rate and channel layout - video streams use the same resolution
To comply with this requirements it is often needed to convert the input files, use -q 1 or similar option to keep the initial quality, details are in the chapter Conversion Between Formats.	

On Windows we can use the **copy** command with a **/B** flag to indicate a binary mode, between the files must be a plus sign. The generic form of the copy command for concatenating N files is:

```
copy /B file1+file2+...+fileN-1+fileN outputFile
```

For example to concatenate files videoclip1.mpg and videoclip2.mpg to the file video.mpg, we can use the command:

```
copy /B videoclip1.mpg+videoclip2.mpg video.mpg
```

On Linux, Unix and OS X we can use the **cat** command in the form: `cat file1 files2 > file3`, therefore we can modify the previous example like:

```
cat videoclip1.mpg videoclip2.mpg > video.mpg
```

Concatenation with concat protocol

Another option is to use a **concat** protocol, prerequisites are like with the **copy** command. For example to modify the previous example utilizing this protocol we can use the command:

```
ffmpeg -i concat:"videoclip1.mpg|videoclip2.mpg" -c copy video.mpg
```

Concatenation with concat filter

Special filter for an audio and video concatenation is a **concat** filter described in the table:

Multimedia filter: concat	
Description	Concatenates audio and video files one after the other. The filter works on segments (files) of synchronized video and audio streams, where all segments must have the same number of streams of each type, for example 1 audio and 1 video, or 2 audio and 1 video, etc.
Syntax	**concat=a=a_streams:v=v_streams:n=segments[:unsafe]** all parameters are optional
Description of parameters	
a	number of output audio streams, default value is 0
n	number of segments, default value is 2
unsafe	safe mode activation, if set, concatenation will not fail with segments of a different format
v	number of output video streams, default value is 1

Prerequisites for a proper filter results:
- all segments must start at timestamp 0
- corresponding streams must use in all segments the same parameters, especially the video size
- recommended is the same frame rate, otherwise the output will use a variable frame rate

Concat filter enables to join various formats, some examples are:

```
ffmpeg -i input1.avi -i input2.avi -filter_complex concat output.avi
ffmpeg -i input1.avi -i input2.avi -filter_complex concat output.mp4
ffmpeg -i input1.avi -i input2.mp4 -filter_complex concat output.webm
ffmpeg -i input1.avi -i input2.mp4 -i input3.mkv -filter_complex ^
concat=n=3 output.flv
ffmpeg -i input1.avi -i input2.avi -i input3.avi -i input4.avi ^
-filter_complex concat=n=4 output.mp4
f -i 1.avi -vf movie=2.avi[a];[in][a]concat a.mp4
```

Other types of joining

- audio merging (several streams to 1 multichannel stream) - described in the chapter Digital Audio
- mixing several audio files to 1 - described in chapter Digital Audio
- multiplex - described in the chapter FFmpeg Fundamentals, section Selection of media streams
- overlay - described in the chapter Overlay - Picture in Picture

Removing logo

Some videos contain a company logo, usually in the top-left corner, common example are recordings of TV programs. FFmpeg contains 2 special filters to remove logos and while the final effect is not always perfect, in many cases is acceptable.

delogo filter

Video filter: delogo	
Description	Hides a TV station logo by a simple interpolation of the surrounding pixels. User sets a rectangle covering the logo and it usually disappears (but in certain case the logo is more visible). The filter accepts parameters as a string of the form "x:y:w:h:band", or as a list of key=value pairs, separated by ":".
Syntax	**delogo=x=0:y=0:w=width:h=height[:t=band:show={0,1}]** parameters in [] are optional, show is 0 or 1
Description of parameters	
x, y	coordinates of the top-left corner of the logo
w, h	width and height of the logo
band or t	thickness of the fuzzy edge of the logo rectangle, default value is 4
show	parameter for locating, default value is 0, if set to 1, a green rectangle shows on the screen as an aid to find the correct x, y, w and h parameters

For example to remove a logo from the top-right corner of 800x600 pixels sized video illustrated on images below at first we estimate the logo position with a show option that will display a green rectangle:

```
ffmpeg -i eagles.mpg -vf delogo=x=700:y=0:w=100:h=50:t=3:show=1 nologo.mpg
```

Now we can precisely specify the position and the logo presence is almost invisible:

```
ffmpeg -i eagles.mpg -vf delogo=x=730:y=0:w=70:h=46:t=1 nologo.mpg
```

Fixing of shaking video parts

Some parts of the video taken without a tripod or from a vehicle usually includes shaking - small changes in horizontal and vertical shift that can be in certain cases corrected with a **deshake** filter:

Video filter: deshake	
Description	Fixes small changes in the horizontal and vertical shift, useful when the video was taken without a tripod or from the moving vehicle.
Syntax	**deshake=x:y:w:h:rx:ry:edge:blocksize:contrast:search:filename** all parameters are optional
Description of parameters	
x, y, w, h	Coordinates and size of rectangular area where to search for motion vectors, x and y are top left corner coordinates, w is width and h is height. These parameters have the same meaning as the drawbox filter which can be used to visualize the position of the bounding box. This is useful when simultaneous movement of subjects within the frame might be confused for camera motion by the motion vector search. If any or all of x, y, w and h are set to -1 then the full frame is used. This allows later options to be set without specifying the bounding box for the motion vector search. Default - search the whole frame.
rx, ry	specify the maximum extent of movement in x and y directions in the range 0 - 64 pixels, the default value is 16
edge	specifies how to generate pixels to fill blanks at the edge of the frame, the value is an integer from 0 to 3: 0 - fill zeros at blank locations 1 - original image at blank locations 2 - extruded edge value at blank locations 3 - mirrored edge at blank locations, the default value
blocksize	specifies the blocksize to use for motion search, the value is from range 4 - 128 pixels, the default value is 8
contrast	Specifies the contrast threshold for blocks. Only blocks with more than the specified contrast (difference between darkest and lightest pixels) will be considered. The value is from range 1 - 255, the default value is 125.
search	specifies the search strategy: 0 = exhaustive search, the default value 1 = less exhaustive search
filename	if included, a detailed log of the motion search is written to the specified file

Parameters can be entered sequentially in the default sequence or specified with their name in any order:

```
ffmpeg -i travel.avi -vf deshake fixed_travel.avi
ffmpeg -i travel.avi -vf deshake=contrast=160 fixed.avi
ffmpeg -i travel.avi -vf deshake=blocksize=4:filename=log.txt fixed.avi
```

Adding color box to video

With a **drawbox** filter we can find precise coordinates for the rectangular area where to search for motion vectors, it is used in the deshake filter. Other use include various diagrams, schemes, etc.

Video filter: drawbox	
Description	Draws a box with specified color and specified size on the selected area of the input.
Syntax	**drawbox[=x:y:width:height:color:thickness]**
Description of parameters	
color, c	standard color name or hexadecimal value in the form 0xRRGGBB[AA]
height, h	height of the box, the default value is 0
thickness, t	thickness of the box edge in pixels, the default value is 4
width, w	width of the box, the default value is 0
x, y	coordinates of the top-left corner of the box, default values are 0

For example to add a yellow box with the size 600x400 pixels on the SVGA sized input 150 pixels from the left and 0 pixels from the top, we can use the command:

```
ffmpeg -i ship.avi -vf drawbox=x=150:w=600:h=400:c=yellow ship1.avi
```

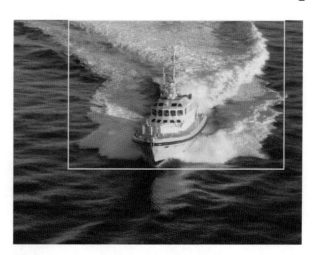

Number of frames detection

If you need to know how many frames contains your video file, you can use the command:

```
ffmpeg -i input.mpg -f null /dev/null
```

The 2 last lines from the displayed output looks like:
```
frame=  250 fps=0.0 q=0.0 Lsize=     0kB time=00:00:10.00 bitrate=   0.0kbits/s
video:16kB audio:0kB subtitle:0 global headers:0kB muxing overhead -100.000000%
```

The number 250 after frames= denotes the total number of video frames, it can be also calculated from the frame rate and duration, but the result is not always exact.

Detection of ads, section transitions or corrupted encoding

Longer video recorded from TV, internet, etc., can contain short parts with advertisement, transitions, incomplete frames and other unwanted content. If this parts include black frames, they can be detected with a **blackdetect** filter that is described in the table.

Video filter: blackdetect				
Description	Detects video parts that are almost completely black and outputs lines containing the time for the start, end and duration of detected black intervals expressed in seconds. Lines are not displayed if the the loglevel is set below AV_LOG_INFO value.			
Syntax	`blackdetect[=d=duration:pic_th=pbr_threshold:pix_th=px_threshold]`			
Description of parameters (all are optional)				
Parameter name	**Unit**	**Description**		**Default**
black_min_duration, d	second	Positive floating-point number determining the minimum duration of the black frames in video.		2.0
picture_black_ratio_th, pic_th	floating-point number between 0 and 1.0	Ratio between fully black pixels and non-black pixels, for example if the frame size is 400x300 (120 000 pixels in total) and 12000 pixels are not black, then the ratio is 0.9.		0.98
pixel_black_th, pix_th	floating-point number between 0 and 1.0	Treshold setting which pixels is taken as black, it equals to the expression: `(absolute_threshold-luminance_minimum_value) / luminance_range_size`		0.1

For example, to detect black frames from the source **mptestsrc**, the command is (console output follows):

```
ffmpeg -f lavfi -i mptestsrc -vf blackdetect -f sdl 'test'
```

Detection with blackframe filter

Another filter that detects dark frames is a **blackframe** filter described in the table:

Video filter: blackframe	
Description	Detects frames that are almost black and outputs lines containing: - frame number of detected frame - percentage of the blackness - position in the file if known or -1 otherwise - timestamp Lines are not displayed if the the loglevel is set below AV_LOG_INFO value.
Syntax	**blackframe[=amount:[treshold]]** all parameters are optional
Parameters	
amount	percentage of the pixels which are under the threshold, default value is 98
threshold	number below which are pixels considered black, default value is 32

Filters blackdetect and blackframe are similar, but each displays different information. The output from the blackframe filter using the same video source as with the blackdetect filter is displayed on the image:

```
ffmpeg -f lavfi -i mptestsrc -vf blackframe -f sdl 'test'
```

Selecting only specified frames to output

Special multimedia filters **aselect** for audio and **select** for video enable to precisely specify which frames will remain and which are excluded from the output.

Audio filter: aselect and Video filter: select	
Description	Selects frames to the output, expression is evaluated for each input frame and the frame is selected if value of expression is non zero, otherwise the frame is skipped.
Syntax	**select=*expression*** default value of *expression* is 1
Variables in expression	
n	sequential number of the filtered frame, starting from 0
selected_n	sequential number of the selected frame, starting from 0
prev_selected_n	sequential number of the last selected frame, NAN if undefined
TB	timebase of the input timestamps
pts	PTS (Presentation TimeStamp) of the filtered video frame, expressed in TB units, NAN if undefined
t	PTS of the filtered video frame, expressed in seconds, NAN if undefined
prev_pts	PTS of the previously filtered video frame, NAN if undefined
prev_selected_pts	PTS of the last previously filtered video frame, NAN if undefined
prev_selected_t	PTS of the last previously selected video frame, NAN if undefined
start_pts	PTS of the first video frame in the video, NAN if undefined
start_t	time of the first video frame in the video, NAN if undefined
pict_type (video only)	type of the filtered frame, can assume one of the following values: I ... intraframe, P ... predictive frame, B ... bidirectional frame, S ...switch frame, SI ... switching I frame, SP ... switching P frame, BI ... special intraframe, that is not a keyframe (VC-1 video codec)
interlace_type (video only)	frame interlace type, can assume one of the following values: PROGRESSIVE, TOPFIRST, BOTTOMFIRST
PROGRESSIVE	frame is progressive (not interlaced)
TOPFIRST	frame is top-field-first
BOTTOMFIRST	frame is bottom-field-first
key	1 if the filtered frame is a key-frame, 0 otherwise
pos	position in the file of the filtered frame, -1 if the information is not available (for example for synthetic video)
scene (video only)	value between 0 and 1 to indicate a new scene; a low value reflects a low probability for the current frame to introduce a new scene, while a higher value means the current frame is more likely to be one

Audio only variables for aselect audio filter	
consumed_sample_n	number of selected samples before the current frame
samples_n	number of samples in the current frame
sample_rate	input sample rate

Because the default value of the **select** expression is 1, the next 2 examples of the **select** filter usage produce the same result - all frames are selected to the output (value 0 will select nothing):

```
ffmpeg -i input.avi -vf select output.avi
ffmpeg -i input.avi -vf select=1 output.avi
```

To select a part from 20 to 25 second, we can use the command:

```
ffmpeg -i input.avi -vf select="gte(t\,20)*lte(t\,25)" output.avi
```

To select intraframes only to the output, we can use the command:

```
ffmpeg -i input.avi -vf select="eq(pict_type\,I)" output.avi
```

Scaling input by changing aspect ratios

Chapter Resizing and Scaling Video described the **scale** filter for resizing the video frame. Another method is to use the **setdar** and **setsar** filters that change the display aspect ratio DAR and sample aspect ratio SAR, their relation is expressed by equation (details about aspect ratio are in the Glossary):

$$DAR = width/height * SAR$$

Video filters: setdar, setsar	
Description	The setdar filter sets the display aspect ratio and setsar the sample aspect ratio.
Syntax	setdar[=r=aspect_ratio[:max=number]] setdar[=aspect_ratio[:number]]
Description of parameters	
r, ratio	aspect ratio, value can be a floating point number or expression, default value is 0
max	maximum integer value for expressing numerator and denominator when rounding the aspect ratio to a rational number, default value is 100

Examples how to use the **setdar** and **setsar** filters:

```
ffplay -i input.avi -vf setdar=r=16/9
ffplay -i input.avi -vf setdar=16/9
ffplay -i input.avi -vf setsar=r=1.234
ffplay -i input.avi -vf setsar=1.234
```

Screen grabbing

To record the display output to the video file, for example to create a tutorial, we can use the **dshow** input device with installed UScreenCapture Direct Show source filter, that can be downloaded from

`http://www.umediaserver.net/bin/UScreenCapture.zip`

To grab the fullscreen content we can use the command:

`ffmpeg -f dshow -i video="UScreenCapture" -t 60 screen.mp4`

If we want to grab a specific screen area, we must use the **regedit** Windows utility to modify certain registry keys, details are in the README file included in the downloaded UScreenCapture.zip file.

Detailed video frame information

To display information for each video frame we can use a **showinfo** filter described in the table:

Video filter: showinfo	
Description	Shows a line containing information about each input video frame, data are in the form of key:value pairs. The filter has no parameters and should be used with -report option.
Syntax	-vf showinfo
Description of displayed parameters	
n	sequential number of the input frame, starting from 0
pts	Presentation TimeStamp of the input frame, expressed as a number of time base units; the time base unit depends on the filter input pad
pts_time	Presentation TimeStamp of the input frame, expressed as a number of seconds
pos	position of the frame in the input stream, -1 if this information in unavailable and/or meaningless (for example in case of synthetic video)
fmt	pixel format name
sar	sample aspect ratio of the input frame, expressed in the form numerator/denominator
s	size of the input frame, expressed in the form **widthxheight**
i	interlaced mode: **P** for progressive, **T** for top field first and **B** for bottom field first
iskey	1 if the frame is a key frame, 0 otherwise
type	picture type of the input frame: **I** for an I-frame, **P** for a P-frame, **B** for a B-frame, **?** for unknown type (more in documentation of the AVPictureType enum)
checksum	Adler-32 checksum (hexadecimal) of all the planes of the input frame
plane_checksum	Adler-32 checksum (hexadecimal) of each plane of the input frame, expressed in the form [c0 c1 c2 c3]

For example the next command produces information printed below, included are the first 3 lines:

```
ffmpeg -report -f lavfi -i testsrc -vf showinfo -t 10 showinfo.mpg

n:0 pts:0 pts_time:0 pos:-1 fmt:rgb24 sar:1/1 s:320x240 i:P iskey:1 type:I
checksum:88C4D19A plane_checksum:[88C4D19A]
n:1 pts:1 pts_time:0.04 pos:-1 fmt:rgb24 sar:1/1 s:320x240 i:P iskey:1 type:I
checksum:C4740AD1 plane_checksum:[C4740AD1]
n:2 pts:2 pts_time:0.08 pos:-1 fmt:rgb24 sar:1/1 s:320x240 i:P iskey:1 type:I
checksum:B6DD3DEB plane_checksum:[B6DD3DEB]
```

Audio frequency spectrum

To visualize an audio frequency spectrum we can use a **showspectrum** filter described in the table:

Multimedia filter: showspectrum	
Description	Transforms an audio input to the video output
Syntax	showspectrum[=s=*widthxheight*[:slide=*number*]]
Description of parameters	
size, s	output video size, default value is 640x480
slide	sets if the spectrum will slide along the window, default value is 0

For example the image below displays the sound spectrum created by the command:

```
ffmpeg -i audio.mp3 -vf showspectrum audio_spectrum.mp4
```

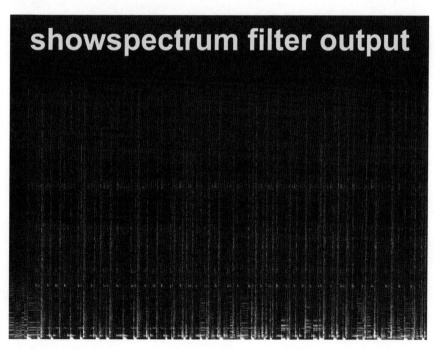

Audio waves visualization

The waves from an audio input can be visualized by a **showwaves** filter described in the table:

Multimedia filter: showwaves	
Description	Converts input audio to the video containing the representation of the audio waves.
Syntax	showwaves[=n=number[:r=rate[:s=video_size]]]
Description of parameters	
n	number of samples printed on the same column, larger value decreases the frame rate, cannot be used in combination with the rate parameter
rate, r	frame rate, default value is 25, cannot be used in combination with the **n** parameter
size, s	video size, default value is 640x480

For example to visualize the waves from the music.mp3 file to waves.mp4 file, we can use the command:

```
ffmpeg -i music.mp3 -vf showwaves waves.mp4
```

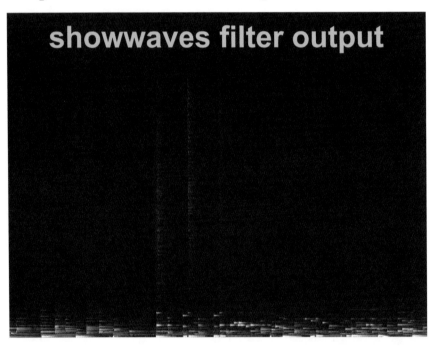

Voice synthesis

With included libflite external library, the human voice can be synthesized with an **flite** audio source that was derived from Flite (Festival Lite) - a small embeddable TTS (Text to Speech) engine. It is developed by the CMU Speech Group on Carnegie Mellon University, USA. Flite is completely written in C language and reimplements the core parts of the Festival architecture for the compatibility between voices designed for each system. Festival Speech Synthesis System from the University of Edinburgh is a framework for building the speech synthesis systems. More details about Flite are on http://www.speech.cs.cmu.edu/flite

Audio source: flite	
Description	Synthesizes a human speech with a selected voice type using the libflite library that is not included in official Windows binaries due to its big size.
Syntax	`flite="text"[:v=voice[:n=n_samples]]` `flite=textfile=filename[:v=voice[:n=n_samples]]`
Description of parameters	
list_voices	if set to 1, displays the list of available voices
n, nb_samples	maximum number of samples per frame, default value is 512
text	source text for the speech
textfile	filename containing the text
v, voice	available voices: female - **slt**, male - **awb**, **kal**, **kal16**, **rms**; the default voice is **kal** and its sample rate (frequency rate) is 8000 Hz, other voices use 16000 Hz

Because flite library adds to the ffmpeg.exe file over 10 MB, it is not in official binaries and the Windows binaries can be downloaded from **http://ffmpeg.tv/flite.php** (Linux and OS X users can compile them). To display a list of available voices we can use the command:

```
ffmpeg -f lavfi -i flite=list_voices=1
```

To let the computer read the text from the Message.txt file with a female voice, the command is:

```
ffplay -f lavfi -i flite=textfile=Message.txt:v=slt
```

For example to save the words "Happy New Year to all" to the file wish.wav we can use the command:

```
ffmpeg -f lavfi -i flite=text="Happy New Year to all":v=kal16 wish.wav
```

If we want to slow down the speech for a better listening, we can use the command:

```
ffmpeg -f lavfi -i flite=textfile=text.txt -af atempo=0.5 speech.mp3
```

Saving output to multiple formats at once

Though it is clear from the command syntax explained in the first chapter, this is a remainder that we can save the result of processing to multiple formats with one command, for example we can save the output from **flite** speech engine to MP3, WAV and WMA formats in one command:

```
ffmpeg -f lavfi -i flite=textfile=speech.txt speech.mp3 speech.wav speech.wma
```

We can also combine audio and video formats, if we specify an audio format from the video input format, only audio stream is included, the file clip.mp3 from the next example contains only audio stream:

```
ffmpeg -i clip.avi clip.flv clip.mov clip.mp3 clip.mp4 clip.webm
```

191

```
Stream mapping:
Stream #0:0 -> #0:0 (mjpeg -> flv)
Stream #0:1 -> #0:1 (pcm_s16le -> libmp3lame)
Stream #0:0 -> #1:0 (mjpeg -> libx264)
Stream #0:1 -> #1:1 (pcm_s16le -> libvo_aacenc)
Stream #0:1 -> #2:0 (pcm_s16le -> libmp3lame)
Stream #0:0 -> #3:0 (mjpeg -> libx264)
Stream #0:1 -> #3:1 (pcm_s16le -> libvo_aacenc)
Stream #0:0 -> #4:0 (mjpeg -> libvpx)
Stream #0:1 -> #4:1 (pcm_s16le -> libvorbis)
```

clip.flv
clip.mov
clip.mp3
clip.mp4
clip.webm

ffmpeg -i clip.avi clip.flv clip.mov clip.mp3 clip.mp4 clip.webm

Additional media input to filtergraph

By default input files are specified before any filters with -i options and the first input is available in the filtergraph with an [in] link label. If we want to filter additional file, we can use an **amovie** source for audio and **movie** source for video files, they are described in the table:

Audio source: amovie & Video source: movie	
Description	Reads audio and/or video streams from a media (movie) container. Required parameter is the filename of the media file and optional key=value pairs are separated by a colon.
Syntax	**movie=*video_name*[:*options*]** **amovie=*audio_name*[:*options*]**
Available key=value pairs in options parameter	
f, format_name	format of the movie - container or input device, if not specified, it is determined from the extension or probed
loop	number of time the stream is read in sequence, if -1, the best video (audio with amovie) stream is selected
sp, seek_point	seek point in seconds, if set, the input starts from the given time
s, streams	- stream to be selected, multiple streams are specified with a + sign, order is important - special names **dv** (movie) and **da** (amovie) specify the default (best) video / audio stream - syntax how to specify particular streams is explained in the first chapter
si, stream_index	index of the stream to read, if -1, the best stream is selected, it is the default value (deprecated, the **s** parameter is preferred)

For example to display a logo on the input video we can use the command:

```
ffmpeg -i video.mpg -vf movie=logo.png[a];[in][a]overlay video1.mp4
```

For instance, with the **sp** (seek_point) option set to 5, the logo will be displayed 5 seconds from the start:

```
ffmpeg -i video.mpg -vf movie=logo.png:sp=5[a];[in][a]overlay video1.mp4
```

24. Video on Web

Due to its omnipresence Internet is the top medium for showing your videos created or edited with ffmpeg. Beside uploading to the popular video sharing websites like YouTube, Vimeo, etc, it is useful to know how to include a media file to the webpage. To make sure, that users with different browsers and media support can listen and see your audio and video, it is recommended to provide your media files in all supported formats for HTML5 and alternatively for Adobe Flash Player.

HTML5 support on main browsers

Adding media files on the web with HTML5 is relatively easy and there are devices that support HTML5, but not Flash Player, so it is useful to learn what media formats are supported in various browsers. FFmpeg is able to convert your audio and video to any of specified HTML5 formats. Files in OGG container format use a Theora video codec and Vorbis audio codec, that are free to use also in commercial projects, the same free use is available with WebM format. Please note that by default ffmpeg encodes the OGG audio with a FLAC codec, that these browsers cannot play, an **-acodec libvorbis** option must be included.

HTML5 Audio Support			
Browser	**MP3**	**OGG***	**WAV**
Apple Safari 5+	yes	no	yes
Firefox 3.6+	no	yes	yes
Google Chrome 6+	yes	yes	yes
Internet Explorer 9+	yes	no	no
Opera 10.6+	yes	yes	yes
Maxthon 3+	yes	yes	yes
HTML5 Video Support			
Browser	**MP4**	**OGG**	**WEBM**
Apple Safari 5+	yes	no	no
Firefox 3.6+	no	yes	yes
Google Chrome 6+	yes	yes	yes
Internet Explorer 9+	yes	no	no
Opera 10.6+	no	yes	yes
Maxthon 3+	yes	yes	yes

HTML5 support for Internet Explorer is available from the version 9, previous versions 6, 7 and 8 can install a Google Chrome Frame plugin from

`https://developers.google.com/chrome/chrome-frame`

An online test how your browser supports particular HTML5 features is located on the web

`http://html5test.com`

Adding audio with HTML5

To provide our audio for the playback on any major browser, the most versatile format is MP3 supported on all browsers except Firefox, and for Firefox we provide OGG or WAV format. The new tag in HTML5 for audio inclusion is <audio> tag described in the table:

<audio> tag all attributes are optional		
Attribute	**Values**	**Description**
autoplay	autoplay	if set, audio starts playing when it is ready
controls	controls	if set, displayed are controls: Play, Pause, Seeking, Volume
loop	loop	if set, audio plays over and over again
preload	auto, metadata, none	auto - entire audio file is loaded metadata - only metadata are loaded none - audio file is not loaded with the web page Do not use it with autoplay attribute; it is recently not supported in IE and Opera.
src	URL	absolute or relative URL of the audio file

Because we want to specify for the same audio at least 2 files in a different format, the **src** attribute of <audio> tag is not used and between opening <audio> and closing </audio> tag are added multiple <source> tags. Browser will scan included media files and select the first one it supports for the playback.

<source> tag src attribute is required		
Attribute	**Values**	**Description**
media	media_query	no browser supports it now, describes type of media resource
src	URL	absolute or relative URL of the audio file
type	MIME_type	MIME type of media resources, recently: audio: audio/mpeg, audio/ogg, audio/wav video: video/mp4, video/ogg, video/webm

The next HTML code includes audio file with displayed controls and looping, it is saved to text file called for example audio.htm with other HTML elements like doctype, head, title, body, div, etc.

```
<audio controls='controls' loop='loop'>
   <source src='music.mp3' type='audio/mpeg' />
   <source src='music.ogg' type='audio/ogg' />
Audio element is not supported in your browser, please update.
</audio>
```

To start an automatic playback, we can add the attribute **autoplay='autoplay'**.

Audio controls in various browsers	
Browser	**audio player**
Firefox 4	
Google Chrome 6	
Internet Explorer 9	
Maxthon 3	
Opera 12	

Adding video with HTML5

The tag for video in HTML5 is a <video> tag and its attributes **autoplay**, **controls**, **loop** and **mute** use the value equal to the attribute name (e.g. loop='loop'), but many browsers accept skipping this value, so for not production usage we can use <video autoplay controls loop>.

<video> tag all attributes are optional		
Attribute	**Values**	**Description**
autoplay	autoplay	if set, video starts playing when it is ready
controls	controls	if set, button controls are displayed: Play, Pause, Seeking, Volume, Toggle fullscreen, Subtitles, etc.
height	*pixels*	height of the video player
loop	loop	if set, video plays over and over again
muted	muted	if set, audio stream is muted, recently not supported in Apple Safari and Internet Explorer
poster	*URL*	URL of image file displayed during video download, if not present, displayed is the first frame of the video
preload	auto metadata none	auto - entire audio file is loaded metadata - only metadata are loaded none - audio file is not loaded with the web page Do not use it with autoplay attribute; now it not works in IE.
src	*URL*	absolute or relative URL of the video file
width	*pixels*	width of the video player

195

To make video visible on all major browsers, we must provide at least 2 different formats, the best choice is MP4 and WEBM. So the **src** attribute of <video> tag is not used and between opening <video> and closing </video> tag are added multiple <source> tags described in the previous section. Browser will scan included media files and select the first one it supports for the playback.

For example to include a video file with displayed controls and looping, we can use the HTML code:

```
<video controls='controls' loop='loop' width='640' height='480'>
  <source src='videoclip.mp4' type='video/mp4' />
  <source src='videoclip.webm' type='video/webm' />
video element is not supported in your browser, please update.
</video>
```

Adding video for Flash Player

For browsers without HTML5 support we can include to the <video> tag an <object> tag for the SWF format (**ffmpeg -f videoclip.mp4 videoclip.swf**). The <object> tag contains <param> tags and <embed> tag for browsers that do not support <object> tag.

```
<object width='400' height='300'>
   <param name='src' value='videoclip.swf' />
   <param name='loop' value='true' />
   <embed src='videoclip.swf' width='400' height='300' loop='true' />
</object>
```

Video sharing websites

Successful introduction of the video sharing service by YouTube was followed by many similar websites in English and other languages. YouTube is still the most popular, but some other servers provide additional features. Almost all video sharing websites support the following media formats: 3gp, avi, asf, flv, mkv, mp4, mpegps, mov, ogg, wmv, etc. The list of most popular video sharing webs is in the table.

Most popular video sharing websites		
Name	**Visitors monthly**	**Description** (monthly visitors count is from USA only and grows)
YouTube youtube.com	800,000,000	- most popular video web, 3rd most visited website overall, over 4 billion video views daily - 1080p HD videos, max. 2 GB and 15 minutes - support for 3D videos and videos in 4k format (4096x3072 resolution) - available on mobile phones, iPod, PlayStation, Xbox, etc. - Flash Player and HTML5 video - video editor, captions, etc. - user comments, rating, video responses, etc. - images and audio files unsupported
DailyMotion dailymotion.com	61,000,000	HD videos, maximum file size 2 GB and 60 minutes, audio 90 kbps MP3 or AAC, Flash Player or HTML5 Users can create slideshows from images, 30 images max, MP4 output
Vimeo vimeo.com	17,000,000	HD videos (1920x1080), max. file size 5 GB, unlimited duration - Flash Player, HTML5 - over 8 million registered users, 65 million unique visitors monthly - bitrate of encoded videos is among the highest (2000 kbps on average, 5000 maximum)
Metacafe metacafe.com	9,200,000	- short entertainment videos (movies, games, music, sport, TV clips, etc.) - max. file size 100 MB, videos are converted to 320x240 FLV, VP6, bit rate 330 kbps, MP3 audio - 17 million views per day, 40 million unique monthly visitors worldwide
Break break.com	6,800,000	- funny videos (pop culture, lifestyle, trasportation, games, etc.) - videos selected to homepage get reward: first $400, second $500, third and all next $600
Veoh veoh.com	6,100,000	- videos can be organized to series and channels - blocked in several countries
RuTube rutube.com	4,000,000	max. file size 300 MB and VGA resolution, Flash Player; in Russian, nice interface, reported 30 mil. unique visitors monthly, also Facebook login
Internet Archive archive.org	1,600,000	- users can upload video, audio, documents, free books, etc. - permanent storage
Multiply.com	695,000	user profiles, very popular
Qik.com	505,000	mobile-based
Phanfare.com	323,000	photos and videos
Sevenload.com	192,000	blocked in several countries
OpenFilm.com	114,000	films, music, community
ScienceStage.com	100,000	science-oriented media portal, users can upload also files in mp3, vob and swf formats

Videoprocessing on webserver

Due to popularity of ffmpeg and video sharing websites some webhosting companies offer the support for videoprocessing on the server with ffmpeg that requires a bigger CPU load than traditional websites. The preview of several webhosts including the parameters they offer is in the table:

Webhosting services with FFmpeg support	
Name URL	**Description**
CirtexHosting www.cirtexhosting.com	Supported: FFmpeg, FFmpeg-PHP, Mplayer + Mencoder + Yamdi + Yasm, flv2tool + GD Library, Xvidcore + Faac + Faad2, Libogg + Libvorbis + Libtheora, Libx264+ Libopencore-amrnb + Libopencore-amrwb, LAME MP3 Encoder
GlowHost www.glowhost.com	Available modules: FFmpeg and FFmpeg-PHP, GD Library 2+, MPlayer and MEncoder, FAAD/FAAC, FLVTool2, Libogg and Libvorbis, LAME MP3 Encoder, x264 / H.264, MPEG-4 AVC
HostUpon www.hostupon.com	All modules to start a video website, Youtube clone or social network with video uploading. Scripts on FFmpeg hosting: Boonex Dolphin, PHPMotion, Social Engine, ABKsoft Scripts, Joomla Video Plugin, Clipshare, ClipBucket, Social Media, Rayzz, Vidi Script etc.
PacificHost.com www.pacifichost.com	Webhosting with option to create and run online video sharing websites like YouTube. They employ software to convert video: ffmpeg-php, mplayer, mencoder, flvtool2, lame, libogg, libvorbis, xvid, theora, faac, phpshield loaders. PacificHost's FFmpeg includes the modules: libfaac, libfaad, libxvid, libamr-nb, libamr-wb, libgsm, libogg, libtheora, and libvorbis.
VPSDeploy https://vpsdeploy.com/whm-cpanel-ssd-hosting.php	Managed hosting with: FFmpeg support, flvtool2, X.264 plugin, libogg, flac and LibTheora for videostreaming

FFmpeg Web Hosting

GlowHost offers FFmpeg web hosting support for your video sharing applications. FFmpeg's popularity stems from its accessibility. Users don't have to know much about multimedia formats. They just upload whatever file they have and FFmpeg automatically converts it to a file format which will play in any web browser that has Flash Player enabled. If you have seen video on YouTube, you have seen the end result of FFmpeg in action. Your app will allow your users to upload video to your web site in all of the most popular video formats, and will pump them out into something anyone can watch, even full High Definition video.

FFmpeg & Associated Modules Include:

- ✔ FFmpeg and FFmpeg-PHP
- ✔ GD Library 2+
- ✔ MPlayer and MEncoder
- ✔ FAAD/FAAC

- ✔ FLVTool2
- ✔ Libogg and Libvorbis
- ✔ LAME MP3 Encoder
- ✔ x264 / H.264
- ✔ MPEG-4 AVC

Monetizing video uploads

Some video sharing websites offer a payment for viewing uploaded videos:

- YouTube Partner Program gives creators tools and programs to build audiences and to monetize their videos. Monetized videos will display adds, more information is on the webpage
  http://www.youtube.com/account_monetization

- Blip.tv pays 50% from included adds, but creator must upload and an original video series and not all series are accepted, more information is on
  http://blip.tv/users/apply

- NowVideo.eu pays $10 for each 1000 video streams (complete visitor views), details are on
  http://www.nowvideo.eu/affiliate.php

- Break.com selects interesting videos from users and includes them to its homepage. Creators of these videos are paid for each video from $200 to $600, the amount depends on the user's decision to sell or to license the video and other conditions, more information is on
  http://info.break.com/break/html/upload_videos.html

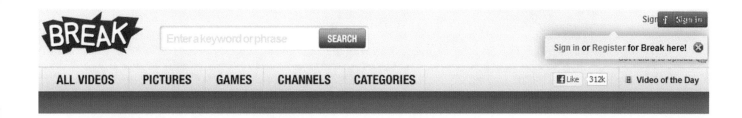

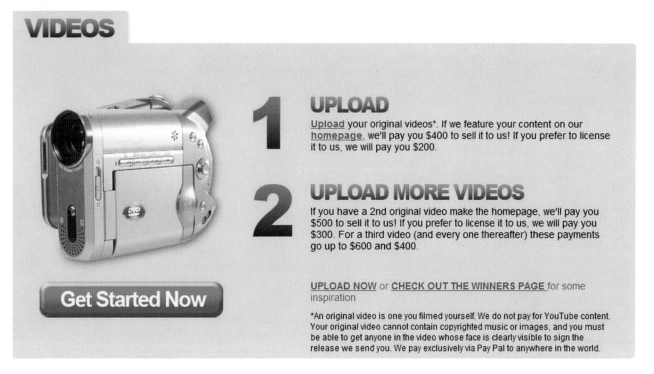

25. Debugging and Tests

To detect errors and to test various inputs, parameters, performance, etc. we can use several FFmpeg filters, options and sources. When the console output is long, the **-report** option will save the test results to the file named **ffmpeg-*yyyymmdd-hhmmss*.log** , where the part in italic typeface denotes the current date and time.

debug, debug_ts and fdebug options

The basic debugging tool in FFmpeg is a **-debug** option that has 17 possible values described in the table:

Option: debug	
Description	Prints specific debugging information about selected audio, subtitle or video stream(s).
Syntax	**-debug[:stream_specifier]**
Description of available values	
pict	picture info
rc	rate control
bitstream	bitstream
mb_type	macroblock (MB) type
qp	per-block quantization parameter (QP)
mv	motion vector
dct_coeff	DCT coefficient
skip	skip
startcode	startcode
pts	presentation timestamp
er	error recognition
mmco	memory management control operations (H.264)
bugs	bugs
vis_qp	visualize quantization parameter (QP), lower QP are tinted greener
vis_mb_type	visualize block types
buffers	picture buffer allocations
thread_ops	threading operations

For example, we save a short output from mptestsrc source to an MP4 (H.264) file with an **mmco** value:

```
ffmpeg -debug mmco -f lavfi -i mptestsrc -t 0.5 output.mp4
```

To the console output were added 12 lines describing individual frames; description of included terms:
- QP - quantization parameter
- NAL - Network Abstraction Layer units
- Slice: B - bi-predictive, I - intra-coded, P - predicted

```
[libx264 @ 03decb60] frame=    0 QP=13.00 NAL=3 Slice:I Poc:0    I:1024 P:0     SKIP:0     size=93 bytes
[libx264 @ 03decb60] frame=    1 QP=31.03 NAL=2 Slice:I Poc:2    I:1024 P:0     SKIP:0     size=1376 bytes
[libx264 @ 03decb60] frame=    2 QP=21.76 NAL=2 Slice:P Poc:10   I:1    P:222   SKIP:801   size=253 bytes
[libx264 @ 03decb60] frame=    3 QP=24.00 NAL=2 Slice:B Poc:6    I:1    P:8     SKIP:1014  size=44 bytes
[libx264 @ 03decb60] frame=    4 QP=21.00 NAL=0 Slice:B Poc:4    I:1    P:2     SKIP:1021  size=26 bytes
[libx264 @ 03decb60] frame=    5 QP=22.94 NAL=0 Slice:B Poc:8    I:1    P:5     SKIP:1018  size=32 bytes
[libx264 @ 03decb60] frame=    6 QP=25.26 NAL=2 Slice:P Poc:18   I:5    P:158   SKIP:861   size=238 bytes
[libx264 @ 03decb60] frame=    7 QP=23.51 NAL=2 Slice:B Poc:14   I:2    P:7     SKIP:1015  size=45 bytes
[libx264 @ 03decb60] frame=    8 QP=23.99 NAL=0 Slice:B Poc:12   I:3    P:6     SKIP:1015  size=46 bytes
[libx264 @ 03decb60] frame=    9 QP=25.47 NAL=0 Slice:B Poc:16   I:1    P:9     SKIP:1012  size=46 bytes
[libx264 @ 03decb60] frame=   10 QP=28.09 NAL=2 Slice:P Poc:24   I:6    P:39    SKIP:979   size=118 bytes
[libx264 @ 03decb60] frame=   11 QP=26.42 NAL=2 Slice:B Poc:22   I:1    P:13    SKIP:1009  size=63 bytes
[libx264 @ 03decb60] frame=   12 QP=25.49 NAL=0 Slice:B Poc:20   I:4    P:9     SKIP:1011  size=62 bytes
```

Another debugging option is **-debug_ts** that prints a timestamp information during processing, for instance we can modify the previous example and use only 0.1 second time (3 frames):

```
ffmpeg -debug_ts -f lavfi -i mptestsrc -t 0.1 output.mp4
```

To the console output are added the next lines:

```
demuxer    ->    ist_index:0    type:video    next_dts:NOPTS    next_dts_time:NOPTS    next_pts:NOPTS
next_pts_time:NOPTS  pkt_pts:0 pkt_pts_time:0 pkt_dts:0 pkt_dts_time:0 off:0
decoder    ->    ist_index:0    type:video    frame_pts:0    frame_pts_time:0    best_effort_ts:0
best_effort_ts_time:0 keyframe:1 frame_type:1
[libx264 @ 023ef4c0] using mv_range_thread = 88
demuxer    ->    ist_index:0    type:video    next_dts:40000    next_dts_time:0.04    next_pts:40000
next_pts_time:0.04  pkt_pts:1 pkt_pts_time:0.04 pkt_dts:1 pkt_dts_time:0.04 off:0
decoder    ->    ist_index:0    type:video    frame_pts:1    frame_pts_time:0.04    best_effort_ts:1
best_effort_ts_time:0.04 keyframe:1 frame_type:1
demuxer    ->    ist_index:0    type:video    next_dts:80000    next_dts_time:0.08    next_pts:80000
next_pts_time:0.08  pkt_pts:2 pkt_pts_time:0.08 pkt_dts:2 pkt_dts_time:0.08 off:0
decoder    ->    ist_index:0    type:video    frame_pts:2    frame_pts_time:0.08    best_effort_ts:2
best_effort_ts_time:0.08 keyframe:1 frame_type:1
demuxer    ->    ist_index:0    type:video    next_dts:120000    next_dts_time:0.12    next_pts:120000
next_pts_time:0.12  pkt_pts:3 pkt_pts_time:0.12 pkt_dts:3 pkt_dts_time:0.12 off:0
decoder    ->    ist_index:0    type:video    frame_pts:3    frame_pts_time:0.12    best_effort_ts:3
best_effort_ts_time:0.12 keyframe:1 frame_type:1
No more output streams to write to, finishing.
[libx264 @ 023ef4c0] scene cut at 1 Icost:252652 Pcost:248376 ratio:0.0169 bias:0.0250 gop:1 (imb:0
pmb:900)
[libx264 @ 023ef4c0] frame=    0 QP=13.00 NAL=3 Slice:I Poc:0    I:1024 P:0     SKIP:0     size=93
bytes
muxer <- type:video pkt_pts:0 pkt_pts_time:0 pkt_dts:-1024 pkt_dts_time:-0.08 size:782
[libx264 @ 023ef4c0] frame=    1 QP=21.48 NAL=2 Slice:I Poc:2    I:1024 P:0     SKIP:0     size=926
bytes
muxer <- type:video pkt_pts:512 pkt_pts_time:0.04 pkt_dts:-512 pkt_dts_time:-0.04 size:926
[libx264 @ 023ef4c0] frame=    2 QP=26.98 NAL=2 Slice:P Poc:4    I:1    P:6     SKIP:1017 size=50
bytes
muxer <- type:video pkt_pts:1024 pkt_pts_time:0.08 pkt_dts:0 pkt_dts_time:0 size:50
```

Option **-fdebug** has only 1 possible value **ts** and is often used together with -debug_ts option for various tests, for instance to debug DTS (decoding timestamp) and PTS (presentation timestamp) relations. Using the modified command from previous example, the console output shows the added lines that are listed after the command:

```
ffmpeg -fdebug ts -f lavfi -i mptestsrc -t 0.1 output.mp4
```

```
[libx264 @ 0206cb00] using mv_range_thread = 88
[lavfi @ 0229c2c0] ff_read_packet stream=0, pts=1, dts=NOPTS, size=393216, duration=0, flags=0
[lavfi @ 0229c2c0] read_frame_internal stream=0, pts=1, dts=1, size=393216, duration=1, flags=1
[lavfi @ 0229c2c0] ff_read_packet stream=0, pts=2, dts=NOPTS, size=393216, duration=0, flags=0
[lavfi @ 0229c2c0] read_frame_internal stream=0, pts=2, dts=2, size=393216, duration=1, flags=1
[lavfi @ 0229c2c0] ff_read_packet stream=0, pts=3, dts=NOPTS, size=393216, duration=0, flags=0
[lavfi @ 0229c2c0] read_frame_internal stream=0, pts=3, dts=3, size=393216, duration=1, flags=1
No more output streams to write to, finishing.
[libx264 @ 0206cb00] scene cut at 1 Icost:252652 Pcost:248376 ratio:0.0169 bias:0.0250 gop:1 (imb:0 pmb:900)
[libx264 @ 0206cb00] frame=   0 QP=13.00 NAL=3 Slice:I Poc:0   I:1024 P:0    SKIP:0    size=93 bytes
[libx264 @ 0206cb00] frame=   1 QP=21.48 NAL=2 Slice:I Poc:2   I:1024 P:0    SKIP:0    size=926 bytes
[libx264 @ 0206cb00] frame=   2 QP=26.98 NAL=2 Slice:P Poc:4   I:1    P:6    SKIP:1017 size=50 bytes
```

Flags for error detection

Detection of errors in ffmpeg processing can be specified by an **-err_detect** option described in the table:

Option: err_detect	
Description	Detects an error, which type is specified by the flag.
Syntax	**-err_detect[:stream_specifier]** *flag*
Description of available flags	
aggressive	consider things that a sane encoder should not do as an error
bitstream	detect bitstream specification deviations
buffer	detect improper bitstream length
careful	consider things that violate the specification and have not been seen in the wild as errors
compliant	consider all specification non compliances as errors
crccheck	verify embedded CRCs
explode	abort decoding on minor error detection

For example, to detect an improper bitstream length we can use the command:

```
ffmpeg -report -err_detect buffer -i input.avi output.mp4
```

Logging level setting

Logging level determines what content is displayed in the console output during processing, available values for modifications are: quiet, panic, fatal, error, warning, info, verbose, debug. To set the logging level we can use option **-v** or **-loglevel** option, for example for a verbose level we can use the command:

```
ffmpeg -loglevel verbose -i input.avi output.mp4
```

Timebase configuration test

Filters **asettb** and **settb** are used to test timebase configuration, **asettb** is for audio input and **settb** for video input. Both filters have the same parameters and are described in the common table:

Audio filter: asettb & Video filter: settb	
Description	Both filters set the time base, that will be used for output frame timestamps. This setting is used to test the timebase configuration and similar features. The syntax and parameters of both filters are the same.
Syntax	**settb=expr** result of **expr** is a rational number, can contain variables described below
Variables available in expression	
AVTB	sets default timebase value (AVTB = default timebase)
intb	input timebase
sr	sample rate, only for asettb

The next examples set the time base, first one to AVTB, second one to 0.3 and third one to 1.5 multiple of the input timebase:

```
ffmpeg input.mpg -vf settb=AVTB output.mpg
ffmpeg input.mpg -vf settb=0.3 output.mpg
ffmpeg input.mpg -vf settb=1.5*intb output.mpg
```

Testing encoding features

To generate various test patterns for a discrete cosine luma, chroma, for frequency and amplitude of the luma and chroma, etc. we can use an **mptestsrc** filter from MPlayer project that is described in the table:

Video filter: mptestsrc	
Description	Generates various tests related to chroma, luma and other video properties. If used without parameters, all test are performed until user stops the process.
Syntax	**mptestsrc[=t=test_type[:d=duration[:r=rate]]]**
Description of parameters	
test, t	- name of the selected test, available tests are dc_luma, dc_chroma, freq_luma, freq_chroma, amp_luma, amp_chroma, cbp, mv, ring1, ring2 - default value is "all"
duration, d	duration of test in seconds or in HH:MM:SS format
r	frame rate, the default value is 25

The next table illustrates the samples of particular test values.

Pattern	Syntax	Picture
DC luma	`mptest=t=dc_luma`	
DC chroma	`mptest=t=dc_chroma`	
luma frequency	`mptest=t=freq_luma`	
chroma frequency	`mptest=t=freq_chroma`	
luma amplitude	`mptest=t=amp_luma`	
chroma amplitude	`mptest=t=amp_chroma`	
Coded Block Pattern (CBP)	`mptest=t=cbp`	
Motion Vector (MV)	`mptest=t=mv`	
test ring 1	`mptest=t=ring1`	
test ring 2	`mptest=t=ring2`	

Test patterns

To detect various bugs and to provide sources for the video tests FFmpeg contains 3 special video sources listed below. Except the **color** parameter they share the same parameters with the **color** source that is described in the chapter Image Processing, section Creating images.

RGB test pattern

To test RGB and BGR color spaces available is the video source named **rgbtestsrc**,

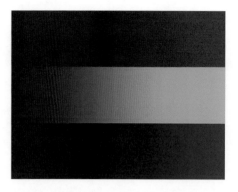

```
ffplay -f lavfi -i rgbtestsrc
```

Color pattern with scrolling gradient and timestamp

To generate a video pattern similar to TV pattern, the testsrc video source can be used with the command:

```
ffplay -f lavfi -i testsrc
```

SMPTE bars pattern

Color bars pattern from the Society of Motion Picture and Television Engineers (SMPTE) can be created with the command:

```
ffplay -f lavfi -i testsrc
```

Simple packet dumping or with payload (hexadecimally)

For more precise debugging also the payload can be dumped with **-hex** option, usually with -report option to save results to the file in the current directory. Using this option, the processing is very slow and the report file is much bigger. The example of the command is:

```
ffmpeg -dump -hex -report -i input.mpg output.flv
```

CPU time used and memory consumption

To display used CPU time and memory consumption during processing we can use a **-benchmark** or **-benchmark_all** options that produce similar output:

- -benchmark option shows results after encoding
- -benchmark_all shows results during encoding, in various steps

The computer systems that do not support maximum memory consumption data will display 0 instead of value. Both options are global options and are entered at the beginning of the command, for example:

```
ffmpeg -benchmark -i input.avi output.webm
```

```
frame=  900 fps= 35 q=0.0 Lsize=      931kB time=00:00:30.00 bitrate= 254.2kbits/s
video:799kB audio:115kB subtitle:0 global headers:3kB muxing overhead 1.579193%
bench: utime=25.849s maxrss=36808kB
```

At the end of the console output is added a line starting with **bench:** and the **utime** denotes the time that was used by the CPU (Central Processing Unit of the computer) during processing. The **benchmark_all** option displays the results during processing, the screen after completing is on the image below.

```
ffmpeg -benchmark_all -i input.avi output.mpg
```

```
bench:        0 decode_audio 0.1
bench:        0 decode_video 0.0
bench:        0 decode_audio 0.1
bench:   468003 flush Video 0.0
bench:        0 flush Video 0.0
bench:        0 flush Video 0.0
bench:        0 flush Video 0.0
bench:        0 flush Video 0.0
bench:        0 flush Video 0.0
bench:        0 flush Video 0.0
bench:        0 flush Video 0.0
bench:        0 flush Video 0.0
bench:        0 flush Video 0.0
bench:        0 flush Video 0.0
bench:        0 flush Video 0.0
bench:        0 flush Video 0.0
bench:        0 flush Video 0.0
bench:        0 flush Video 0.0
bench:        0 flush Video 0.0
bench:        0 flush Video 0.0
bench:        0 flush Video 0.0
bench:        0 flush Video 0.0
bench:        0 flush Video 0.0
bench:        0 flush Video 0.0
bench:        0 flush Video 0.0
bench:        0 flush Video 0.0
bench:        0 flush Video 0.0
bench:        0 flush Audio 0.1
bench:        0 flush Audio 0.1
bench:        0 flush Audio 0.1
bench:        0 flush Audio 0.1
bench:        0 flush Audio 0.1
frame=  900 fps= 21 q=0.0 Lsize=      931kB time=00:00:30.00 bitrate= 254.2kbits/s
video:799kB audio:115kB subtitle:0 global headers:3kB muxing overhead 1.579193%
```

Glossary

4cc or fourcc

fourcc (also FourCC - **Four C**haracter **C**ode) is an identifier for a video codec, compression format, color or pixel format used in media files. A character means a 1 byte (8 bit) value, so fourcc always have 32 bits (4 bytes) in a file. 4 characters in a fourcc is generally limited to be within the human readable characters in the ASCII table, so it is easy to convey and communicate what the fourccs are within a media file. AVI files is the most widespread, or the first widely used media file format, to use fourcc identifiers for the codecs used to compress the various video/audio streams within the files. Some of the more well known fourccs include DIVX, XVID, H264, DX50, etc. Examples of using fourcc in FFmpeg:

- **-vtag** (or **-tag:v**) option sets the fourcc value for the video stream
- **-atag** (or **-tag:a**) option sets the fourcc value for the audio stream
- **-tag** option sets the fourcc value for all streams

Aspect ratio

Aspect ratio is a ratio between the width and height of an image or a video frame.

Types of aspect ratio		
Type	**Abbreviation**	**Description**
Display Aspect Ratio	DAR	Aspect ratio of images and videos as displayed. Alternative names are Image Aspect Ratio (IAR) and Picture Aspect Ratio.
Storage Aspect Ratio	SAR	Aspect ratio in which an image or video frames are stored, depends on the video source.
Pixel Aspect Ratio	PAR	Ratio of a pixel width to its height, in most LCDs it is 1:1, but some analog devices use the rectangular pixels.
Original Aspect Ratio	OAR	Term from Home Cinema standard, denotes the aspect in which the video was originally created, many films has wide aspect like
Modified Aspect Ratio	MAR	Home Cinema standard term, means the aspect to which the OAR was adjusted to conform with aspect ratio of output screen available, usually 4:3 or 16:9.

The relation between DAR, SAR and PAR can be expressed by equation

$$DAR = PAR \times SAR$$

In ffmpeg there is an **-aspect** option that can be used to specify an output video:

```
-aspect[:stream_specifier]
```

Thomas Alva Edison and William Dickson created in 1892 an universal standard with the film of 35 mm width, where perforations determine a frame size of 24.89x18.67 mm, it is approximately a 4:3 or 1.33:1 ratio. Since then many aspect ratios where created and some of them are described in the next table.

Common aspect ratios	
1.33:1 or 4:3	Original film aspect ratio widely used today for LCD monitors, TV screens, camcorders, etc. It is also a standard for MPEG-2 compression.
1.618:1	Golden ratio, FFmpeg contains it as a built in constant PHI, where PHI=(1+sqrt(5))/2
1.77:1 or 16:9 (also 1.78:1)	Widescreen standard used for High Definition TV, LCD monitors, camcorders, etc. It is one of 3 aspect ratios in MPEG-2 standard. Ratio 16:9 can be derived from 4:3, where 4^2 = 16 and 3^2 = 9.
1.85:1	Widescreen cinema standard in US and UK introduced in 1953.
2.2:1 or 11:5	70 mm film standard developed in 1950s, it is also a part of MPEG-2 standard with the value 2.21:1.
2.37:1	New standard introduced in 2010 in so called "21:9 cinema displays". The ratio is derived from 4:3, where $4^3:3^3$ = 64:27 = 2.37.
2.39:1	35 mm film standard that is anamorphic and is used from 1970 as 'Scope' or Panavision format. Blu-ray discs utilize this ratio as 2.4:1 and record films in resolution 1920x800.

CIE

International Commission on Illumination (in French CIE - Commission internationale de l'éclairage) is an institution and authority on light, illumination, color spaces etc., more in the chapter Color Corrections.

Color depth, bit depth, bits per pixel

Color depth, bit depth and bits per pixel are terms describing how many bits are used to specify color properties of each pixel components from the image. The most used color depths are in the table:

Common color depths		
Bits per pixel	**Number of colors**	**Corresponding pixel formats available in ffmpeg**
1 (B&W)	$2^1 = 2$	monob, monow
2 (CGA)	$2^2 = 4$	no pixel format (2 bpp was used in early computers)
3	$2^3 = 8$	no pixel format (used in early home computers with TV display)
4 (EGA)	$2^4 = 16$	rgb4, rgb4_byte, bgr4, bgr4_byte
8 (VGA)	$2^8 = 256$	gray, pal8, bgr8, rgb8
12	$2^{12} = 4096$	yuv420p, yuv411p, yuvj420p, nv12, nv21, rgb444be, rgb444le
16 high color	$2^{16} = 65,536$	yuyv422, yuv422p, yuvj422p, yuv440p, yuvj440p, rgb565be, etc.
24 true color	$2^1 = 16,777,216$	rgb24, bgr24, yuv444p, yuvj444p, gbrp, 0rgb, rgb0, yuva422p, etc.
32 true+alpha	24-bit with alpha	argb, rgba, abgr, bgra, yuva444p, yuv422p16be, yuv422p16le
30 deep color	$2^{30} = 1,073,741,824$	yuv444p10be, yuv444p10le, gbrp10be, gbrp10le
36 deep color	$2^{36}=68,719,476,736$	yuva444p9be, yuva444p9le, gbrp12be, gbrp12le, yuv444p12be etc.
48 deep color	over 280 trillion	rgb48be, rgb48le, bgr48be, bgr48le, yuva422p16be, yuva422p16le

Color models and color spaces

Color space is derived from a color model. Color models describe the methods that can be used to model the human vision. When such mathematical model describing how to represent the colors as numbers is supplemented with a precise definitions for the interpretation of these numbers, such set of colors is regarded to be a color space. Numeric color representations commonly use 3 or 4 components to describe each color. More precise specification requires bigger numbers, details are in the previous section. 5 color models are considered major: CIE, CMYK, HSL/HSV, RGB and YUV and video technologies utilize commonly RGB and YUV. Computer monitors use pixels to display information and color spaces are implemented as the pixel formats, their list is in the second chapter.

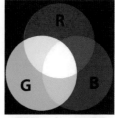
RGB color model

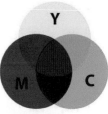
CMYK color model

Color vision

While human ear is sensitive to the vibrations with the frequency from 16 to 20,000 Hz, human eye is able to perceive electromagnetic waves with the frequency from about 405 THz (740 nanometres) to 789 THz (380 nanometers). The dark light without a color is perceived with the special eye cells called cones and the trichromatic vision is provided by the rod cells. 3 different types of rod cells are sensitive to 3 basic colors: red, green and blue:

- L (long waves) rods - sensitive to waves from about 564 to 580 nm - red color
- M (medium waves) rods - sensitive to waves from about 534 to 545 nm - green color
- S (short waves) rods - sensitive to waves from about 420 to 440 nm - blue color

The peak sensitivity of the rods is for the waves of about 498 nm, therefore the green color is the perceived better than the red color and even better than the blue color, more details are in the chapter Interlaced Video.

DCT - Discrete Cosine Transform

Discrete cosine transform is used in compression of audio and visual data with lossy codecs, where it reduces the amount of stored data several times. It transforms a complex signal to its complex spectrum using a sum of cosine functions that oscillate at different frequencies. DCT is a special type of a discrete Fourier transform (DFT), where input and output samples are real numbers (DFT works with complex numbers). Examples of DCT use with ffmpeg:

- option -dct[:stream_specifier] to set DCT algorithm for any codec
- option -idct[:stream_specifier] to set DCT implementation for any codec
- value ildct (use interlaced DCT) in -flags option for any codec
- value dct_coeff in -debug option for any codec
- value dct (sum of absolute DCT transformed differences) and value dctmax in -cmp, -subcmp, -mbcmp, -ildctcmp, -skipcmp and -precmp options for any codec
- option -skip_idct[:stream_specifier] option for any codec

Decoder

During transcoding, decoder processes encoded data packets from the demuxer and produces uncompressed frames for the next processing. Definition from FFmpeg documentation:

"Decoders are configured elements in FFmpeg which allow the decoding of multimedia streams."

The list of decoders can be displayed with the command:

```
ffmpeg -decoders
```

Demuxer (demux)

In transcoding process, demuxer (also demux and demultiplexer) reads the input file(s) and produces encoded data packets that are sent to the decoder for decoding.

Definition from FFmpeg documentation:

"Demuxers are configured elements in FFmpeg which allow to read the multimedia streams from a particular type of file."

Demuxers are listed among available formats, details are in the second chapter. Information about a particular demuxer can be displayed with the command:

```
ffmpeg -h demuxer=demuxer_name
```

Encoder

During transcoding encoder processes uncompressed frames and encodes them according to the selected codec to the data packets that are sent to the demuxer, usually with some compression, lossy or lossless.

Definition of the encoder from FFmpeg documentation:

"Encoders are configured elements in FFmpeg which allow the encoding of multimedia streams."

The list of encoders is in the second chapter and can be displayed with the command:

```
ffmpeg -encoders
```

To display a detailed information about a particular encoder we can use the command:

```
ffmpeg -h encoder=encoder_name
```

FFmpeg configuration

The possibilities of a native FFmpeg source code are improved by including the code of additional software libraries from other open source projects. These libraries are included before the compilation using an **--enable-*library*** option to the configuration file named **configure**. With every console usage of ffmpeg, ffplay and ffprobe tools is displayed the actual FFmpeg configuration with enabled additional libraries, like in the next console output:

```
configuration: --enable-gpl --enable-version3 --disable-pthreads --enable-
runtime-cpudetect --enable-avisynth --enable-bzlib --enable-frei0r --enable-
libass --enable-libcelt --enable-libopencore-amrnb --enable-libopencore-amrwb
--enable-libfreetype --enable-libgsm --enable-libmp3lame --enable-libnut
--enable-libopenjpeg --enable-librtmp --enable-libschroedinger --enable-
libspeex --enable-libtheora --enable-libutvideo --enable-libvo-aacenc
--enable-libvo-amrwbenc --enable-libvorbis --enable-libvpx --enable-libx264
--enable-libxavs --enable-libxvid --enable-zlib
    libavutil      51. 73.101 / 51. 73.101
    libavcodec     54. 56.100 / 54. 56.100
    libavformat    54. 27.101 / 54. 27.101
    libavdevice    54.  2.100 / 54.  2.100
    libavfilter     3. 16.104 /  3. 16.104
    libswscale      2.  1.101 /  2.  1.101
    libswresample   0. 15.100 /  0. 15.100
    libpostproc    52.  0.100 / 52.  0.100
```

Displayed are also versions of FFmpeg native libraries: libavutil, libavcodec, etc.

JPEG

JPEG has usually 2 meanings:

- Joint Photographic Experts Group that is a predecessor of Moving Pictures Experts Group (MPEG). JPEG group was founded in 1986 and created JPEG, JPEG 2000 and JPEG XR standards.
- lossy compression method for images and video frames with about 10:1 compression without a visible decreasing of quality, it is used in many image formats including JPG images that are widely used on the webpages and in digital cameras.

Due to the lossy compression JPEG format is not suited for multiple editing and certain technical tasks. Segments that create the JPEG image are delimited with various markers (SOI, SOF0, SOF2, DHT, etc.). During encoding the content is converted to the YCbCr (YUV in FFmpeg pixel formats) color space, where Y denotes the luminance channel and Cb and Cr two chrominance channels. Chrominance channels are optionally downsampled and each channel is split to 8x8 blocks that are converted to the frequency domain by a normalized 2-dimensional discrete cosine transform (DCT) of type II.

Examples of using JPEG and derived standards in FFmpeg:

- mjpeg2jpeg bitstream filter converts MJPEG/AVI1 packets to complete JPEG/JFIF packets
- mjpegadump bitstream filter is used for conversion to MJPEG file format
- decoders and encoders based on JPEG: jpeg2000, jpegls, ljpeg, mjpeg, mjpegb (only decoder), nuv (RTJPEG), sp5x (Sunplus JPEG), adpcm_ima_smjpeg (audio, only decoder)
- file formats: ingenient (raw MJPEG, only decoding), mjpeg, mpjpeg (MIME multipart, only encoding), smjpeg (Loki SDL MJPEG)

Macroblock

Division of image or video frame to the macroblocks is a part of encoding using the discrete cosine transform (DCT). In FFmpeg are macroblocks used in various AVC codec context options, H.263 encoder options, ProRes encoder options, libx264 options, libxavs options, etc.

Coding of Macroblocks for DCT
(JPEG images and video frames)

ADDR	TYPE	QUANT	VECTOR	CBP	b0	b1	...b5

ADDR - address of a block in the image (frame)
TYPE - macroblock type: intra, inter (predicted), inter (bidirect.)
QUANT - quantization parameter
VECTOR - motion vector (2D vector for inter prediction)
CBP - Coded Block Pattern (bit mask for blocks coefficients)
b0...b3 - 4 Y blocks for luminance
b4 - 1 block for Cr
b5 - 1 block for Cb

Motion vector

Motion vector represents a macroblock in a picture according to the position of macroblock in another picture (reference picture). Motion vector is the main element in the motion estimation during video compression. The official definition from the H.264 standard is:

A two-dimensional vector used for inter prediction that provides an offset from the coordinates in the decoded picture to the coordinates in a reference picture.

Examples of motion vector use in FFmpeg:

- value mv4 (use four motion vector by macroblock (mp4)) in -flags option for any codec
- value guess_mvs (iterative motion vector (MV) search) in -ec (error concealment strategy) option for any codec
- value mv (motion vector) in -debug option for any codec
- -vismv[:stream_specifier] (visualize motion vector) option for any codec
- -me_range[:stream_specifier] (limit motion vectors range) option for any codec
- -bidir_refine option for any codec (refine 2 motion vectors used in bidirectional macroblocks)
- deshake filter uses x, y, w and h parameters to specify a rectangular area to search for motion vectors

MPEG

MPEG (pronunciation "em-peg") stands for Moving Pictures Experts Group, what is a team of multimedia experts established by ISO/IEC in 1988 to develop standards for audio and video compression and transmission. MPEG standards include:

- MPEG-1
- MPEG-2
- MPEG-4
- MPEG-7
- MPEG-21

MPEG is divided to the teams called working groups.

MPEG-1

Official definition of the standard is: "Coding of moving pictures and associated audio for digital storage media at up to about 1.5 Mbps." It was standardized in 1993 and the primary target was to encode video and sound for a storage on the Compact Disc. MPEG-1 is used on Audio CD, Video CD and optionally on SVCD and low quality DVD. Before MPEG-2 it was also used on digital satellite and cable TV networks. The part of the standard is a popular audio format MP3, what is abbreviation of MPEG-1 Audio Layer III. In ffmpeg you can select this format with the option **-f mpeg1video**, for example:

```
ffmpeg -i input.avi -f mpeg1video output.mpg
```

MPEG-2

MPEG-2 standard official definition is: Generic coding of moving pictures and associated audio information (ISO/IEC 13818). This wide standard was released in 1995 and contains transport, video and audio specifications for broadcast TV. Its compression scheme is used for:

- terrestrial digital TV, namely ATSC, DVB and ISDB
- satellite digital TV, e.g. Dish Network
- digital cable TV
- Super Video CD, DVD Video and occasionally on Blu-ray Discs

In ffmpeg you can select this format with the option **-f mpeg2video**, for example:

```
ffmpeg -i input.avi -f mpeg2video output.mpg
```

MPEG-4

The official definition of the standard by ISO/IEC is: "Coding of audio-visual objects". It was standardized in 1998 and the main features are:

- new encoding algorithm ACE (Advanced Coding Efficiency), that enables about 11 times less data storage/bandwidth than MPEG-2
- decoder is a rendering processor and the compressed bitstream describes 3D shapes and surface texture
- supports MPEG-J (Java API), what is program solution for developing of custom interactive multimedia applications
- supports IPMP (Intellectual Property Management and Protection) for the use of proprietary technologies to manage and protect content like DRM (Digital Rights Management).

For output files with MP4 extension ffmpeg automatically selects h264 encoder and yuv420p pixel format.

Muxer (mux)

During transcoding muxer (also mux or multiplexer) processes encoded data packets and produces a file of the specified format. Definition of the muxer in FFmpeg documentation:

"Muxers are configured elements in FFmpeg which allow writing multimedia streams to a particular type of file."

The list of muxers is in the second chapter among available formats. To display details about a particular muxer we can use the command:

```
ffmpeg -h muxer=muxer_name
```

Pixel

Pixel or pel is derived from **pic**ture **el**ement and represents the smallest controllable element of the digital image or video frame. The shape of the pixel is usually a square, but some frame resolutions use rectangular pixels. The ratio between pixel width and height is a pixel aspect ratio, often abbreviated PAR. ffmpeg contains pixel formats that contain 1, 3 or 4 components and are displayed with the command:

```
ffmpeg -pix_fmts
```

Protocol

The term protocol in computer terminology usually means a set of communication rules for data receiving and transmitting. Definition of the protocol in FFmpeg documentation:

"Protocols are configured elements in FFmpeg which allow to access resources which require the use of a particular protocol."

The list of available protocols is in the second chapter and can be displayed with the command:

```
ffmpeg -protocols
```

Examples of protocols are http (Hypertext Transfer Protocol), rtmp (Real-Time Messaging Protocol), tcp (Transmission Control Protocol), udp (User Datagram Protocol), etc.

Quantization

Quantization of digital signal involves reducing a range of values to a representative single value. Media processing includes audio and video quantization, in audio are quantized sound amplitudes and video encoding involves color and frequency quantization. Both audio and video quantization can utilize the DCT transform. Examples of ffmpeg options related to quantization:

- value naq (normalize adaptive quantization) in -flags option for any codec
- qp (quantization parameter) and vis_qp (visualize QP) values in -debug option for any codec
- -trellis[:stream_specifier] (rate-distortion optimal quantization) option for any codec

Sampling and sampling rate

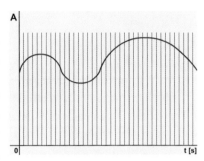

To sample a continuous (analog) signal means to reduce it to a discrete signal, for instance sound waves (illustrated on the image) are converted to a sequence of samples. Values of these samples are expressed in numbers and this digital form can be saved to computer files. Sampling rate (or frequency rate) determines the number of samples per second, typical audio sample rates are multiples of 8000 Hz and 11025 Hz. Human ear sensitivity range is from 16 Hz to 20 kHz and due to sampling theorem at least 40 kHz frequency is needed to represent all audible sounds, selected was 44,100 Hz as a standard for CD audio.

Video

The term video was created when television was invented and denotes a technology for manipulating of moving pictures in an electronic form (compares to the film - a photochemical form) , what can include:

- capturing
- recording
- compressing
- encoding
- decoding
- transmitting (broadcasting) etc.

The main video features are:

- frame rate
- aspect ratio
- storage type (analog or digital)
- color space
- interlaced or progressive
- quality (perceived by users)
- bits per pixel (color depth)
- codec (digital video only)
- 3 dimensional (3D)

Video represents still images that are projected in a fast sequence specified by frame rate to make an illusion of a continuous motion, the minimal frame rate when human eyes see a continuous scene is about 15 images (frames) per second. Video is derived from the film that is a mechanical technology for processing moving pictures and was developed initially for the cinema and television, which used interlacing to eliminate flickering. FFmpeg works with many video formats, that are listed in the second chapter. Some formats enable to store multiple different sequences of moving pictures and these sequences are called **video streams**; their numbering is zero-based, the first stream is numbered 0, the second is numbered 1, etc.

Video filters

Filters in FFmpeg are implemented via libavfilter library. For optimal performance they are often used in filterchains (comma-separated filter's descriptions) and filtergraphs (semi-colon separated filterchains). With filtergraphs can be used the labeled links that can substitute an input in the filterchains that follows, a special [in] link label is created by default and denotes the input entered with -i option. Combining filters to filterchains and filtergraphs is more preferred than repeated processing that involves slight changes caused by compression algorithms. The list of filters is in the 2nd chapter and is showed by: `ffmpeg -filters`
Video filters can be divided according to several criteria and the general classification is in the next table:

Video filters (general classification)		
Filter type	**Description**	**Examples**
Prefilters	used before encoding	contrast adjustment
		deflicker
		deinterlace
		denoise
		scale (downsample, upsample)
Intrafilters	used in encoding (usually part of a video codec)	deblock
Postfilters	used after decoding	deblock, deinterlace, dering
Note: Some filters like deinterlace are listed in 2 categories because the modification of input video stream depends on a software implementation.		

Video pipeline

Video pipeline describes the processing of video frames from a raw video input to the final output on a display device, a simplified video pipeline is illustrated on the diagram. ffmpeg contains 2 special input devices **dv1394** and **iec61883** that enable to record directly from the FireWire port used by digital videocameras.

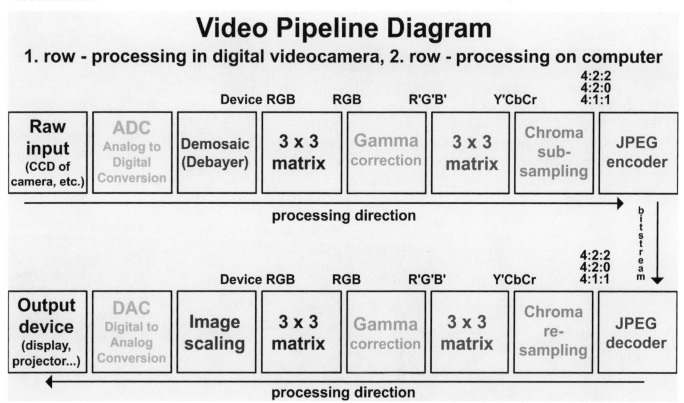

About the author

Frantisek Korbel is a Zend Certified Engineer and his work includes programming, video editing and web design. In 2004 he created a First Aid Basics freeware using Macromedia Flash and since then he often works with animations and video. Using Adobe AIR in 2009 he developed a Learning Periodic Table of chemical elements. Big part of his activities is devoted to the volunteering, mainly for educational and community projects in developing countries (Africa – nkolfoulou.org, oyoko.org), India (kidedu.org), etc. He participates in various projects by UN Volunteering and on WaterWiki.net website design coordinated by United Nations Development Programme. For this book he created a supporting website ffmpeg.tv.

Links

Book homepage: http://ffmpeg.tv
Facebook: http://ffmpeg.tv/facebook
Twitter: http://twitter.com/FFmpeg
YouTube: http://youtube.com/FFmpegTv